EMOTION, DEPTH, AND FLESH

A Study of Sensitive Space

Reflections on Merleau-Ponty's
Philosophy of Embodiment

SUE L. CATALDI

STATE UNIVERSITY OF NEW YORK PRESS

Permission for use of copyright material has been granted by: Routledge & Kegan Paul Ltd. and Humanities Press International, Inc., Atlantic Highlands, New Jersey, for the extracts from *Phenomenology of Perception* by Maurice Merleau-Ponty, English translation copyright © 1962 by Routledge & Kegan Paul Ltd.; Northwestern University Press for the extracts from *The Visible and the Invisible; Followed by Working Notes* by Maurice Merleau-Ponty (English Translation copyright © 1968 by Northwestern University Press); Lawrence Erlbaum Associates, Inc. for the extracts from *The Ecological Approach to Visual Perception* by James J. Gibson, copyright © 1986 by Lawrence Erlbaum Associates; Glen Mazis for the extracts from *Emotion and Embodiment: Fragile Ontology* (forthcoming with Peter Lang Publishers, 1993); and Princeton University Press for the extracts from *Justice and the Politics of Difference* by Iris Marion Young, copyright © 1990 by Princeton University Press. Excerpts from *Nineteen Eighty-Four* by George Orwell, copyright 1949 by Harcourt Brace Jovanovich, Inc. and renewed 1977 by Sonia Brownwell Orwell, reprinted by permission of the publisher.

Published by
State University of New York Press, Albany

© 1993 State University of New York

For information, address State University of New York Press,
State University Plaza, Albany, N.Y. 12246

Production by M. R. Mulholland
Marketing by Theresa A. Swierzowski

Library of Congress Cataloging-in-Publication Data

Cataldi, Sue L., 1951–
    Emotion, depth, and flesh : a study of sensitive space :
reflections on Merleau-Ponty's philosophy of embodiment / Sue L.
Cataldi.
        p.   cm.
    Includes bibliographical references and index.
    ISBN 0-7914-1651-8 (cloth : alk. paper). — ISBN 0-7914-1652-6
(pbk. : alk. paper)
    1. Emotions (Philosophy)   2. Depth (Philosophy)   3. Body, Human
(Philosophy)   4. Ontology.   5. Merleau-Ponty, Maurice, 1908–1961.
I. Title.
B105.E46C37   1993
128'.3—dc20
                                                    92-36052
                                                    CIP

10 9 8 7 6 5 4 3 2 1

To my parents

When we say that the perceived thing is to be grasped 'in person' or 'in the flesh,' this is to be taken literally.

—Maurice Merleau-Ponty, "The Philosopher and His Shadow"

Contents

Acknowledgments

Many persons helped me to complete this book by generously providing me with emotional and intellectual support. I wish to take this opportunity to thank them:

Bruce Wilshire, Ed Casey, and Glen Mazis, for their encouragement in the early stages of this project and for the conversation and commentary that strengthened and clarified my thought.

Joyce Tigner, Eileen Digrius, and Patricia Murphy, for the stability of their friendships and for sharing their intelligences with me through so many heartwarming hours of camraderie.

For innumerable kindnesses and her sisterly support, I am indebted to Linda Laba. I am also grateful to Michael Laba, for his extensions of brotherly love and logical guidance.

Gail and Tom Stepka provided countless occasions for laughter in the midst of their special hospitality. Stellar communications with Jeffrey Laba helped me to think in terms of black holes and light years. I also thank Regina Laba for inspiring me with her observation that time is what keeps everything from happening at once.

For her constant provisions of wisdom and solace, humor and love, and food, for thought, I am most grateful to my mother, Ann B. Laba.

Finally, I wish to acknowledge the spiritual support of my aunt, Sophie Zablana Bilek—who came to me in a picture frame, in the nick of time and in an opening of space.

Without these persons and their caring, I could not have written this book. I am deeply grateful.

Introduction

one in a state of 'deep despair in his soul' can experience some sensuous pleasure and enjoy it...One can also drink a glass of wine while being unhappy and still enjoy the bouquet of the wine....Expression also participates in this difference. A careworn face remains that, even in a smile. A serene face remains serene, even while crying. The fact that there is no blending into one feeling, as is the case in [the] feeling of such diverse *levels of depth*, points to the fact that feelings are not only of different qualities but also of different levels of *depth*.

—Max Scheler, *Formalism in Ethics and Non-Formal Ethics of Values*

While working at a psychiatric hospital several years ago, I noticed how summarily and frequently patients' "affects" were recorded as being "flat." At the time and given the context, the only significance I attached to this expression was the inference that a "flat" affect is indicative of emotional disturbance. Normally, emotional responses are differentiated in depth. We expect or suppose them to be.

Implicitly, we sense that our emotions are not all "on a level." Some appear to be "deeper" than others. For example, we think of love, rage, wonder, or remorse, as being respectively "deeper" than liking, irritation, curiosity, or regret. Implicitly, we also seem to sense that the divergencies in their "depths" are related to our own and to pronounced alterations in our ways of perceiving. For example, after a "deep emotional experience," we may say that we are "not the same person" or we may realize that we are beginning to see things in a different "way" or in a different "light."

We also tend to expect there to be a certain "fit" between emotional and evocative depths; and when there is not, we are surprised. It would appear just as peculiar and inappropriate, or overexaggerated and "shallow," for someone to be deeply emotionally responsive to *everything* as it would appear if he or she were deeply emotionally responsive to nothing. In both cases, the affect would appear to be "flat."

Despite our implicit understandings of the phenomenon of emotional depth, there is next to no philosophical literature devoted

to the topic.[1] This lacuna in philosophical literature on emotions and
my puzzling over the various meanings of *depth*, the various "levels"
of emotional depth, and the ways in which they appear to intertwine
with personal and perceptual depth led to the present study. Its
purpose is twofold.

   One of its objectives is to explicitly thematize our implicit
understandings of emotional depth. This I do through examples,
phenomenological description and analysis, and by comparing and
extending the insights of Maurice Merleau-Ponty[2] and James J. Gibson[3]
on the nature of perceived depth into the realm of emotional
experience. The other purpose of this study is to show how, through
its radically unified accommodation of distance/difference, Merleau-
Ponty's 'Flesh' ontology of perception[4] affords a nondichotomous
philosophical setting in which the complex phenomenon of emotional
depth can, theoretically, be.

   Since we do not experience "deep" emotions over things that
are manifestly superficial, I assumed when I began this project and
I take the position throughout it that emotional and perceptual depths
are intertwined, and that the meanings of *depth* are, in both cases,
essentially the same. My study of "sensitive space" can be read as
an attempt to apply literal senses of depth to emotional experience in
order to 'Flesh' out these assumptions.

   The text is divided into two parts. Except for the opening chapter,
Part I is the more theoretical because it is composed of Gibson's and
Merleau-Ponty's commensurable insights—on depth perception and
on the role of the body in perception. These insights are specifically
and concretely applied to emotional experiences in Part II. The
connection between emotional depth and perceptual depth and the
bearing of emotions on identity are also discussed in the second part
of the text.

   I begin with a collage of examples, culled from literary art,
personal experience, and ordinary language. These are intended,
initially, simply to informally focus some attention on what we already
seem to know about emotional depth. I refer back to these examples,
for illustration and analyses, throughout the course of the book. Some
of the preliminary findings later analyzed and set in the context of the
Flesh ontology are that the "deeper" the emotion, the more appropriate
it is to describe ourselves as being "in" it; that literal senses of "depth"
can be attached to certain emotions and emotional experiences; that
deeper emotions are "blind"; and that emotional well-being appears

EMOTION, DEPTH, AND FLESH

A Study of Sensitive Space

to depend upon the maintenance of *some* distance, some "happy medium"—between ourselves and others, and between ourselves and the world.

Depth is ambiguous; and its two primary meanings are ordinarily thought apart from each other: depth in the sense of "distance" and depth in the sense of thickness or occlusion. In Chapters 2 and 3, as I trace Merleau-Ponty's phenomenological thought on depth through its "metaphysical" culmination in the Flesh ontology's idea of "proximity through distance" and its thesis of (incomplete) "reversibility," I show how Merleau-Ponty thinks these two senses of depth together as mutually synonymous.

In their criticism of what they call *air* or *empty space* theories of depth perception and their objections to traditional philosophical dichotomies that separate the "subjective" from the "objective," Merleau-Ponty and Gibson both fault the empiricist tradition for distorting our understanding of depth perception by failing to take occlusions and embodied, ecologically niched, and mobile perceivers into account; and they both develop an account of "lived" distance. Interpreting depth as a reciprocity or "reversibility" between observer and environment, perceiver and perceived, they both came to re-vision depth as distance along the Ground of a recessed Surface. This elemental surface of sensibility is what Merleau-Ponty came to mean by *Flesh.*

Flesh incorporates our bodily being, but is not confined to it. It is a surface to which we, as embodied perceivers, always already belong or are "of," a surface from which we cannot be thought as entirely separated. I argue that 'Flesh' and Depth cannot be thought apart from each other. The Flesh ontology is a Depth ontology.

Chapter 4 is a brief, but pivotal chapter—a "turning point" in the text, as it depends upon the discussion of depth in Chapters 2 and 3 and anticipates themes in the following chapters. In it, I interpret depth as a "break/brake," as a "medium" or a "midway." By means of an ambiguous cube drawing, the phenomenon of perceptual reversibility is illustrated, and I explain the sense in which Depth is neither here nor there, neither past nor future, but the bond that lies between them and the source of their "reversibilities." Depth is not simply the "background"; and neither is it simply a "hidden dimension." It is best understood as a source of "reversibilities," as the process that generates that backgrounding of the foreground and that foregrounding of the background we can perceive whenever we perceive one or another of the ways in which ambiguous figures can come to the fore or unfold.

DEPTH AS A SOURCE OF REVERSIBILITIES.

A formal discussion of emotion and emotional depth begins in Part II. By *emotion* I mean to refer to phenomena such as hatred, fear, joy, anger, pride, love and so forth. My discussion of emotion focuses on their depthful, embodied, and perceptual dimensions, and is critical of purely "cognitive" or purely "subjective" approaches to the study of emotional experience.

By interpreting the felt phenomena of being emotionally moved as being-distanced or dis-oriented with respect to a prior orientation, I develop, in Chapter 5, a core or prototypical sense of emotional depth. I also explain Merleau-Ponty's view of emotions through an elaboration of his claims that emotional meanings are conveyed and comprehended through "blind" recognitions and in the process of our bodies' overlapping with or "inhabiting" a spectacle.

Chapter 6 is the heart, so to speak, of the text. In it, emotion and emotional depth are examined in the context of the Flesh ontology. I apply its "reversibility" thesis to emotional experience and connect the sense of "in" we apply, in ordinary language, to emotional experience (when we say, for instance, that we are "in love" or "in awe" or "in shock"), to the sense of "en" in the Flesh ontology's "*en-être*" thesis.

Other aspects of embodied emotional experience are also examined in Chapter 6. Overlaps between touch and emotional feeling are explored; and a discussion of the body's relation to group or social identities is situated in the context of social, political, and economic oppression.

Chapter 7 focuses specifically on the relation of emotional depth to alterations in personal identity. Here, the depth of an emotion is connected to the depth of a person; and the interminglings of personal, perceptual, and emotional depths become evident.

In Chapter 8, I show that a sufficient condition for the experience of a deep emotion is a perception of depth.

My hope is that this work sheds some light on hidden dimensions of emotional experience. I also hope that it will be found to be compatible with postmodern and feminist projects of thinking through the body to think beyond traditional philosophical dichotomies.

I

DEPTH AND EMBODIMENT

1

Flat Affects vs. Deep Emotional Experience

Introduction

A series of examples are presented in this chapter—from ordinary language, personal experience, and literary art—that contrast "flat" or superficial affect with deep emotional experiences. All examples are intended, simply or initially, to informally focus some attention on what we already implicitly seem to know about emotional depth.

That emotional and perceptual depths are intervolved (that we do not experience deep emotions over the manifestly superficial) is a part of my thesis. Some of the following examples are illustrative of these intervolvements in that they begin to show how the depth of an emotion appears to vary with the depth of the target of the emotion and illustrate that there is a certain appropriateness or "fit" between the two forms of depth.

Linguistic Distinctions

In our ordinary language, emotions are differentiated in depth. In some cases, we use the term *deep* explicitly and, presumably, to offset some relatively significant difference, say, between love and deep love. In other cases, particularly when we consider clusters of related kinds of emotional experience—those that bear a close family resemblance to each other—presumably significant differences in depth are implicit in the choice of word used to describe an emotion: *loving* instead of *liking*, or *rage* instead of *anger*.

Remorse, rage, and agony are (respectively) deeper than regret, anger, or pain—just as cruelty is deeper than spite, awe is deeper than admiration, sorrow is deeper than sadness, joy is deeper than gladness, reverence is deeper than respect; and so forth. Within emotion clusters, vectors of significance appear to exist so that the relation of emotional depth between them is asymmetrical. For example, irritation or indignation may deepen into anger or into outrage; but we never speak of rage "deepening" into anger or of anger "deepening" into irritation.[1]

Neither do we speak of being "deeply irritated." If we are "deeply irritated," we say that we are irate or angry. By the same token, if we are "deeply angry," we say that we are enraged, or furious.

Irritation or annoyance is the relatively superficial member of this emotion cluster. Irritation just scratches our surface. If we are irritated, something is "rubbing us the wrong way" or "grating" on us. If we are annoyed, we are "bugged." "Abrasive" personalities are, naturally, irritating. So is monotonously senseless repetition: the dripping of a leaky faucet, an attack of hiccups, the recurrent lighting of a fly, the skipping of a broken record, or nervous habits like the drumming of fingers on a table—all are irritating, annoying.

There is more (moral and cognitive) sense to anger than there is to irritation. To experience anger, I must believe that I have been, deliberately, wronged or harmed, and I will usually want, at least, to move toward the source of anger and *do* something. To experience irritation, I need not believe anything; and often I simply want to walk away from its source. Although we may, when irritation wears through our patience, become angry, it is somewhat misguided or inane to become angry at a source of irritation. For example, I may become angry at the plumber for not fixing my faucet properly, but it is ludicrous to become angry at the dripping drops of water—just as it seems to me absurd to become angry over a bout of my own hiccups, irritating though they are. In any case, the differences in depth between irritation and anger seem to be related to anger's ability to engage us cognitively and morally in a way that irritation does not.

Rage is deeper still. We speak of being "in" a "blind" rage ("en"-raged). We never say that we are "in" an irritation. Similarly, it is appropriate to speak of being "in" love (but not "in" liking) and of love as "blind." It is also commonly thought that the proper object of love is a person—not a superficial or "surface" trait of a person. I may love the color of your eyes, for example, but I would not say that I was "in" love with them.

By the same token, hatred or loathing is deeper than dislike; and although I may dislike your hairdo or your tie, the proper object for my hatred is you or "your guts."

We have a complex vocabulary for sadness. We may feel glum, dismal, dissatisfied, distressed, disappointed, dejected, depressed, sorry, sorrowful, despondent, miserable, wretched, melancholy, nostalgic, hurt, bitter, "brokenhearted," grim, distraught, grievous, mournful, tormented, in agony, anguished, or in despair. Many of these emotions may be deep, and some are deeper than others. We construe sorrow and despair, for example, as being deeper than just feeling sad or glum. If we are tormented, we are deeply distraught. We can be more or less deeply disappointed or distressed, but we cannot mean that we are anguished or in despair unless we also implicitly mean to say that we are in some way "deeply" affected. There are some "blind" aspects to grievous misery. In depression, for example, we experience a "darkening" of our world.

We also tend to regard the sadness cluster of emotions as being "heavy." Perhaps we differentiate their depths on the basis of this "weight" or "heaviness."

Honoring is a deep respect. We can respect just about anything we perceive as having value; but we customarily honor the cherished (deeply valued) shared ideals of social traditions (like "Truth, Justice and the American Way"). For example, we honor honesty and regard practices of deception and miscarriages of justice as scandalously dishonorable—not just disrespectful.

Honor has a social dimension; respect is more individual. We understand the notion of self-respect, and we may either respect or honor each other. But do we understand the notion of "self-honor"? I may be or feel "honored," it seems, only by others and "honored" only for doing, or embodying, something of social value.[2]

If honor has a social dimension that accounts for its depth, then reverence has a divine dimension and is in this sense deeper. Reverence is reserved for that which is held in deepest[3] esteem. We may respect or even honor the Reverend, but it would be irreverent (in the same sense as the misplaced reverence of idolatry is) to revere him instead of that for which he "stands."

Is it irreverent to revere Mother Teresa? My own attitude toward her borders on reverence. Those who might feel reverently toward her do so, I suspect, because they view her as a holy person, a living saint. It is then her holiness or saintliness and not she, herself, who is revered.[4]

All forms of respect suggest the keeping of a deferential *distance—and* an observance of *tact*. That is, in this value-rich and ethical cluster of emotions, we see to our touch and keep our distance in an especially thoughtful manner.

We teach children respect for life by teaching them to handle living beings (their pets, their baby brothers) in nonabusive ("make nice") ways. If we honor human rights, we do not like to see them "tampered" with. I disrespect you "as a person" if I coerce you or treat you ("handle" or "manipulate" you) merely as an instrumental "means" to my own "ends"—instead of acknowledging that you have "ends" of your own—purposeful and personal desires, goals, or interests different or *removed* from mine, by denying you the "space" or depriving you of the "room" to carry them out.

Distance is kept and social standing is secured by setting aside "places" of honor. A respect for "ends" (purposes) in the form of a special "handling" also plays a role at the level of reverence. To use a chalice as a spittoon or a crucifix as a doorstop is as irreverent as "making ourselves at home" or "setting up shop" in a church. The pope's ring is kissed; the pope is not. In the "observance" of holy days, rituals, and decorum, there is an implicit keeping of distance—from the commonplaces of the everyday.

Awe is deeper than admiration. We can express admiration but not awe in the form of a compliment. I admire newborns; I am awed by life itself. We tend to stand back or stand apart when or as we admire something or someone. But awe, like reverence, is an experience we describe ourselves as standing "in."

We emotionally experience (some) disbelief whenever we are startled, surprised, amazed or astonished by something. To emotionally experience disbelief in the "deepest" way is to be shocked, or "in shock."

Can we be deeply curious? We usually regard curiosity as a superficial interest. Curiosity may momentarily invite or distract our attention, but interest, which is deeper, holds it. Curiosity is like glancing—sliding or skimming over a surface; interest is like peering. We peer at or into things, to try to "grasp" them. We never glance into things—we only glance onto them—and we cannot grasp very much, even in a "sweeping" glance.

If curiosity is a glance and interest a peering into or at, then fascination is somewhere in between—a sort of spellbound staring. If I find something interesting, I experience myself as motivated to take some further, more comprehensive "hold" or "handle" on it. However, if I find myself fascinated by something (say, the shimmering plays of light on a body of water or the gracefully erotic sensuality of ballet movements), then I experience the object of fascination as spell*binding*, trans*fixing me*—by catching and holding my attention, but not, as in interest, by inviting or motivating it to further "grasp." The fascinating "captures" my attention, but it does not do so in a way that invites my involvement; and, although there is something very "up front" about the fascinating, the fascinating is not superficial—in

Orange

By the firmly intentional way that he blocked my path, I begin to sense in a fuzzy, inchoate way that something is "wrong." I feel vaguely threatened—like "something funny is going on."

[Hindsight reflections: My "situation" is beginning to alter itself. There are differences in my spatial orientation: in what I perceive as being "there" in relation to my "here" and in what I perceive as being near and far. My house, at the same "objective" distance is not my primary focus (it is not "there") any more—this man is. Although he was nearer to me (in "objective" space) than it, he was further away from me (in "lived" space) before he started blocking my path. He and the house "reverse" with respect to how my heres and theres are unified. Also, his crossing the street (from there to here) is now a unified stretch of time-space (with a different *sens* or meaning) which is beginning to intermingle with my own time-space, as I live and experience them. (In Minkowskian terms, there is a clear space/dark space dynamic at play. I am (just) beginning to "slip" from "clear" or indifferent space into "dark space.")

Another depth—where am I? I am somewhere in-between the dissipation of the pleasure of walking in the dusky air and the nightmare that is about to begin. This breach, this break— this "inter-ruption" in the continuity of our activities—this is that sense of a "felt hiatus" that is crucial to an understanding of emotional depth. It can be linked to Merleau-Ponty's notion of the 'chiasm' and to Gibson's notion of the 'occluding edge'. (I am averse to using the expression *readjusting* to describe this experience. For one thing, it is too mechanical. For another, it is too "active." It is not what is felt. Immediately or directly. I prefer de-adjusting; or de-situating because what one immediately or directly feels is "un-hinged." That is, one feels "at a loss" with respect to a prior ground of support; to the "hold" one had on one's ecological space. We can feel this "grip" slipping away sometimes; feel like we are losing ground—and it seems to happen *before* anything like "readjustment" takes place.)

As I now *think* back on it, I think of other path-blocking experiences with people. These may occur in a fooling-around, teasing way that can be comical (Marx Brothers) or as sport ("blocking" in basketball) or spontaneously and inadvertently— when, for example, one has that silly little dance with a stranger on a street as you both take a couple of stabs at trying to walk around each other. In this case, neither person is maliciously meaning to block the other's path. In the situation I am describing, my movements were being anticipated in order to prevent them; and his "blocking" them was not—in the least—funny. I perceive that there is a "motive" behind his actions. It has something to do with me. What it is I do not yet know. But I am picking up on there being something "behind" what he is doing. (The perceiving of something "behind" something else is a perception of depth.) In thinking back on it, I can say that I did experience an incipient real-eye-zation (cf. Daly) that he was not out for a stroll. I sensed a danger or threat in his movements. I sensed that he was not "fooling around."]

I still feel confused about being so abruptly "thrown off track"; but my sense that I am in danger becomes more keen, as he taunts me for a time or two more by continuing to block my movements. He is stalky/stocky. The wool of a ski mask pulls over my eyes; and I see that I can't walk through him, and I can't walk around him. ("This is real; really happening," I think.)

[The thought that this was real or "really" happening was a part of this experience; usually we do not explicitly notice to ourselves that things are real or that things are really happening. James and Husserl talked about "the feeling of the depth of reality." This was a part of what I felt—this is another depth.]
I feel *sealed* into the "situation." Scared.

[I never think of walking backward. The space behind us is "dark space" it is not space we move around in.]
He has my attention. I am "set"—"set up." Cornered. Then, he says,

very thick black magic marker: **Give me your purse**.

Ordinary Paper

I think: ("What?")

[Hindsight Reflections: I am momentarily dumb-founded, as though I do not understand what he is saying; and I have no inclination whatsoever to give him my purse.

I continue to marvel at this—at why I felt no inclination to simply hand over my purse. I never even considered it. Apart from the fact that I am not in the habit of handing my purse over to strangers on the street (any more than I am accustomed to walking backward) and the fact that I had no *time* to think about what was going on or what might happen, perhaps what is also true is that my purse is usually not experienced as an "object" apart from my body. It is in some sense a bodily belonging—not just an object, separate from me that I "have" or "possess." Or, if it is, then it is one to which I am (in a meaningful sense) "attached." Because]

Red

In a flash, I become FURIOUS as he tries to yank its strap from my shoulder. (Thinking something like "How DARE this punk.")

Before I "know" what I am doing, I'm beating him back with all my might, tearing at wool and wildly vacuous (drugged?) eyes. The 'strongest' obscenities I know are hurling from my mouth. I hear myself calling him a motherfucker. I cannot believe my mouth, his mouth. All I see are teeth: squared, spaced.

[Gray Dull Cardboard: There is no color for this experience; I use gray, dull cardboard; this seems right. Dulling the pain?]

I only realize that I am no match (and that he is no "punk") when I feel the blunt of a blow coming down hard on my head. It felt like a rock in a fist. He steps back and shows me a skinny silver knife. He twists it. Focusing on the knife and stunned by the blow to my head, I am slackened out of my righteous rage and in the next sliver of a second, skewered to the ground beneath my feet by a profound feeling lasering its way down the length of my body. A living steel beam thread spliced right in the middle of my slackening movements, and sheared them, stopped them, short. [A flurry of "close" expressions come to my mind here; like close shave, close call, too close for comfort.] I am stayed,   still,   standing on end. I experience this crystalized hair's breadth of a feeling as a ridge-id (l)edge of sheer terror.

Sheer terror. As in, I felt "nothing but" (this feeling of terror and myself to hang onto); as in, the opaque weight of the blow and the blade of the knife making it *transparently* "clear" (to my body) that my very life was "at stake." I must emphasize, 'I' did not tell my body what to do. Through the way this feeling felt, she told me: Don't move; stop moving; you are overpowered; this man might kill you. This experience of terror was also sheer in the sense that I was standing on the only safe ground to be had—that between my feet. All of the rest, for all practical purposes, had (simply?) steeped into space.

On the basis of this felt feeling,[9] I believe that the same sense of "sheer" as is applied to cliffs or (l)edges can be applied to (the depth of) the emotion of terror.

The sense of "sheer" I am relating to terror in this example is also and obviously related to the "shearing" of my movements: to my "staying still" and to my "standing on end." This is apparently as it should be. Terror is, after all, an emotion we also describe ourselves as "freezing in."

We will review this example and analyze the sense of this "freezing" and the sense of this "in" later, in the context of the Flesh ontology and its conceptions of "Depth."

Literary Depictions

The Stranger

> He went on to ask if I had felt grief on that 'sad occasion.' The question struck me as an odd one; . . .
> I answered that, of recent years, I'd rather lost the habit of noting my feelings, and hardly knew what to answer. . . . Anyhow, I could assure him of one thing: that I'd rather Mother hadn't died.
> The lawyer, however, looked displeased. 'That's not enough,' he said curtly.

We expect people to be deeply emotionally affected when their mothers die. This is one reason why, from the very first page of Camus's novel, we disconcertingly detect that something is very "wrong" with its protagonist, Meursault. He is not deeply emotionally affected by his own mother's death. Or, seemingly, by anything else. To Meursault, everything is "all one" or "all the same." Nothing matters or "makes a difference." He says, for example, that he loved his mother and loves his lover, Marie, "like everybody else."

Meursault's is a model flat or "cardboard" affect. His evocative landscape is not differentiated into levels of depth; and he is "strange" or a "stranger" to us because of it.

Meursault's appearing "devoid of the least spark of human feeling"[10] is related to his appearance of being wholly without a moral sense[11]—another "strange" aspect of this character. For much of the novel, he refrains from making moral or value judgments[12]—especially with respect to his own complicity in morally reprehensible situations. He never assumes anything more than a "legal" responsibility for the murder he commits, for instance.[13]

Meursault recovers the habit of noting his feelings and begins to develop in emotional and moral depth only after he is imprisoned for murder and placed on trial for his life. Until he is fleshed out in emotional depth in the second part of the novel—a development that coincides with alterations in his experiencing of space and time—deep emotional experiences "do not mean anything" to Meursault.

For example, when the emotionally flat Meursault is asked if he regrets killing a man, he says: "that what I felt was less regret than a kind of vexation—I couldn't find a better word for it."[14] During his trial, though, his lack of remorse is explained by his wishing to explain "in a quite friendly, almost affectionate way, that I have never been able really to regret anything in all my life. I've always been far too much absorbed in the present moment, or the immediate future, to think back."[15]

The shallow present in which he lives, his unremitting *absorption* in the present *moment*—that is, the way in which he experiences his space and his time—is an important aspect of what else is "wrong" or "strange" about Meursault. His temporal structure is not three dimensional. He simply "is where he is"—at the moment. He does not think back or look ahead. His "here and nows" are isolated from each other and from his "there and thens." Because these punctiform presents are not lived as having future and past horizons, his life, composed of his "fusion" with or absorption in them, appears "all the same" to him.

Meursault's all-the-same here-and-now spatiotemporality is related to the leveling of his evocative landscape and the flattening of his emotional character. The emotional responses we expect from him cannot take root. There is no room for them—no room for grief or remorse or guilt in a time that does not retain the past in the present.

Meursault does not appear to be living in a "living present"—one that "holds the past and future within its thickness."[16] When he does begin to live in this living present though, he does begin to experience "deep" emotions.

These are precipitated by his becoming less "absorbed" in his surroundings and by his grasping "how days could be at once long and short...so distended that they ended up by overlapping on each other." Eventually, Meursault "learned the trick of remembering things,"[17] and he stopped thinking in terms of punctiformly present "days": "only the words 'yesterday' and 'tomorrow' still kept some meaning."[18]

The only incident that later "stands out" in Meursault's recollection of his trial is a deeply emotional one, evoked by the memory of his memories and their overlapping on his present situation.

> toward the end, while my counsel rambled on, I heard the tin
> trumpet of an ice-cream vendor in the street, a small shrill sound
> cutting across the flow of words. And then a rush of memories

went through my mind—memories of a life which was mine no longer and had once provided me with the surest, humblest pleasures: warm smells of summer, my favorite streets, the sky at evening, Marie's dresses and her laugh. The futility of what was happening here seemed to take me by the throat, I felt like vomiting,...[19]

Meursault's development in emotional depth also coincides with a growing awareness of his intervolvement with others—of the social dimensions of his own identity—a dimension that is revealed as Meursault is exposed to "significant" others who are, from a distance, directing or expressing deep emotional feelings toward him. Meursault, eventually, "gets the message"; that is, emotions begin to take or have a depthful "affect" on him. Things begin to "matter" to him, they do begin to "make a difference." At the trial, for example,

- When, "for the first time," he realizes "how all these people loathed" him, it matters. "I felt as I hadn't felt in years. I had a foolish desire to burst into tears";[20]
- When, feeling "a sort of wave of indignation spreading through the courtroom" at hearing of the sort of vigil he kept beside his mother's body, it matters: "for the first time, I understood that I was guilty";[21]
- When, reading the moist eyes and trembling lips of a person who has taken the witness stand in his defense as saying "Well, I've done my best for you, old man. I'm afraid it hasn't helped much. I'm sorry." It matters. It makes a difference: "I didn't say anything, or make any movement, but for the first time in my life I wanted to kiss a man."[22]

It is as though Meursault is learning, for the first time, the ways in which people do "matter" or "make a difference" to each other; and learning, through the emotional expressions of people who matter to his fate, how, himself, to respond with a measure of emotional depth. He "catches on" to their meanings; and he responds to them, emotionally and appropriately.

After being sentenced to public decapitation, "the Stranger" is no longer emotionally "strange" to us. He has precisely the sorts of deep emotional responses we would expect (and some which we would not) from a person sentenced to death and waiting for the sentence to be carried out. His incarceration, his own impending death, the time he has left to live—these matters are eventually and emphatically *not* "all the same" to Meursault. The sealing of his fate makes, in Meursault, an emotional difference: "Try as I might, I couldn't stomach this brutal certitude."[23] At the thought of a future possibility, when he dares to hope that his appeal will be successful, he finds that "the trouble was to calm down that sudden rush of joy racing through my body and even bringing tears to my eyes."[24]

On the eve of his execution, Meursault is "emptied of hope" but he does not despair. He is calm. He is so calm that he appears to be returning to the indifference of a "flat affect." However, this later calm is another "first" for Meursalt; and it is deep:[25] "gazing up at the dark sky spangled with its signs and stars, for the first time, the first, I laid my heart open to the benign indifference of the universe. To feel it so like myself, indeed, so brotherly, made me realize that I'd been happy, and that I was happy still."

Through the stars and in the mournful solace of the dusk, Meursault even begins to identify with his mother—with what she must have felt "in that home where lives were flickering out."

Through the course of this novel, Meursault—who appears initially as a model "flattened affect"—develops an emotional character. As he develops in emotional depth—a development that appears to be related to Camus's fleshing him out spatiotemporally into a living presence and interpersonally into an acknowledgement of his social dimensions—the Stranger becomes more familiar.

Other instances and attributing factors of flat affects can be found in "negative utopian" literature.

Brave New World

Despite their being conditioned to the belief that "Everybody's Happy Nowadays," the emotionally infantile members of Aldous Huxley's *Brave New World* seem to have no deep or genuine emotional experiences. Such experiences appear either to have been trained out of them or artificially induced into them.

For their all-the-same "happiness," they depend on habitually frequent ingestions of "soma," an ideal tranquilizing stimulant, which instantly raises "a quite impenetrable wall between the actual universe and their minds"[26] and produces a refreshing sense of euphoric well-being. Soma takes them "away from it all"—away from their own spatiotemporal existence. However, the planners of this society recognize that these excursions into "happiness" are insufficient. So, for "perfect health," they supplement the soma rations with a chemically simulated form of "emotional depth" on a routine, compulsory basis. "Violent Passion Surrogate. Regularly once a month. We flood the whole system with adrenin. It's the complete physiological equivalent of fear and rage. All the tonic effects of murdering Desdemona and being murdered by Othello, without any of the inconveniences."[27]

All the same, we get the feeling that they are not really emotionally feeling. What they are feeling is either "all in their minds" or "all in their bodies" and not related to emotionally evocative situations—and there seems, to us, to be something "wrong" with these chemically induced short circuits. When emotions are unhinged from the "inconveniences" and depths of an actual situation, the important sense of emotions as responses—as a form of communication, as a contact, between us and the (actual) world—is lost. Furthermore, our ability to behave responsibly and maturely in that world is radically undermined.

ACTION

Bernard Marx and the Savage are the "strangers" in this society. Unlike Meursault, though, the Savage is deeply distressed and grieved by his mother's death.[28] But the society (which decants or man-ufactures babies—"Mother" is apparently the only obscenity in this womb-envious fantasy) is "not accustomed to this kind of thing."

The Savage also argues with the director of this society, which rules by providing constant and dubious forms of diverting pleasures, for the right to be *un*happy; and Bernard Marx longs "to know what passion is." He wants "to feel something strongly"—"all the emotions one might be feeling if things were different."[29]

If things *were* different in this society, its members would not be so stunted in their growth—physically and psychologically. As it is, they do not age or mature.

What is also missing in this society is privacy—the space and the time alone to develop and enjoy intimacy with oneself and with "significant" others. Solitude is suspect; and emotionally "long-drawn" relations, the growth or maturing of emotional feelings between members, is considered "indecorous."

Except for those experienced by the nonconforming characters, emotions in the *Brave New World* are like their tactually titillating movies—"feelies." The (all-male) "Alphas," who "are so conditioned that they do not *have* to be infantile in their emotional behavior" must make "a special effort to conform."[30] Emotional depth is arrested. Refusing to be emotionally infantile is a crime. Those (few) who are incorrigible in this regard are sent, as though they are children being sent to their room, to an "island."

That the depth of an emotion depends on its maturity—its growth over time—and that the unfolding of this depth depends for its existence on the (spatial) allowance or accordance of privacy (which is a form of distance from others) *and* intimacy (which is a form of closeness with others) is what we learn, at least, from the *Brave New World*.

Nineteen Eighty-Four

George Orwell also depicts a society ruled by privacy deprivation. However, the members of *Nineteen Eighty-Four* are not, even superficially, "happy nowadays." Under the constant surveillance of Big Brother, they know that persons who were caught behaving in any unorthodox manner "simply disappeared and were never heard of again."[31]

Unorthodox behavior included "thought-crime"—thinking for oneself. This was detectable through "face crime": "It was terribly dangerous to let your thoughts wander....The smallest thing could give you away...to wear an improper expression on your face...was itself a punishable offense."[32]

A substitute form of emotional depth is also dispensed in *Nineteen Eighty-Four*. The Orwellian analogue to the *Brave New World*'s Violent Passion Surrogate is a daily "social" ritual called "Two Minute Hate":

> The horrible thing about the Two Minute Hate was not that one was obliged to act as a part, but that it was impossible to avoid joining in. Within 30 seconds, any pretense was always unnecessary. A hideous ecstasy of fear and vindictiveness, a desire to kill, to torture, to smash faces with a sledge hammer, seemed to flow through the whole group of people like an electric current, turning one even against one's will into a grimacing, screaming lunatic. And yet the rage that one felt was an abstract, undirected emotion which could be switched from one object to another like the flame of a blowlamp.[33]

Ostensibly, the contagious two-minute experience of expressed "hatred" is directed toward the poster face of Big Brother's enemy. However, as Winston Smith, the protagonist of the novel, realizes: "Your worst enemy...was your own nervous system. At any moment the tension inside you was liable to translate into some visible symptom."[34]

Orwell highlights the perverse state of emotional affairs in this society by focusing on Winston's remembrance of his mother's death:

> The thing that now suddenly struck Winston was that his mother's death, nearly 30 years ago, had been tragic and sorrowful in a way that was no longer possible. Tragedy, he perceived, belonged to the ancient time, to a time when there were still privacy, love, friendship....His mother's memory tore at his heart because she had died loving him...and because somehow, he did not

remember how, she had sacrificed herself to a conception of loyalty that was private and unalterable. Such things, he saw, could not happen today. Today, there were fear, hatred, and pain, but no dignity of emotion, no deep or complex sorrows.[35]

We later see how true these reflections of Winston's are. We see, after he betrays his lover, Julia, that it is impossible for him to die loving either Julia or his mother and that his conception of loyalty—to them and to himself—is neither private nor unalterable. We also see that his torturers have a certain understanding of emotional depth.

Caught in the act of criminal behavior (making love and enjoying it), Winston and Julia are separated from each other and taken to be tortured in the "Ministry of Love." Nevertheless, and for some time, Winston manages to sustain a deep feeling of love and loyalty towards Julia:

he had not stopped loving her; his feeling for her had remained the same.. .[36]

For a moment he had had an overwhelming hallucination of her presence. She had seemed to be not merely with him, but inside him. It was as though she had got into the texture of his skin. In that moment he had loved her far more than he had ever done when they were together and free.[37]

As a last resort and to "minister" to these deep feelings of love, Winston is taken "many meters underground, as deep down as it was possible to go"—to the dreaded Room 101—where the "worst thing in the world" is waiting.[38] There, Winston is exposed to his deepest fear: of rats. He is strapped to a chair, helplessly vulnerable as a cage of them is brought nearer and nearer to his face and is told:

You understand the construction of this cage. The mask will fit over your head, leaving no exit. When I press this other lever, the door of the cage will slide up. These starving rats will shoot out of it like bullets. Have you ever seen a rat shoot through the air? They will leap onto your face and bore straight through it. Sometimes they attack the eyes first. Sometimes they burrow through the cheeks and devour the tongue.[39]

During this dreadful emotional ordeal, face to face with his deepest fear, Winston understands that the only "tiny fragment of hope" of saving his own skin is to interpose Julia's body between himself and the rats. He betrays her. ("Do it to Julia...I don't care what you do to her. Tear her face off, strip her to the bones. Not me! Julia! Not me!"[40]) After he peels this layer of himself-herself off, he experiences himself

> falling backwards, into enormous depths, away from the rats. He was still strapped in his chair, but he had fallen through the floor, through the walls of the building, through the earth, through the oceans, through the atmosphere, through outer space, into the gulfs between the stars—always away, away, away from the rats.[51]

We would say that Winston underwent a "deep emotional experience" during his dreadful ordeal with the rats. Why?

One obvious reason is that he is confronting some of his deepest, in the sense of undermost or underlying, emotions—his love and loyalty for Julia and his fear, presumably, of rats. Orwell emphasizes this sense of emotional depth by situating Room 101 "as deep down as it is possible to go."

Another reason is the way in which Winston's emotional experience, of fear, is intertwined with a spatial one, of distance. This is as it should be, for deep fear or dread is not just a "feeling" about some dangerous or threatening "object"— it is as much a longing to be spatially-distanced from that object: a desire to keep some dreadful happening in the future from "closing in." Because Winston cannot physically flee the situation, his only recourses are to his imagination or to "blacking out," to insert distance between himself and that which he fears.

However, there are paradoxical interplays of distance and proximity (what we will later analyze as "reversibilities") to be noted here, for Winston has not really gotten himself "away, away, away" from the rats. After this experience, he is "closer" to the "rats" than he ever was (and further away from Julia). That is, Winston has only gotten "away" from the rats, is no longer plagued with the fear of them, by *identifying* with them, by becoming one himself—by "ratting" on Julia.

In Room 101, the worst thing in the world happens. One's deepest fears are realized. Winston's deep*est* fear, we later realize, was not "of rats." His deepest fear was of becoming one himself, which he does.

So, the enormous distance is not a distance between Winston and the rats. The depths are really between who, before this experience, Winston *was* and who, after this experience, he later *is* or *becomes*.

After undergoing this experience, Winston *has* "lost face"—his capacity for face crime. He no longer appears to be the person he was,

and there is no longer a "mask" between him and "the rats"—a mask
that he must struggle with to "keep up the appearance" that he is "one
of them." After he betrays Julia, he becomes "one of them." He knows
it and so do others. The knowledge seems to vaguely "gnaw at him"—
"hovering close to his face" and in "a smell that clung to his nostrils."
Other members of the society (who are still deeply fearful of "rats")
do not care "to be seen sitting too close to him";[42] and the "thought
police" no longer bothers to "watch" him.

After their respective betrayals, Winston and Julia admit to each
other that it is impossible to feel the same way. No longer "under his
skin," Julia's body appears to Winston to have been changed into
something "corpse-like," rigid and awkward to handle: "more like stone
than flesh."[43] At the thought of sexual intimacy with her *now*, Winston's
own flesh freezes "with horror."

Winston's face is bloated and colored by the effects of an alcohol
addiction that also blocks his capacity to "fix his mind on any one
subject for more than a few moments at a time" so that he cannot
sustain, differentiate between or even understand the emotions that
simply "flare up and fade" within him.[44] And he can no longer tell,
when he experiences "successive layers of feelings" which layer was
"undermost," struggling inside him.[45]

The cessation of Winston's emotional struggles is precipitated by
his gazing up at the "enormous face" of Big Brother at the very end
of the novel. The "long hoped-for bullet" deadens his brain; and as
Winston finally stops "thinking for himself" a new "undermost" or
deepest emotional layer—a *love* of Big Brother—surfaces.

What we cannot help but notice in this text is that the emergence
of this emotional depth coincides with the coming to the fore of a
perceptual depth: the seeing of his malefactor in a new and benevolent
light. Winston says that it has taken him forty years to see "the loving
breast" and "what kind of smile" was "there" all along, hidden *beneath*
Big Brother's moustache.

The "final, indispensable, healing change" in Winston is his
betrayal of (which is described as a "victory over") himself. In a tragically
dramatic act of self-deception, he participates in his own destruction.
Ultimately, he loves Big Brother—and—as the novel comes to a close,
Winston Smith, as the character that we knew him to be "simply
disappears and is never heard from again."

We commonly use the expression *deeply emotionally affected* to
connote some perceptible and relatively longstanding transformation
in identity. Any emotional experience about which it seems appropriate
to say that the emotional experiencer is "not entirely the same person"

afterward is a "deep emotional experience." Winston Smith in *Nineteen Eighty-Four* has a "deep emotional experience" in this important sense.

Sophie's Choice

The deepest emotional experience in *Sophie's Choice* is her being forced, against her will, to "choose" (quickly and before they both are) which one of her two children will be sent to a Nazi crematorium in order to spare the life of the other. The situation is anguishing and unbearably "heavy"; Sophie is "crushed": "Her thought processes dwindled, ceased. Then she felt her legs crumple." She screams that she "cannot choose" and "She could not believe any of this. She could not believe that she was now kneeling on the hurtful, abrading concrete, drawing her children toward her so smotheringly tight that she felt that their flesh might be engrafted to hers even through layers of clothes. Her disbelief was total, deranged."

But she does "choose." She wrenches her daughter's body away from her own in order to save the life of her son.

> She would forever retain a dim impression that the child had continued to look back, beseeching. But because she was now almost completely blinded by salty, thick, copious tears she was spared whatever expression Eva wore, and she was always grateful for that. For in the bleakest honesty of her heart she knew that she would never have been able to tolerate it, driven nearly mad as she was by her last glimpse of that vanishing small form.[46]

Sophie's (lifelong) gratitude over being blinded by tears and consequentially spared the articulation of expression on her daughter's face reminds us (as the notion of "face crime" does in *Nineteen Eighty-Four*) how visibly apparent emotional expression can be and how painfully a sight can "tear at our hearts."

Sophie's choice torments her for the rest of her life, and she is altered by the experience. No longer "the woman she was," she eventually becomes, as an emotionally feeling person, numbed. Her heart—"outraged as desperately as the mind can conceive"—is hardened: "It has been hurt so much, it has turned to stone."[47] Years later, in remorseful despair, she commits suicide.

It is also noteworthy that Sophie's first response to the "choice" she is compelled to make is that of a total disbelief. ("She could not believe any of this.") This shock to the system of our beliefs—to the extent that one questions the reality "behind" them—appears to me to be another characteristic of deep emotional experience. Sometimes, it is as though sleep and waking space are intermingled. A particularly unpleasant experience is "like a nightmare"; a particularly pleasant one is like a "dream come true."

Another typical response to the emotionally overwhelming situation is to faint or "pass out." This caving-in of perceptual experience serves the same purpose, in cases of extreme emotional distress, as the hardening or numbing of Sophie's heart does. It prevents us from thinking or feeling at all. Just as there are limits to physical pain, there are limits to our perceptual capacities and our emotional endurance. If one experiences too much, one winds up or "crosses over" into not perceiving, not feeling anything at all. or · · ·

Depth carries the meaning not only of distance, but also of an occlusive or obstructive thickness—a "stopping" of sight or touch. Emotional experiences in which we are feeling so much that we cannot feel at all are "deep" in this sense. They return us, perceptually and spatially, to the realm of a tangibly "dark" space—a space in which we "black out" and in which we are, so to speak, "beyond feeling."[48]

At its most glaring, reality can blind us and erode our sensitivities. This "dark" dimension of emotional experience is epitomized by Oedipus in *Oedipus Rex*.

Oedipus Rex

Oedipus, discovering that he has, in truth though in ignorance, murdered his father and married his mother, experiences deep remorse or sorrow. He does not just feel his past actions to be superficially embarrassing. He experiences his own identity, in the light of his sexual intimacies with his mother, to be deeply shameful.

The first move that he makes to "do" something about it, is to violently blind himself. Oedipus never regrets this move. He contends that it was a "good design," that it is better, as he says, "to stuff the senses of my carcass dumb."[49]

It is unbearable or "too much" for Oedipus to see his wife as his mother, his mother as his wife, just as it was "too much" for Sophie to be forced to choose between her children. Both are "torn." Like Sophie's heart, which has "turned to stone" and "crosses over" into feeling nothing at all, Oedipus stops up his sight and "crosses over" into seeing nothing at all.

In dashing out his eyes, Oedipus makes a sight, a *spectacle* of himself. His (simultaneously) seeing *and* not seeing becomes what is seen. Blind, Oedipus is a spectacular reminder that there are invisible, hidden dimensions to everything we see and all we claim to clearly "know," and that the ex-posures of some of reality's hidden dimensions are frequently evocative of deep emotional experiences.

We shall return to this "dark" dimension of lived obscurity, and we shall analyze the emotionally depthful significances of Oedipus blinding himself in more detail later. We can mention here, however, that sight is connected, to and through our visibility, to shame[50] and that eyes are thought to be revealing of who we are. In the course of blinding himself, Oedipus undergoes an alteration in identity, a change in his sense of self.

It is also noteworthy that sight is the mode of perception most related to distance, and the transgression of incest is precisely a violation of distance. In blinding himself, "all incest sealed" in Jocasta's womb, Oedipus "reflects" this breach of intimacy: his failure to maintain a proper or socially prescribed distance between himself and his mother.

Summary

In contrasting flat affects with deep emotional experiences, we find that we already seem to know quite a bit about "emotional depth."

From the analysis of experienced terror (and of reverential "observance" and Winston's dread of the rats in *Nineteen Eighty-Four*), we have seen that literal senses of "depth"—real "distances" can be attached to certain emotions and emotional experiences. There are, in lived space-time, literally "depthful" aspects to emotions.

We have noted some "dark" dimensions to emotional experience— some space of nonfeeling; and we have seen that certain emotions (like shock, love and rage) are regarded as "blind." We have also seen that "deeper" emotions (wonder and anger vs. curiosity and irritation) engage us cognitively and morally in a way that the more superficial ones do not.

From our ordinary speech, we have discovered that the "deeper" the emotion, the more appropriate it is to apply the locution *in* to it. We say, for example, that we are "in love" or "in mourning," "enraged," "in wonder," or "in terror."

In later chapters, I distinguish this sense of *in* from the *in* of a "container" view of space by calling it "the in of in-mergion." I do this in an attempt to identify this sense of *in* with the sense of *en* in Merleau-Ponty's "en-être" (being-of) thesis and to connect it to what I will be calling "e-mergions" of perceived or evocative depths.

The "dark" aspects of emotional experiences will eventually be connected to the Flesh ontology's thesis of the invisible ground of visibility and its notion that all feeling takes place through what is, on principle, unfeelable.

As we shall see, the maintenance of distance is a crucial element of the Flesh ontology. That differentiations in emotions and emotional "depths" are related to divergencies in distance (and to the maintenance of some happy "medium")—between our selves and the world and between our selves and others—is a recurrent theme in several of the examples. It appears that there can be too much of this lived distance, and there can be too little.

(Phenomenologically, our sense of "self" is that we are *simultaneously* open to and closed off from others; simultaneously intermingled with *and* distanced from them. Similarly, our "lived" experience of the world is that we belong to it or are of it, but are not it.)

With his ontology of "Flesh" and its conception of depth as a distanced contact, Merleau-Ponty tried to make some philosophical sense of this. After discussing the ways in which it does, we will return, in Part II, to the task of analyzing what is meant by emotional depth.

2

Depth: Recovering the Hidden Dimension

Four centuries after the 'solutions' of the Renaissance and three centuries after Descartes, depth is still new, and it insists on being sought, not 'once in a lifetime,' but all through life.

—Maurice Merleau-Ponty, "Eye and Mind"

Introduction

Depth perception, our ability to see at a distance and in the bounty of the "third" dimension, is puzzling. Because my thesis involves the claims that perceived and emotional depths are interrelated and that some literal senses of depth can be found to apply to emotional experience, this chapter and the next are devoted to explanations of what and how we can perceive in depth.

The present chapter consists of summary descriptions of the commensurate ways in which James J. Gibson ecologically revisions[1] and Maurice Merleau-Ponty phenomenologically "resuscitates"[2] the vision of depth. As we shall see, both thinkers stress the role embodiment plays in our understanding of space and are extremely critical of "air" or empty-space theories of depth perception. Further continuities between Gibson's 'Ground' or 'Surface' theory of perception and Merleau-Ponty's 'Flesh' ontology of perception are noted throughout the text and are summarized at the end of the next chapter, which is devoted to the Flesh ontology and its conceptions of depth.

Although some of their affective applications are mentioned in this theoretical, "groundwork" on Depth and Embodiment, the notions of embodiment and the several senses of depth gathered in this first part of the text are more specifically and concretely applied to emotional experience in the second.

Depth as the Perception of Ecological "Affordances"

(To perceive the world is to coperceive oneself.). .The awareness of the
world and of one's complementary relations to the world are not separable.

—James J. Gibson, *The Ecological Approach to Visual Perception*

How we—and even if we—visually perceive depth is a matter of
controversy. The empiricist tradition has maintained that depth,
construed as relative distances or the "thick" third dimension, is not
directly or immediately visible. In developing Berkeley's position in *A
New Theory of Vision* of distance as "a line endwise to the eye," registering
at only one point on the retinal surface, empiricists thought it necessary
to "add" depth to a primarily flat and static image, produced by a two-
dimensional array of radiant energy on the retinal surface, through the
"association" of learned, nonvisual cues with tactile and kinesthetic
information. Empiricism, that is, conceived visual depth as being
derivatively perceived.[3] James J. Gibson's reinterpretation of visual depth
from an ecological perspective[4] challenges critical aspects of the
empiricist account.

Gibson contends that the assumption that perception begins with
a flat-form retinal picture is fallacious and that, accordingly, the notion
that "cues" add the third dimension is "worthless" and reliant on a
"mythical" distinction between two-dimensional and three-dimensional
vision.[5]

He affirms that as a line endwise to the eye, distance "as such,"
"of itself," or "extending through the air" is invisible. He denies,
however, that distance is a line endwise to the eye and names his
ecological approach to space perception the "ground theory" to
distinguish it from traditional "air theories." Regarding distance as a
line, he contends, confuses "abstract geometrical space with the living
space of the environment."[6] According to him, "the third dimension
is not lost in the retinal image since it was never in the environment
to begin with."[7]

A Gibsonian environment consists of a medium (air for terrestial
creatures), substances (solids and liquids), and surfaces, which separate
substances from the medium.[8] The medium, not to be confused with
abstract empty space, is filled with illumination, an omnidirectional,
steady-state, reverberating flux of light, bouncing back and forth
between surfaces, called _ambient light_[9]. Ambient light, coming to every

point, environing or surrounding at every point "could not exist in empty space, but only in an environment of reflecting surfaces."[10] That is, ambient light, depends on surfaces and is thus of a second order—an effect of radiant light. Whereas radiant light is a set of rays, diverging and propagating from an energy source, not different in different directions and unstructured, ambient light can be thought as a set of solid angles, converging to a point of observation, different in different directions, having a structure, and as "simply there"—all around. The import of these differences, in Gibson's view, is that, while radiant light is energy, "ambient light can be information."[11]

Gibson conceives distance as extending along the ground (the surface of the earth) and contends that recession along the ground is directly visible.[12] It is "projected as a *gradient* of the decreasing optical size and increasing optical density" of the ground's features.[13] Thus, one Gibsonian reinterpretation of depth is *a directly visible surface recession*.

We find other senses of depth in Gibson's ecological approach. As Gibson remarks, depth is a "loose term."

> If *depth* means the dimension of an object that goes with height and width, there is nothing special about it. Height becomes depth when the object is seen from the top, and width becomes depth when the object is seen from the side. If depth means distance from *here*, then it involves self-perception and is continuously changing as the observer moves about.[14]

A distinguishing aspect of ecological optics is that points of observation are to be thought of as moving. Depth as *distance from here* is an intrinsically dynamic concept. Because animals are mobile observers, observation implies movement.[15] Gibson's experiments are designed to study invariants in the changing array of "ambulatory vision."[16]

We walk around. We also walk back and forth. Our locomotion is thus reversible. From this reversibility of locomotion, Gibson develops his general principle of *reversible occlusion*, a principle that involves *the interchangability of the hidden and unhidden* as observers move. According to this principle, "Any movement of a point of observation that hides previously unhidden surfaces has an opposite movement that reveals them."[17]

Occlusion is a key term in the Gibsonian approach and underlies another of Gibson's criticism of traditional optics. Their projective geometry leaves occlusion out of account. According to Gibson, this fallacious omission "lies deep in our conception of empty space, especially the so-called third dimension of space."[18] His principle of occlusion leads Gibson to another reintepretation of visual depth: "What we see is not depth as such but *one thing behind another.*"[19]

How we can see something behind something else or how we can see covered, as well as covering, surfaces is puzzling in its implication that we can see what is (partially and temporarily) hidden. Gibson does not mean that we can see the unseen. He does, however, suggest that ("one can perceive surfaces that are temporarily out of sight" and that information for covered and covering surfaces "is implicit in the edges that separate the surfaces" and presumably "becomes evident over time, with changes in the array."[20])

Occluding edges are those taken with reference to an observer that cause surfaces to hide one another.[21] An occluding edge has a paradoxical status: "It both separates and connects the hidden and unhidden surface, both divides and unites them."[22] (We will later refer to this paradox of depth as a "unity through disparity.") In Gibson's view, the hidden and the unhidden, the invisible and the visible, are continuous. "To perceive the persistences of surfaces that are out of sight is also to perceive their coexistence with those that are in sight."[23]

Gibson believes the discovery of occluding edges to be "radically inconsistent" with traditional depth theory in its implication of the temporal-perceptual persistence of occluded surfaces. For traditional theories, a *hidden* surface cannot be *perceived*: "it can be recalled, imagined, conceived, or perhaps known, but not perceived."[24] To counter this assumption, Gibson describes an experiment[25] wherein

> the surface that was being covered was seen to persist after being concealed, and the surface that was being uncovered was seen to pre-exist before being revealed. The hidden surface could not be described as remembered in one case or expected in the other. A better description would be that it was perceived retrospective and prospectively. It is certainly reasonable to describe perception as extending into the past and future, but note that to do so violates the accepted doctrine that perception is *confined* to the present.[26]

So depth has, in Gibson's view, a temporal extension.

Gibson distinguishes *the occlusion of superposition,* a surface covered by something placed in front of it, from the *self-occlusion of solidity or voluminosity.* The *continuity* of surfaces "extending behind" or "bending under" others is *localized at* an occluding edge. The perception of superposition involves a *disruption* of the adjacent surface being covered or uncovered (through deletions or accretions in the structure of the array); whereas, as evidenced, for example, in the interchangability of width and depth, the perception of solidity or voluminosity involves the *transformation* of *near sides turning into far while far sides are turning into near.*[27]

Near-far visual perceptions have anchoring limits: "The nose projects at the maximum of nearness just as the horizon projects at the maximum of farness."[28] An occluding edge, the edge of the nose, provides an absolute "distance from here."[29] The horizon, although it is not an occluding edge, is analagous to it "in being one of the loci at which things go out and come into sight."[30] Gibson provides evidence to show that "even when the earth-sky horizon is hidden," an implicit horizon is "always there," wherever one goes, as an invariant feature of terrestial, ambulatory vision. Thus, even the anchoring near-far limits are continuous and related in a mutual, linked complementarity.[31]

This linked complementarity finds expression in Gibson's theory of affordance. In its hypothetical implication "that the 'values' and 'meanings' of things in the environment can be directly perceived,"[32] this theory is the most philosophically interesting (and radical) aspect of his ecological approach to perception.

Affordance is a doubly-referential expression coined by Gibson and is "wholly inconsistent" with any form of psychophysical dualism.

> The *affordances* of the environment are what it *offers* to the animal, what it *provides* or *furnishes*, either for good or ill. The verb *to afford* is found in the dictionary, but the noun *affordance* is not. I have made it up. I mean by it something that refers both to the environment and the animal in a way that no existing term does. It implies the complementarity of the animal and the environment.[33]

> An important fact about the affordances of the environment is that they are in a sense objective, real and physical, unlike values and meanings, which are often supposed to be subjective, phenomenal and mental. But, actually an affordance is neither an objective property nor a subjective property; or it is both if you like. An affordance cuts across the dichotomy of subjective-objective and helps us to understand its inadequacy. It is equally a fact of the environment and a fact of behavior. It is both physical and psychical, yet neither. An affordance points both ways, to the environment and to the observer.[34]

For example, the well-known visual cliff experiments[35] are ordinarily interpreted as suggesting that depth perception is innate. For Gibson, however, "the sight of a cliff is *not* a case of perceiving the third dimension" but a case of perceiving its affordance. Gibson has us notice "that the perception of the ground and the co-perception of the self are inseparable in this situation. One's body *in relation to the ground* is what gets attention." A cliff is "a falling-off place. . .a negative affordance for locomotion, a place where the surface of support ends."[36] Gibson reinterprets perceptions of depth as perceptions of affordances.

> An affordance is for a species of animal, a layout *relative to* the animal and commensurate with its body. A cliff is a drop-off that is large relative to the size of the animal, and a step is a drop-off that is small relative to its size. . . .What animals need to perceive is not layout as such but the affordances of the layout. . . .Consider the difference between the edge of a horizontal surface and the edge of a wall. You go *over* the former whereas you can *go around* the latter. Both are dihedral angles, and both are occluding edges. But the meanings of the two kinds of 'depth' are entirely different.[37]

Subtly, with his theory of affordances, Gibson has transformed depth into *meaning*. We do not perceive "depth as such." What we perceive is *the significance of surfaces in relation to our body*.

Gibson admits that his ecological approach to visual perception is undeveloped and radically controversial. However, by reinterpreting, from an ecological and ambulatory perspective, what and how we see in depth, Gibson has nevertheless provided an account of "lived depth" or lived distance to contrast with traditional, Berkeleyian-based accounts—those that attempt to build visual depth out of points and "lines endwise to the eye" by adding "cues."

It is true, however, even in Gibson's view, that "depth as such" is *not* directly visible. However, the invisibility of an isolated, abstract, objectified depth—depth as "distance in the air"—is considered irrelevant at the ecological level of a "cluttered" substance-medium-surface environment filled with the accessible, available information provided by ambient light.

What is important about Gibson's ecological approach is that surfacings of depth are thought to be directly visible as observers move around in the living space of their ecological habitats. These surfacings of depth, temporally extended into the past and future, become directly visibly apparent through surface recessions, through the interchangably linked dimensions of near-and-far, at occluding edges and through the reversible occlusions of solidity and superposition, and finally, through the direct, nondichotomous perception of one's body in relation to the ground; that is, through affordances.

In Gibsonian optics, an exemplary, extraordinary affordance is the terrestrial horizon. "This stationary great circle. . .is neither subjective nor objective, it expresses the *reciprocity* of observer and environment."[38] As optimal distance from there, invariantly anchoring and inextricably linked to the movements of our body's distance from here, it affords visual depth perception.   *HORIZONAL FOCUS ASPECT   — ECOLOGICAL AS PERCEPTUAL Δ AGENT.*

Depth as Copresent Implication

In the *Phenomenology of Perception*, Merleau-Ponty approaches the problem of the visibility of depth through the problem of oriented space: the problem of how we can "take the world's bearings," of how "an object can appear to us as the 'right way up' or 'inverted' and what these words mean."[39]

Citing experiments wherein these spatial levels disintegrate (when special glasses or mirrors invert or slant the visual field) and rematerialize (when "motor intensions and perceptual field join forces"[40]), he argues: "We cannot understand. . .the experience of space either in terms of the consideration of contents or that of some pure unifying activity. We are confronted with a third spatiality. . .which is neither that of things in space, nor that of spatializing space. . . .We need an absolute within the sphere of the relative. . . ."[41]

This "absolute within the sphere of the relative" is space regarded as a precession, as essentially preceding itself or "always already constituted."[42] Like the terrestial horizon in Gibsonian optics, this space is invariantly "there." *(Arcté)*

If space is essentially a precession, then one level will always presuppose some other.[43] But Merleau-Ponty does not regard his account of how perception can come by absolute directions, viz., an account that presupposes them at the source of spatial experience, as "a mere expression of defeat."[44] For inquiries into "why being is oriented, why existence is spatial," and why our body's "co-existence with the world magnetizes experience and induces a direction in it"[45] are without sense in Merleau-Ponty's phenomenology of perception. Merleau-Ponty regards spatial orientation as an *essential* aspect of every (meaningful) perception. We cannot step beyond spatial orientation to understand spatial orientation. For one thing, there is no beyond.[46] For another, orientation is connected to sense. "Thus, since every conceivable being is related either directly or indirectly to the perceived world, and since

WHAT IS THE SOURCE OF PERCEPTION?
THE BODY → mind/BODY (M/B)
'SENSORIUM/SENSE'

the perceived world is grasped only in terms of direction, we cannot dissociate being from oriented being, and there is no occasion to 'find a basis for space' or to ask what is the level of all levels."[47]

On principle, the primordial spatial level, "on the horizon of all our perceptions," can never be reached. As the first level, it cannot be spatially particularized, because it cannot be referred to a preceding anchoring setting *"anywhere"* to be expressly perceived. The primordial spatial level is always already there, but it is in no *particular* place. So, although it is "behind" all our observations, or is presupposed in every perception, it cannot, itself, be expressly perceived or "grasped."

Because this primordial level cannot be oriented "in itself," spatial orientation is presupposed in the body's "marking out" a place in the world from the time of its coming-to-Be. According to Merleau-Ponty, our first "hold" on the world is that of *blind adhesion*. Although we lose sight of this "contingency" as we take our succeeding bearings, it is nevertheless passed on to each and "endows every subsequent perception of space with its meaning." Existentially then, in our blind occupation of it, space has a basis in our "facticity." "Space and perception generally represent, at the core of the subject, the fact of his birth, the perpetual contribution of his bodily being, a communication with the world more ancient than thought. That is why they saturate consciousness and are impenetrable to reflection."[48]

This obscure "communication with the world more ancient than thought" is occasioned by our coming to *perceptible*-bodily being. As Merleau-Ponty later put it (when he "reverses" his body-"subjective" perspective), it is occasioned by our coming to "belong to" or be "of" the 'Flesh' of the world.

According to Merleau-Ponty, "The possession of a body implies the ability to change levels and [in its ancient communication with it] to 'understand' space."[49] He also interprets the orientation experiments to highlight the critical role the "lived" moving body (the body as a system of possible actions or an "I am able to") plays in establishing spatial orientation. In his view, once the embodied subjects *inhabit their spectacle*, once their actions coincide with their objectives, a new orientation, a new *sens*, can be said to fall, magnetically, into place. A newly positioned spatial level is thus or then defined by Merleau-Ponty as "a certain hold of my body on the world." This "holding" can be thought, without question begging, in terms of direction.

An inverted visual field that a person does not live in, cannot get involved in, cannot move about or manipulate objects in, appears "unreal." One reason for the visual unreality is because inverted objects are deprived of their significance or *sens** for a gaze. That is, a *moving gaze*, favoring certain directions and angles, does not recognize a visual object "unless it comes up against its details in a certain irreversible order," unless it takes "a certain hold on it," unless it is "able to follow on its surface a certain perceptual route."[50]

An upside-down world is a novel perceptual experience. That we can eventually find our bearings in such a world so that even it can be "set right" and eventually inhabited or "lived in" is the startling finding of the orientation experiments. The disoriented subjects in the orientation experiments are of course not returned to the novelty of being born—primordially encountering Being or the onset of perception. However, the experiment does obviously disrupt innumerable "perceptual routes" and learned bearings since then. It is therefore not unreasonable to suppose that in its initial "sens"-lessness, the experimental conditions return the subjects to a visual space or a visual orientation experienced during a much earlier time of their lives. If we think of how babies must struggle before they achieve a balanced upright posture or note how toddlers must make a concerted effort simply to grasp certain objects as they coordinate with the world— how difficult it is for them to grasp a cup and learn to drink from it, for example—we begin to get the picture here.

Although he critiques other interpretations of the orientation experiments, Merleau-Ponty never really spells out his own. He just offers his thesis that space is essentially precessive and that, because there is always another spatial "level" to fall back on, any being, through its participation in space in coming-to-Be, is always, already "oriented" being. His point appears to be that these experiments should not be interpreted as though the subjects are ever *non*oriented, for being oriented or being situated in relation to an environment is thought by Merleau-Ponty, as it is in Gibson, as an essential structure of embodied being.

This essential structure of situated embodiment is also expressed in emotional experience.

> Between our emotions, desires and bodily attitudes, there is not
> only a contingent connection or even an analogical relationship:
> if I say that in disappointment I am downcast, it is not only

---

*The French expression *sens* is ambiguous. It means direction or way, sense (in the sense of "sense" experience— sentience or feeling); and sense (in the sense of significance or meaning). Merleau-Ponty intentionally exploits this ambiguity.

because it is accompanied by gestures expressing prostration in virtue of the laws governing nervous mechanisms, or because I discover between the objects of my desire and my desire itself the same relationship as existing between an object placed high above me and my gesture toward it. The movement upwards as a direction in physical space, and that of my desire toward its objective are mutually symbolical because they both express the same essential structure of our being, being situated in relation to an environment, of which we have already stated that such structure alone gives significance to the directions up and down in the physical world.[51]

Merleau-Ponty also links the sense (*sens*) of objects to the orientation or direction of a body's habitual "hold" on them.[52] Again, he appears to be subscribing to a view similar to Gibson's; namely, that the "affordances" or meanings of things in our "habitats" are perceptible (for moving gazes in ambulatory vision) through the significances of surfaces in relation to our body, the *sens* of our body in relation to the surface/ground. We may apply some of these thoughts to an example from Chapter 1, that of Oedipus coming to the awareness, the climactic realization, that his wife, Jocasta, is his mother.

The body's habitual orientation or "hold" on the body of a wife differs from the body's prenatal "hold" in the body of a mother. Oedipus apprehends the "sens" of Jocasta as his mother by dashing out his eyes and enveloping himself in the darkness of a womblike "ground." The act of blinding himself is his symbolic return to that state of blind adhesion—to the fact of his birth. Assuming the (fetal) position of himself as her son, he inhabits the spectacle of Jocasta as his mother. Thus he comes to the "blind" and embodied apprehension of the "sens" of his "situation" in relation to her and the "sens" of his own identity.

To return to the *Phenomenology*; Merleau-Ponty is led, from his discussion of a primordial spatial level and the orientation experiments, directly into a detailed discussion of depth perception.[53] In this section of the text, he critiques Berkeley's conception of depth as a "line endwise to the eye" and argues for depth's visibility as a "hold" on a bodily and temporal basis. We shall defer, for the time being, the question of whether Merleau-Ponty regarded depth as the primordial spatial level.[54]

Merleau-Ponty's most forceful objection to the invisibility of Berkeley's "objectified" depth is that, in tacitly equating depth with breadth seen from the side, depth is deprived of its "originality"—its originality not in the sense of its being the primordial level but in the sense of its differentiation from length and breadth.

Berkeley's argument, made quite explicit, runs roughly like this. What I call depth is in reality a juxtaposition of points, making it comparable to breadth. I am simply badly placed to see it. I should see it if I were a spectator looking on from the side....What makes depth invisible for me is precisely what makes it visible for the spectator as breadth: the juxtaposition of simultaneous points in one direction which is that of my gaze. The depth which is declared invisible is, therefore, a depth already identified with breadth and, this being the case, the argument would lack even a semblance of consistency.[55]

(The argument also begs the question of whether space is isotropic.[56])

Merleau-Ponty does not mean to argue that the depth-breadth equivalence is "objectively" incorrect. But he does mean, as a phenomenologist, to "bracket" this assimilation of depth to breadth to discern its "originality"; and he does, as we have already seen, object to any approach to spatial perception that would dissociate being from oriented being.

In order to treat depth as breadth viewed in profile, in order to arrive at a uniform space, the subject must leave his place, abandon his point of view on the world, and think himself into a sort of ubiquity. For God, who is everywhere, breadth is immediately equivalent to depth. Intellectualism and empiricism do not give us any account of the human experience of the world; they tell us what God might think about it.[57]

It is clear that Merleau-Ponty is discussing depth as we experience it, a depth in which a perceiver is implied and one that is therefore akin to Gibson's sense of depth as "distance from here." Straightaway, Merleau-Ponty asserts that depth "announces a certain indissoluable link between things and myself by which I am placed in front of them."[58] This initial description of depth is put into service in his critique of traditional cue theory.

Merleau-Ponty does not, as Gibson does, regard the "cues" for perceptual depth as "worthless." Instead, he points out that interpretations of the significance of the cues are always already spatially informed. For example, they are generally conditioned by the knowledge of my body's "standing in front of this world like a mirror"; or, more specifically, in eye convergence, by presupposing "an orientation toward an object placed at a distance."[59] So, "The 'signs' which *ex hypothesi*, ought to acquaint us with the experience of space can, therefore, convey the idea of space only if they are already involved in it."[60]

Circularity notwithstanding, cues for depth are interestingly problematic for Merleau-Ponty. As a phenomenologist, he is supposed to describe depth just as it appears in our experience. As it happens, cues do not expressly appear when we are perceiving at a distance. As a psychologist, aware of stereoscopic experiments and illusions of depth, he must nevertheless acknowledge that cues are present in the experience of depth. As a philosopher, he is obliged to make sense of all this, but he wants to avoid regarding cues as either "causes" or "signs" of an invisible depth. So he concludes that we experience cues "non-thetically"; that is, they are withdrawn to an "implicatory" status.

According to Merleau-Ponty, the relationship between cues and depth is one of reciprocal significance. Cues imply and are implied by distance. Cues tacitly "motivate" or express our vision of depth (they are "already certain ways of looking at a distance"); and are motivated by depth (as "they already contain it in their significance"). Cues and distance are not independently definable, but, in the experience of depth, they are "mutually synonymous"—"not because the subject of perception posits objective relations between them, but on the contrary, because he does not posit them separately and therefore has no need to unify them expressly."[61]

He exemplifies this by reconsidering size constancy.[62] At the (primary) level of experienced perceptual depth, "apparent size" is not apparent as a size, as a measurable dimension, not even one of equality. I might "cause size to appear where hitherto it had no place," but only by violating the unity of the perceptual field by isolating some object from the perceived context and measuring it against some other object. For example, unless isolate him in order to measure his "apparent size," a person walking away from me is not "smaller" or even the "same size." All we can say of the experience as we perceptually live it is that he is "the same man seen from further away"—he becomes progressively less distinguishable, less articulate. My gaze has a less of a "hold" on him—"he presents fewer and less identifiable points on which my gaze can fasten..." Because none of the various "apparent sizes" is ever posited at the level of the lived experience, "it is not necessary to link them together in a synthesis." "If we want to talk about a synthesis, it will be, as Husserl says, a 'transition synthesis,' which does not link disparate perspectives, but brings about the 'passage' from one to the other."[63] For we " 'have' the retreating object, we never cease to 'hold' it and to have a grip on it..." To Merleau-Ponty, increasing distance "expresses merely that the thing is beginning to slip away from the grip of our gaze and is less closely allied to it. <u>Distance is what distinguishes this loose and approximate grip from the complete grip which is proximity.</u>"[64]

In considering stereoscopic images and ambiguous figures<u>(depth</u> ✳ is further described as a moment "<u>in arriving at a perceptual faith in one single thing.</u>"[65] <u>Depth effects or achieves a "unity through disparity."</u>)

In the following demonstration one can, if one sets one's *eyes* to it, experience this fusing in depth. This is what I call a *unity through disparity.* Depth is already implicitly there in the monocular images that replicate the distance of our eyes from each other and in our holding the images in front of them. Note especially how it takes time for your eyes to "take up" or achieve this unity and how, from the "moment" you grasp it, it is "held." (While I am in the midst of this experience, I can also detect some wavy or diffuse voluminosity. Can you?)

THE DEPTH/METAPHOR
RELATION

FIGURE 2.1

Demonstration
A Stereoscopic Picture

Take a piece of blank cardboard that is about 20 cm wide and line it up along the dotted line in the figure. Rest your nose on the cardboard edge that is the closest to you. Each eye should stare at just the one figure on the appropriate side fo the cardboard. Try to fuse the two separate images into a single, unified image. You may find it helpful to try converging your eyes by looking slightly cross-eyed. When you achieve a single image, it should look three-dimensional.

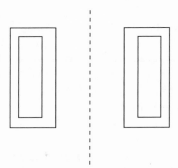

Finally, Merleau-Ponty is ready to "resuscitate" the originality of
depth. Whereas length and breadth are dimensions of juxtaposition,
depth is not built up "partes extra partes," but reveals itself in an
implicatory copresence:

> This being simultaneously present in experiences which are
> nevertheless mutually exclusive, this implication of one in the
> other, this contraction into one perceptual act of a whole possible
> process, constitute the originality of depth. It is the dimension
> in which things or elements of things envelop each other, whereas
> breadth and height are the dimensions in which they are
> juxtaposed.[66]

The originality of depth therefore consists, for Merleau-Ponty, in its
being the dimension by which things or elements of things simultaneously envelop or *copresently implicate* each other.
The "simultaneous presence in experiences which are nevertheless
mutually exclusive" about which Merleau-Ponty speaks is to be
construed spatio*temporally*.

> When I say that I see an object at a distance, I mean that I already
> hold it, or that I still hold it, it is in the future or in the past as
> well as being in space. . . . Perception provides me with a 'field of
> presence' in the broad sense, extending in two dimensions: the
> here-there dimension and the past-present-future dimension. The
> second elucidates the first.[67]

Phenomenologically, we see (or our gaze "holds") something (in
front of us) from *here* at its place *there—at the same time*. The here and
the there are contemporary in our experience. Provided we do not
conceive either space or time atomistically or either apart from the other,
Merleau-Ponty contends (evidently following Erwin Straus), that the
visibility of depth is not problematic.
Straus reasoned as follows:

> Measured against the logical order of the geometrical space, the
> phenomenon of distance is paradoxical. [But] The structure of
> experienced space does not conform to that of geometrical
> space. . . . The particularity of the 'there' arises from the fact that
> I can grasp it 'here'; to be more exact, that I can grasp it from here
> as a different spot. . . . As a body I am limited to one location at

any given time; as I seeing being, however, I can reach out beyond myself . . .

'Here' and 'there,' in their visibility, are joined in time.[68]

A physicist working with an atomistic conception of space and time, must separate the here from the there, both spatially and temporally, in explaining how light there at location A at time t strikes the eyes here at location B at time t_1. But then it is physically impossible to shift the location B back to that of A. For it would mean that one and the same event takes place at two different locations.[69]

A perceptual "field of presence" in the broad sense and especially a "living present" is believed to obviate this theoretical difficulty. "The lived present holds a past and a future within its thickness."[70] Merleau-Ponty, Straus before him (and Gibson after him), "resuscitate" the visual experience of depth in a living spatiotemporal present. It is possible to see things from here over there at the *same* time because they, and we, are held (together and apart) in the thickness, in the depth, of the same "living present."

If Merleau-Ponty is correct in his view of depth as a space of copresent implication, then space is not isotropic. It is the begging of this question, the assimilation of a unified space of implication to a linear space of juxtaposed points and a "flat" or punctiform conception of time that drives a theoretical wedge between the unity of the here and the there. The phenomenological logic is pragmatic: If it's not broken, don't fix it.

This pragmatic logic is applied to emotion in Part II. As we shall see, depth as copresent implication has an interesting application in affective experience—in the uniting and the subsequent "reversals" of emotional dimensions "here" (serenity, fear, boredom, curiosity) with evocative dimensions "there" (tranquility, danger, monotony, novelty).

Lived Distance and Living Movements

The third dimension of spatial depth is not a purely optical phenomenon. The subject who sees is a being who moves. Only to such a being will space appear as articulated into regions of removedness.

—Erwin Straus, *The Primary World of Senses*

Merleau-Ponty, Gibson, and Straus all emphasized the "living movements" of a "body in relation to the ground" and believed that near-far perceptions stood "in relation to the extent of reach."

EXTENSION AS A QUALIFYING METAPHOR.

For Straus, the extent of reach that articulates distances is intrinsically personal (dependent on "my state of being, on my Here and my Now"[71]) and determined by one's "potentiality." It is also explicitly affective.

Whereas Merleau-Ponty focused on the vision of depth and defined *increasing distance* as "expressing merely that the thing is beginning to slip away from the grip of our gaze," Straus defined the *remote* as "that which is removed from my longing or that which is beyond the reach of my desire":[72]

> Distance opens up to me and articulates itself to me in remoteness and nearness only as long as I am directed toward my world, only as long as I, as a sensing being, move in it and, as a mobile being, sense in it in uniting and separating.

DISTANCE
R/T.
POTENTIALITY
+
EFFORT,
SKILL

> Distance is therefore relative to a becoming, desiring being. It is *his* reach which determines the articulations of distance into the near and the far....What is decisive is not the objectively measured distance but the relation of such distance to potentiality.... [For example, a] poor swimmer finds the sandbar upon which he can touch bottom and rest much further away than the skilled swimmer.[73]

This distance, which is relative to a becoming, desiring being and which can be contrasted with an "objective" or an "indifferent" space is what Merleau-Ponty calls *lived distance.* It is a distance that "binds me to things which count and exist for me" and that "measures the 'scope' of my life at every moment."[74]

Lived distance is an emotional depth—a sensitive space. It is a space of personal "outlook" in which we orient ourselves situationally.

There are "living movements" in lived distances. In his recent work on the dynamics of being affectively moved and re-moved, turned and re-turned in directions of personal significance, Glen Mazis has captured their sense as "e-motions." " 'To be moved' means to come to a different position *in regard* to one's situation. It is to experience a change in one's Being-toward something or someone or things in general....Actually, emotions *are* themselves this kind of motion, hence the name 'e-*motion*.' "[75]

One emotional "position" in lived distance is joy, with its spirited, carefree sense of lighthearted elevation—of being "on top of the world." In contrast, the weight of our troubles can be felt, sorrowfully, as a burden, "on our shoulders." We see this position embodied in the

PSYCHO-STRUCTURAL BODY   (E-MOTION) < BEARINGS
                                          < POSITIONS

downturned head and the slouch and sagging of postures. In contempt, we may find ourselves "looking down" on someone or something, as ✱ though we are not on the same "level," as though they are "beneath us." Then again, we may be "looking up" to others, in admiration.

Of course, we cannot "move" (or "e-move") without it, so some distance, or depth, is essential to any sensing of emotion. According to Straus: ("Distance is a primal phenomenon. . . .There is no distance without a sensing and mobile subject; there is no sentience without distance."[76])

As we saw in several of Chapter 1's examples, some understanding of space, some sensing of distance, is implicit in our understanding of emotional experience. In addition, there is the experience of love, which suggests closeness and proximity—a gentle binding to those we care for most,[77] and hatred, with its forces of repulsion and separation. When I am feeling overwhelmed, the world is experienced as too close; when I am withdrawn, it appears to recede, it is too far away. There is a despondent sense of isolation, a sharp sense of disconnection, of being "severed" or "cut off" in the experience of loneliness; and if others exclude us often enough, we may come to the "position" of feeling "left out" or "marginalized."

As we proceed, we shall see in more detail how the different emotional "bearings" can be thought, situationally, as "positions" and as diverse "holds" of our body on the world. We shall also see how the different "levels" of emotional depth can be articulated as diverse regions of removedness.

To this point, we have been following Merleau-Ponty by viewing depth as a spatial dimension or level—as an orientation according to which we acquire a bodily "hold" by "grasping" or being "linked" to what is in front of us. Depth has also been distinguished from length and breadth as being—in its "originality"—a unified, enveloping space of copresent implication. As it is lived, depth is the dimension that contemporaneously unites and separates. That is, although my here is "linked" to a there, I also see, at the same time, from here, that the there is a place in which I am not. To preserve this paradoxical unity through disparity, Merleau-Ponty follows Straus in appealing to a living present (a "thick" or three-dimensional view of time). The unity of the here and the there is therefore attributed to their being "*present* to the same perceiving subject and enveloped in one and the same temporal wave."[78]

Finally, we are ready to introduce yet another sense of depth as we address the question (which becomes, so to speak, retrospectively significant in the light of Merleau-Ponty's *Visible and Invisible* thoughts on depth) of whether, in the *Phenomenology*, Merleau-Ponty regarded depth as the primordial spatial level.

Although it is tempting to interpret him this way, if we try to do so only on the basis of his focused discussion of depth, we are faced with a number of perplexities and inconsistencies. For a start, he himself has reasoned, from his view of space as a precession, that the very question "What is the level of all levels?" is senseless. We cannot, in some foundational sense, "base" space because we cannot get beyond space to do so. Space is always already there; and since the time of our coming to bodily be, we are always already caught up in the "thick" of it.

Furthermore, if the perceived world is grasped or understood only in terms of the (significant) directions of our holding of its levels and if space is essentially precessive, each level would presuppose some other, as each of our orientations toward the world would be preceded by some other. Because the first level, as a *first* level (conceived ontologically an essential precession or regarded existentially as our first and blindly adherent hold upon the world) could not be anchored in a prior level that would enable us to "grasp" it, it follows that the first level could no longer be either reachable or graspable and, so, not even a level. So, even apart from its supposed senselessness "on principle," the first problem we encounter in trying to interpret depth as the primordial spatial level—as that "absolute within the sphere of the relative"—is that Merleau-Ponty has depicted depth precisely in terms of an in-front-of grasping or holding; and the primordial level, he thinks he has reasoned, can*not* be grasped.

A second, related problem is of course that Merleau-Ponty has taken pains to show how, contra Berkeley and if we understand it spatiotemporally, depth is directly and immediately visible. He has also, however, just as emphatically asserted that the primordial spatial level is visually imperceptible and that our first hold upon the world is one of "blind adherence."

So we wonder, at this stage in the text; is "blind adherence" the primordial spatial level? Or, because all being is presumed to be oriented, is the primordial spatial level simply "that of being situated in relation to an environment?"[79] It would appear that the "situation" of blind adherence must precede any situated establishment of spatial orientation. If so, then what prevents this blind adherence from serving as its "basis"? Why can it not be "the level of all levels"—"the dimension of all dimensions"?

Finally, although Merleau-Ponty begins his discussion of depth by describing it as the 'most existential' of all dimensions,[80] he later

[margin annotations:] PRimoRDIAL + PRe-eXiSTENT NOT AS eSSeNCe oR FOuNDATIONAL THe Re·ARCHe

retracts this setting of depth "over against the other dimensions" because they are all ultimately definable as the best hold of our body on the world.[81]

As I mentioned earlier, Merleau-Ponty's focused discussion of depth immediately follows discussion of the primordial spatial level and leads a reader to believe that there is some connection between these two discussions. However, he does not refer back to the earlier section until the very end of his focused depth discussion and then he uses, for the first time, the expression *primordial* in connection with depth. This primordial depth, he says "confers upon the other its significance."

Regrettably, the *other* is ambiguous. Reading what comes before, it apparently refers to "objectified depth"; that is, to Berkeley's sense of depth as "a line endwise to the eye." If, however, one focuses on what immediately follows, the *other* may also be read as the "distance" sense of depth developed up to that point in the text. For we find (on page 266) that Merleau-Ponty has, quite abruptly and without preparing his readers in any way, suddenly changed the sense of depth to "the thickness of a medium devoid of anything." It is as though, after reminding us that time is thick, he remembers, almost as an afterthought, that space is too. He contends that we must rediscover a "voluminosity" beneath depth "as a relation between things or even between planes," a sort of atmospheric diffusion that can be penetrated and that we can experience "when we allow ourselves to be in the world without actively assuming it."[82] *(experience . . .)*

This "primordial depth"— which is "a depth which does not yet operate between objects, which, *a fortiori*, does not yet assess the distance between them, and which is simply the opening of perception upon some ghost thing as yet scarcely qualified"—is scarcely developed beyond the language quoted here. Instead, in closing his focused discussion of depth after introducing this provocative meaning, he retreats back to the sense of depth as a bodily hold on its surroundings and says that distance is "rooted" in this surrounding. We are, however, expecting him to "root" our bodies, our surroundings, and even distance in this other voluminous "medium," this "primordial depth," and we are surprised when he does not.

There is a real loose end here in the text. This new depth, this "primordial depth," is evidently the "absolute within the sphere of the relative" he begins his chapter on space by telling us that we need. However, it is still—to this point in the text, not expressly "taken up."

We do, however, seem at least to pick up this obscure thread of Merleau-Ponty's thought later in this chapter when he begins to discuss "pure depth." So, we now turn to this new sense of depth and to that discussion. A primordial plane

'whereas the play of all is enacted'

Depth as the "Dark Space" of Occlusive Permeation

clarity is not the only fundamental substance of life; we also live in the night. Isn't it necessary, perchance, to turn our eyes toward it? But I no longer have the black night, complete obscurity *before me*; instead, it covers me completely, it penetrates my whole being, it *touches* me in a much more intimate way than the clarity of visual space.

—Eugene Minkowski, *Lived Time*

"Pure" depth is depth without distance from here; it is not the spatial dimension added to length and breadth. Dark space or pure depth is a space of intimacy and is exemplified by our experience of the night. Darkness evolves a spatiality without things.

Night is not an object before me; it envelops me and infiltrates through all my senses, stifling my recollections and almost destroying my personal identity. I am no longer withdrawn into my perceptual lookout from which I watch the outlines of objects moving at a distance. Night has no outlines; it is itself in contact with me and its unity is the mystical unity of the *mana* . . . it is pure depth without foreground or background, without surfaces and without any distance separating it from me.[83]

Because it is so difficult to regard depth in its sense of distance as "primordial" in Merleau-Ponty's view, this "pure" depth presents itself as a candidate for the "absolute" space.

For one thing, it is clear that the primordial depth first mentioned by Merleau-Ponty is a medium of thickness with a tangibly diffuse materiality that is not "held" at a distance. The night or dark space qualifies in this regard. Moreover, Merleau-Ponty is evidently following Minkowski in this later discussion; and Minkowski explicitly disqualifies the "depth" of dark space from being a spatial level or orientation.

Minkowski also explicitly contrasts two ways of living space: the distance of a visually "clear" or indifferent space with the "lived obscurity" of dark space. Minkowski also contends that there is no distance in dark space[84]—nothing separating me from an object—and so it is a more "personal" space. As Merleau-Ponty points out, the depth of darkness is not perceived at a distance, as something I hold "in front of" me. Nevertheless, it is perceived as a sort of density, a sort of materiality, a sort of tangibility—one in which I am enveloped and by which I am immediately, and intimately, touched. I quote Minkowski:

> Certainly, the dark night is not taken here in the sense of absence of light or the impossibility of seeing; it is taken in its positive value—in its materiality, we would almost like to say—and as such it is much more material, much more tangible, and even more penetrating than the limpid clarity of visual space....The dark night also has something more personal about it...it is more 'mine' than clear space...penetrating to the very depths of our being...[85]

> But does this obscure night which we are describing have anything to do with space? I believe so, but this space will be a particular kind of space. Obviously, it will not be an analytic space. Contrary to light space, it will have no 'besides' or distance, no surface or extension, properly speaking; but there will nonetheless be something spatial about it; it will have depth—not the depth which is added to length and height but a single and unique dimension which immediately asserts itself as *depth*. It is like an opaque and unlimited sphere wherein all the radii are the same, all having the same character of depth. And this depth remains black and mysterious.[86]

Minkowski also contends that "I will not situate myself in this space" in relation to sounds or objects. This is significant because it portrays darkness as a space that precedes situated orientation.

If in clear space we grasp, in dark space we grope. We live obscurity whenever we experience ourselves as dis-oriented, trying to find or recover our "bearings"—whenever we feel ourselves to be "lost" or "in a fog." We may say that the subjects in the orientation experiments are thrown, temporarily, into dark space as their goggles dis-lodge them from the ingrained "sens" of an upright visual field. We may also say that what is happening to them is not so very different from what happens to us in some of our "deeper" emotional experiences—when the "sense" of our world is turned "upside down." We may live the confusion of this obscurity at the sudden passing or parting of a loved one, for instance, in those times when we are feeling "lost" without them, and do not know "which way to turn."

For Minkowski, the essence of dark space is mystery:[87] "In dark space everything is obscure and mysterious. One feels as if in the presence of the unknown, in its positive value, and the phenomenon of 'mystery' seems the best and most immediate way to express this characteristic trait of lived obscurity."[88]

Epistemologically, Merleau-Ponty's conception of pure depth comes to the same thing as Minkoswki's dark space—along a different route. For space without distance is a space without direction. Without direction or "sens," we lack understanding. So, whether we call it pure depth or dark space, if it is "without distance," it will be mysterious.

For both Minkowski and Merleau-Ponty, an important difference between the depth of distance and the depth of darkness is that we can be "at one" with the dark.[89] The unity of dark space is not that of a unified holding-what-is-apart-together but is that of a pervasive, confused comingling.

Another difference between these two ways of living space is that we see at a distance in the light, but we *feel* the depth of the darkness. That is, dark space is a more tactile, tangible space. Its presence is *felt*. In its obscure materiality, dark space

> does not spread out before me but touches me directly, envelops me, embraces me, even penetrates me, completely passes through me, so that one could almost say that while the ego is permeable by darkness it is not permeable by light. The ego does not affirm itself in relation to darkness but becomes confused with it, becomes one with it. In this way we become aware of a major difference between our manners of living light space and dark space.[90]

It is interesting that both thinkers relate this depth to that of our personal identity. Merleau-Ponty regards it as "almost destroying" his. For Minkowski, because the self is "confused" with it, dark space is "more personal"; more "mine" than clear space is. He explicitly connects it to the "depth of our being."

Minkowski's discussion of dark space is evidently related to an earlier passage in his text that describes the "dimension in depth of the ego"—a "kind of subterranean gallery," a depth that "seems to go beyond the ego." This is felt to be "the true source of our life" and behind "the so-called elements of our mental life."

> This depth is not like a well whose bottom could never be reached. No, there is only something infinitely moving and living there, something which palpitates at the base of our being, which gives depth to our being. There is something elusive which always escapes the curious looks of knowledge; like a fine spider web,

Pure depth, a space of lived obscurity, without any "distance from
 here" and apparently modeled after Minkowski's notion of dark
space. Dark space contrasts with "clear," indifferent or geographical
space and is thought as a tangible and occlusively permeating space
intimate "oneness." It is characteristically mysterious.

have also tried to show that, although he has not discussed it
great length in the *Phenomenology*'s chapter on space and
standing his own reservations about the sensibility of inquiring
"level of all levels," it is compelling to interpret Merleau-Ponty
regarded dark-depth rather than depth in its sense of distance
rimordial" space—as "the absolute within the sphere of the

re moving into the Flesh ontology of *The Visible and the Invisible*,
leau-Ponty's essays deserve mention. They serve as a bridge
thought on depth.
Eye and Mind" discussion of depth is brief—but pivotal.
au-Ponty begins to think aloud about whether depth should
as a first dimension. We also find him discussing eclipsings
g to define *depth* as "the experience of the reversibility of
This is significant because the notion of "reversibility" is
is later notion of 'Flesh' and because we see that Merleau-
nning, as Gibson does, to take depth's occlusions more
account. Finally, he acknowledges that depth is enigmatic.

lies in the "bond" of the near and the far, in what
y emphasis] them. The enigma consists in the fact
ings, each one in its place, precisely because they
nother, and that they are rivals before my sight
use each one is in its own place. Their exteriority
eir envelopment and their mutual dependence in
y. Once depth is understood in this way, we can
it a third dimension. In the first place, if it were
would be a *first* one; there are forms and definite
is stipulated how far from me their different parts
mension that contains all the others is no longer
east in the ordinary sense of a *certain relationship*
ch we make measurements. Depth thus under-
e experience of the reversibility of dimensions,
ty'—everything in the same place at the same
n which height, width and depth are abstracted,

it is reduced to dust as soon as we think we have it between our
fingers; fleeing, it seems to go beyond the ego, yet we feel it to
be the true source of our life. Taken in itself, this depth appears
to have something impersonal in it; however, it is, above all, when
we strive to give to the world what is most personal in us that
we feel our *elan* coming from the depths of our being. This
depth—and it is scarcely necessary to say it once again—belongs
much more to becoming than to being. Consequently, we have
preferred to speak of the dimension (going) *in* depth rather than
simply depth.[91]

Minkowski's reflections on dark space were inspired by his
reflections on the spatial experiences of patients suffering from
schizophrenia, hallucinations and paranoid delusions. Such persons
experience coincidental occurrences in the distance of clear space as
though they are happening in dark space. That is, every occurrence
is interpreted as being personally relevant, as though it is directly
touching, affecting, or rooted in them.

To grasp this point about dark space, think back to *The Stranger*
and Meursault, to whom nothing matters or makes a difference.
Minkowski is thinking of the reverse of this situation, of persons who
experience events in their surroundings so that *everything* appears to
matter or make a difference. The problem is that it is just as "strange"
for everything to be infused with personal significance as it is for
nothing to be. Normally, we occupy both spheres of space: a "clear"
space of indifference and a "lived" space in which the closeness of
events matters, personally to us, and makes a "difference" in our lives,
in our selves.

The lesson to be learned from Minkowski is that there are
normative and pathological dimensions to the ways in which we live
space, to the keeping of distance. *Some* lived distance appears to be
desirable, even essential.[92] However, to entirely inhabit a space of
personal concern is as precariously "unbalanced" as exclusively
occupying an "objective" space of total indifference. As we saw in several
of our earlier examples, emotional well-being appears to depend on
the establishment of some happy medium between these two extremes.

His reflections lead Minkowski into wondering about the relation
between clear and dark space. Does one surround the other? Do they
overlap? Rather than answering these questions, he tells us that his
study has the sole purpose of throwing "certain ideas into the
discussion," grounding a possible direction of psychological research.[93]

Merleau-Ponty advances Minkowski's discussion somewhat. His response to Minkowski's questions about the relation between clear and dark space appears to be the following:

> Clear space, that impartial space in which all objects are equally important and enjoy the same right to existence is not only surrounded, but also thoroughly permeated by another spatiality thrown into relief by morbid deviation from the normal....This second space which cuts across visible space is the one which is ceaselessly composed by our own way of projecting the world, and the schizophrenic's trouble consists simply in the fact that the permanent project becomes dissociated from the objective world as the latter is presented to perception and withdraws, so to speak, within itself. The schizophrenic no longer inhabits the common property world, but a private world, and no longer gets as far as geographical space: he dwells in the 'landscape space', and the landscape itself, once cut off from the common property world, is considerably impoverished.[94]

Merleau-Ponty also extends the discussion of "dark space" into the realm of mythical and schizophrenic space.

> What protects the sane man against delirium or hallucinations, is not his critical powers, but the structure of his space: objects remain before him, keeping their distance....What brings about both hallucinations and myths is a shrinkage in the space directly experienced, a rooting of things in our body, the overwhelming proximity of the object, the oneness of man and the world, which is, not indeed abolished, but repressed by everyday perception or by objective thought, and which philosophical consciousness rediscovers.[95]

These latter claims of Merleau-Ponty's are interesting because they appear to relate back to an earlier passage about a "lived distance" that can be "both too small and too great": a space in which the nearness of events "obsesses" and "enshroudes" me "like night."[96] They are also interesting in their linking of dark space to the experience of a felt oneness with the world, a oneness "repressed" by mundane perception and objective thought.

A sense of "oneness" with the world and a dwelling in the "landscape space" is also characteristic of mystical and religious experience. Of course, the line between mysticism and hallucination

is a difficult one to draw, but religious experiences emotional'" and to make "deep'" or longlastin

I believe that there is also some sense of space,'" whenever we experience a disorientin or a change in the emotional "direction'" or also believe that, as we are being emotionally ourselves as "slipping'" into a dark, or relativ In this affective space, this space of felt f its repressive "hold" on proximity—and obj in restraint, at a distance. They touch u

In Chapters 3 and 4, we will think as a "blind spot" and as a "break/brak Merleau-Ponty's notion of the "chiasm "occluding edge." In Part II, we will ε emotional feelings and will reconsid the light of Merleau-Ponty's notion of and his view of emotions as "carn without a sensible "screen."

Su

In this chapter's exegesis Ponty's phenomenological app to show that there are sever; elicit some understanding o

1. Depth as distance fror changes as observers

2. Distance as a spatial (in front of.

3. Depth as the perce

4. Depth as the tra "turning into" ea

5. Depth as meanir in relation to o

6. Depth as spac juxtaposed sp disparities.

7. Lived distan the space ir in which l'

I at any notwith into the as having as the "p relative."

Befo two of Me to his later

His " Here, Merle be regarded and beginni dimensions.' definitive of Ponty is begi explicitly into

The enigma is *between* [n that I see th eclipse one precisely bec is known in t their automo no longer call a dimension, it planes only if it are. But a *first* d a dimension, at according to wh stood is, rather, t of a global 'locali time, a locality fror

of a voluminosity we express in a word when we say a thing is
there.[97]

Another essay that anticipates the Flesh ontology is "The
Philosopher and His Shadow." The following passages are of interest
because they show how Merleau-Ponty is beginning to modify his
conception of the lived body as "a system of possible actions or
movements" by *meshing* this body (-"subject") into the *perceptible* world.
Merleau-Ponty's later view of the body as "perceptible-percipience" is
just beginning to take shape here.

This text is also interesting in its claim that "space itself is known
through my body" because of the "sort of reflection" accomplished
through the "reversibilities" of touched and touching hands. In addition,
we see that Merleau-Ponty is beginning to use the word *flesh*.

> my body must itself be meshed into the visible world; its power
> depends precisely on the fact that it has a place *from which* it sees.
> Thus it is a thing, but a thing I dwell in....The relationship
> between my body and things is that of the absolute here to the
> there, of the source of distances to distance....There is a relation
> of my body to itself which makes it the *vinculum* of the self and
> things. When my right hand touches my left, I am aware of it as
> a 'physical thing.' But at the same moment, if I wish, an
> extraordinary event takes place: here is my left hand as well
> starting to perceive my right....The physical thing becomes
> animate. Or, more precisely, it remains what it was (the event does
> not enrich it), but an exploratory power comes to...dwell in it.
> Thus I touch myself touching; my body accomplishes "a sort of
> reflection." In it, through it, there is not just the unidirectional
> relation of the one who perceives to what he perceives. The
> relationship is reversed, the touched hand becomes the touching
> hand, and I am obliged to say that the sense of touch here is
> diffused into the body—that the body is a 'perceiving thing,' a
> 'subject-object.'

It is imperative that we recognize that this description also
overturns our idea of the thing and the world, and that it results
in an ontological rehabilitation of the sensible. For from now on
we may literally say that space itself is known through my body.
If the distinction between subject and object is blurred in my
body..., it is also blurred in the thing, which is the pole of my
body's operations, the terminus its exploration ends up in, and

which is thus woven into the same intentional fabric as my body. When we say that the perceived thing is grasped "in person" or "in the flesh" (*leibhaft*), this is to be taken literally: the flesh of what is perceived, this compact particle which stops exploration, and this optimum which terminates it all reflect my own incarnation and are its counterpart.[98]

3

Depth and Flesh

That every being presents itself at a distance, which does not prevent us from knowing it, which is on the contrary the guarantee for knowing it: this is what it not considered. That the presence of the world is precisely the presence of its flesh to my flesh, that I "am of the world" and that I am not it, this is what is no sooner said than forgotten: metaphysics remains coincidence. That there is this thickness of flesh between us and the 'hard core' of Being, this does not figure into the definition [of philosophy].... More often than not the idea of fusion or of coincidence serves as a substitute for these indications.... We shall have to return to this idea of proximity through distance, of intuition as auscultation or palpation in depth, ...a view which calls 'coincidence' in question.

—Merleau-Ponty, *The Visible and the Invisible*

Introduction

Merleau-Ponty had only begun to develop his Flesh ontology of perception in one chapter, "The Intertwining—The Chiasm," of an incomplete manuscript. This manuscript was published posthumously together with his working notes under the title *The Visible and the Invisible*.[1] A new sense of depth emerges in this text.

Without understanding its idea of proximity through distance, we cannot understand the Flesh ontology. For this new sense of depth (to which I will sometimes refer as *the depth of distanced contact*[2]) is related to Merleau-Ponty's revised conception of the body as a "perceptible-percipient" and to his notion that these two "sides" of Perceptibility, of the Flesh, are incompletely "reversible."

In this chapter, I show how the Flesh ontology was informed by Merleau-Ponty's thinking about depth to, or through, its connotation of distanced contact. I also show in this chapter how the reversibility thesis can be identified with this new conception of depth—with this idea of proximity through distance. It is my belief that once Merleau-Ponty had developed this idea of "proximity through distance," his work on depth was essentially complete. By *complete* I mean the following.

With this new conception of depth, Merleau-Ponty was able to resolve a conflict between two of his philosophical objectives: (1) to think through embodiment beneath subject-object dualism by developing a radically unified ontology; and (2) to accommodate difference (between perceptible phenomena themselves and between that which is perceiving and that which is perceived) and distance (as the "form" or possibility of perceiving) in an ontology of perception.

That the Flesh ontology was informed by Merleau-Ponty's thinking about depth can be seen by the fact that he critiqued other philosophical systems for their mishandling of Depth[3] before introducing his own philosophy in *The Visible and the Invisible*. It is also important to realize that at this "metaphysical" stage in Merleau-Ponty's career, he did not consider phenomenology's intentionality thesis, the view that consciousness is always 'of' an object, to be the ultimate truth.[4]

In the *Phenomenology of Perception*, Merleau-Ponty construed intentionality as a subject-object correlative or coincidental "fusion." In *The Visible and the Invisible*, he considered this to be a mistake—for "metaphysics to remain coincidence"—and we see him speaking in terms of "overlapping" and "fission" instead of "fusion."[5] In fact, several of the unusual expressions which appear in *The Visible and the Invisible* (hollows, folds in the "fabric" of Flesh, the "pulp" of the sensible, chiasms, écart, dehiscence) are suggestive of distance and depth, with its surface recessions, overlapping protrusions, and its hidden dimensions.

As a mental activity of "consciousness," intentionality tends to overlook its own (passive) belonging to the unity of a field or "fabric" of Perceptibility: "the *intentional* analysis that tries to compose the field with intentional threads does not see that the threads are emanations and idealizations of one fabric, differentiations of the fabric"[6] and its own, embodied "ground":

> It is the body, and it alone, because it is a two-dimensional being, that can bring us to the things themselves, which are themselves not flat beings, but beings in depth, inaccessible to a subject that would survey them from above, open to him alone that, if it be possible, would coexist with them in the same world...if it touches and sees, this is not because it would have the visibles before itself as objects: they are about it, they even enter into its enclosure, they are within it, they line its looks and its hands

inside and outside. If it touches them and sees them, this is only because, being of their family, itself visible and tangible, it uses its own being as a means to participate in theirs, because the body belongs to the order of the things as the world is universal flesh.[7]

Furthermore, as Merleau-Ponty noted in "The Philosopher and His Shadow," because of the "reversibilities" between touched and touching hands, there is not, as intentionality would have it, "just the unidirectional relation of the one who perceives to what he perceives." In addition, insofar as it "directs" us to frontal "objects," intentionality invariably tends to flatten or narrow our "perspective," blinding us to the lateral or hidden dimensions of these "objects" and to the extent of their embeddedness, in each other and in us.

Merleau-Ponty did not think it false that we are confronted with objects in our experience. However, as one commentator puts it:

With the focus of our attention only on the frontal aspects of appearing reality, we only see the opposition between the subject and object. Our eyes thus close to what Merleau-Ponty considers the most essential truth, viz., the instrinsic connection between subject and object. The term 'connection' is ambiguous, since every philosopher who accepts a doctrine of intentionality will admit that subject and object are connected. Merleau-Ponty means something more. According to him the connection consists mainly in the fact that the opposed terms belong to one and the same reality. The opposition is not just a kind of unity, of togetherness, but takes place within a unity which precedes and exceeds the opposition. This unity cannot be directly observed. It is not an object itself, since it involves the subject also. It is not a phenomenon, but it co-appears in all phenomena and makes phenomena possible. It is the 'quasi-object' of lateral awareness.[8]

This "quasi-object" of lateral awareness is the invisible depth "behind" the Flesh Ontology and its Reversibility thesis, which, as I shall argue, is "this idea of proximity through distance."

Merleau-Ponty's ontology of perception and the language of its articulation will probably appear strange to those accustomed to the polarity of opposition and to the law of the excluded middle in traditional Western philosophy. According to its exclusionary logic, proximity and distance are contradictory ideas: No sense can be made of a "distant contact"; and Merleau-Ponty's attempt to think them together as "mutually synonymous"—to "deconstruct" them, if you will—may appear far-fetched.[9]

Be that as it may, I believe that the Flesh ontology needs to be grasped and appreciated in the unique terms of Merleau-Ponty's novel, and metaphorically technical, vocabulary. So I use it to explicate his thought. For simplicity's sake, the import of the Flesh ontology to an understanding of emotional depth and concrete descriptions of its application to emotional experience are deferred until Part II.

The Flesh Ontology

Flesh as a Medium

By *Flesh* Merleau-Ponty intended to indicate something which had no name in traditional Western philosophy.[10] Flesh, he says, might be understood in the ancient sense of "element" as a wholly generalized manner of Being "that brings a style of Being wherever there is a fragment of being."[11] It is also his (explicit) expression for the fundamental unity permeating all interrelated, interwoven things.

Flesh, in its elemental sense, is precessive and progenitive. That is, Flesh is always already There; and it functions in the ontology as a source, as "the formative medium of the subject and object" and "the inauguration of the where and the when."[12]

As an elementally *voluminous* medium, Flesh is *un*differentiated, dense, "dark." It is obscure, mysterious, close or closed to itself. It is self-permeating, but insofar as it antedates percipience (as its source), it is (entirely, I should think) self-occluded. Flesh is not stagnant or inanimate "matter," but it is carnal in the sense of being a texture (cf. *Phenomenology*, "the texture of a medium devoid of any thing"). It is not "mind," for without percipience, it is mute, dumb. The Flesh of 'Wild' Being (*Être Sauvage*), as a *medium*, is, I believe, an ontological reworking of the "primordial" depth of the *Phenomenology*. That is, the "dark space" of occlusive permeation is regarded as the "absolute space;" and Flesh, as a voluminous medium, is a "pure" depth—a depth without any distance on itself.

As a *formative* medium, Flesh in its inaugural sense, Flesh creates some distance on itself by folding over (and over. . .) upon itself and "hollowing out" some clearing to make room, so to speak, for an adherent Percipience. In this first, or primordial, "reversibility" of the Flesh, Flesh becomes self-regarding and less self-occlusive.

That is, after a long maturation process of "laboring on itself," this "interiorly-worked over mass" self-diverges—opens itself up—through a self-distancing, an *"écart"* (a stepping aside or a deviation) as it begins to hollow itself out or "coil over" on itself to create an "other" side to its own, occluded Being. Percipience is then imaged as a "dehiscence"— simply bursting forth or splitting open, as seed capsules do. Presumably, this "dehiscence" occurs because of the animation or motion of these "folds" or "fissures" in the "fabric" of "Flesh."

We can construe Merleau-Ponty's account of the origin of percipience as the insertion of clear space into dark space—the insertion of depth in perception.[13] By somewhat (and somehow!) distancing itself from its own occlusive Voluminosity, Flesh (in its formative or inaugural sense—as the generative Body of Being) begins to touch, see, hear, smell, and taste itself; and, eventually, begins to understand or become aware of itself.[14]

This metaphysical account of the "opening of perception" in the element of Flesh sets the stage for the "flesh" of the world and its "overlapping" with the flesh of "perceptible-percipients."

The Flesh of the World

The flesh of the world refers to "the perceptibility which characterizes all worldly reality—which is actualized but not created by human perception."[15] Perceptibility is that surface of sensibility which is passively "there"—before the activation or the exploratory movements of my perception. Because it is our bodies that perceive and because, as enfleshed beings, we are "of" or "belong to" perceptible reality, in the radically unified Flesh ontology, perceptible reality perceives itself. Perceptibility and percipience are of a piece. The perceiving "subject" and a perceived "object" are not thought as entirely separate from each other.

In *The Visible and the Invisible*, perception is, generally speaking, a relationship of the perceptible to itself. That is, the phenonemon of perception is thought on a grand scale as animate Flesh seeing, touching, tasting, hearing, smelling itself. So, in the Flesh ontology, no sense can be made of a disembodied percipience. Percipience is *always* construed as opening up onto from out of the perceptible[16] and as always involving a passive "element"—a circumstance that Merleau-Ponty will sometimes characterize as "the passivity of our activity."

Percipient-Perceptibles

Percipient-perceptible is Merleau-Ponty's new name for the body as a perceiving thing, a body-subject-object. It refers to the two "sides" of bodily being: to the "intertwining" or the "adherence" of a self-sentient "side" of Flesh to its sensible other "side."

Incidentally, I will use the expression "side" because it has an implicit reference to another "side." But the "sides" of Flesh are not sides in the sense of a buttered side of bread or an aluminum side of a house—in the sense in which one thing is layered or placed over something else.

Merleau-Ponty will sometimes also use the expressions *leaves* or *layers*, but even he is dissatisfied with those. If percipient-perceptibles are properly "thought together," then

> one should not even say. . .that the body is made up of two leaves, of which the one, that of the 'sensible' is bound up with the rest of the world. There are not in it two leaves or two layers; fundamentally it is neither thing seen only nor seer only; it is Visibility sometimes wandering and sometimes reassembled. . . .To speak of leaves or layers is still to flatten and to juxtapose, under the reflective gaze, what coexists in the living and upright body. If one wants metaphors, it would be better to say that the body sensed and the body sentient are as the obverse and the reverse, or again, as two segments of one sole circular course, which goes above from left to right and below from right to left, but which is but one sole movement in its two phases. . . .There is reciprocal insertion and intertwining of one in the other. Or rather, if, as once again we must, we eschew the thinking by planes and perspectives, there are two circles, or two vortexes, or two spheres, concentric when I live naively, and as soon as I question myself, the one slightly decentered with respect to the other.[17]

The "wandering" Perceptibility about which Merleau-Ponty speaks in *The Visible and the Invisible* is reminiscent of the *Phenomenology's* mentioning of a "diffuse voluminosity": a voluminosity we experience "when we allow ourselves simply to be in the world without actively assuming it"; a voluminosity with which we are slightly decentered but to which we nevertheless still belong as our percipient focus draws something perceptible out of it from within it. As it does so, Perceptibility "reassembles" itself into its active and passive "sides" (into, for instance, a seeing-being seen or a listening-being heard relation). Neither side is intelligible without the other; they are intelligible only insofar as they are regarded as "sides" of the same unified body.[18]

The ontological significance of a percipient-perceptible is of great consequence. Our reach, our perceptual "grasp" is extended in the Flesh ontology. Because our sentient bodies belong to the same Flesh as non-self-sentient sensibility and because it is self-evident that our sentience belongs to our sensibility, then it is possible for the perceiving side of our flesh to maintain, through transitivity, a *real* contact with a subtended, perceptible order of Flesh.

So Merleau-Ponty has managed to blur, with his conception of percipient-perceptibility, the body-world boundary.[19] However, since *all* of the perceptible flesh of the world (which includes our own—this is the radically unified point) is manifestly *not self*-sentient in the way that percipient flesh is, he has also managed to preserve it, maintaining, therefore, through the flesh of percipient-perceptibles, some thickness of "flesh," some *distance* or difference between the flesh of the world and our own which is essential to perception. That is why, or how, Merleau-Ponty's metaphysics of perception does *not* "remain coincidence."

The En-Être Thesis

En-être refers to the situation of percipient flesh with*in* perceptible flesh and to an underlying unity before the "consciousness of" and "object" dichotomy. The relation suggests that percipience is (in a deeper sense of *of* than the *of* of intentionality) "of" or "belongs to" or is "in" the perceptible.[20]

Merleau-Ponty's working notes show that he was (as Gibson was) reinterpreting depth in terms of surfaces or surfacings. Consider the beginning of a note on "Ontology" (dated October 1959), where Merleau-Ponty indicates that he is taking topological, rather than Euclidean, space as a model of being. He calls this elemental Surface of Sensibility *Flesh*. However, that Merleau-Ponty was just as interested in the "pulp" of the perceptible as he was in its "skin" or "pellicle" or surface is revealed in another note (dated October 27, 1959), which says that "the primordial space as topological" means "cut out in a total voluminosity which surrounds me, in which I am, which is behind me as well as before me. . . .This is right."[21]

This primordial space, this total voluminosity in which topological space is differentially articulated or "cut out," is "pure" Depth. A belonging to the Flesh (or the Surface, of visibility, tangibility, audibility, etc.) is necessarily a belonging to, a being of, this Depth.[22] As perceptible-percipients, we are never (entirely) with-"out" it.

In the Flesh ontology, the visible and the invisible are thought in a manner similar to the way in which Gibson thinks of the unhidden and the hidden; namely, as continuous and connected. That is, the perceptible and the imperceptible (like the percipient and the perceptible) are not regarded as two ontologically distinct orders. They are two "sides" "of" the same Reality. It is just that the relation of "en-être" thinks the former, to some extent, as always "belonging to" the latter.

In effect, Merleau-Ponty uses the en-être thesis to say that we see because we are ("of" the) visible, touch because we are ("in" the) tangible, and so forth. These are alternative ways of saying that sentience belongs to the more primordial order of the sensible; and that the former is "of" the latter—as its source and as its limit.

Ultimately, it is our "blind adherence" to the Depth of Flesh which explains why Merleau-Ponty's is ontology from within. This adherence is the en-être relation—a relation that situates our sensitive flesh and therefore our "mentality" as "close" to this Depth as it can be; that is, without our being completely "reduced" to it or entirely identified or "coinciding" with it, viz., "of" or "belonging to" It—as a circumscribed "openness."

The Openings of Perception

Merleau-Ponty defined *the mind* as "the other side of the body"— not opposed to the corporeal, but another side "of" it: "We have no idea of a mind that would not be *doubled* with a body, that would not be established on this *ground*—"[23]

Through its adherence to the density of the flesh of the world, the sensible side of my body, is a "thing among things." The sentient side is "born by segregation" from the sensible density and "remains open" onto it.

The percipient "other side" of bodily flesh (seeing, touching, tasting) is deeply embedded in or meshed with the density of its perceptibility (visibility, tangibility, tastability). This perceptibility is its source—its "ground." However, because percipience is thought to be generated through the process of Flesh folding over upon itself and creating an opening of and for percipience, this "other side" of the body also has its source in the distance*d* depth of a divergency and is identifiable with an opening—an opening up onto from out of perceptibility.[24]

In this section, I try to be as "one-sided" about this segregated "side" of Merleau-Ponty's ontology as I can be, by construing percipience, literally, as an opening. According to Merleau-Ponty: "The other side [is] to be understood not, as in objective thought, in the sense of another projection of the same flat projection system, but in the sense of *Ueberstieg* of the body toward a depth, a dimensionality that is not that of extension..."[25] *Ueberstieg* is a metaphorical expression; and it connotes a certain depth. It means a stepping over; a going up to and jumping or "skipping" over an obstacle.

We might interpret this "Ueberstieg" as a sur-mounting or an over-lapping; and as referring to the 'écart'—the "stepping a-side" of Flesh in the dehiscence of percipience. This expression may refer to the way in which Flesh sur-mounts the "obstacle" of its own occlusion, creates surface recessions, and finds itself within some slack, with some distance on itself—so that it can begin to sense itself.

What is clear is that this created distance should *not* be thought as "distance in the air." It should be thought as a distance along the ground of a recessed surface. Merleau-Ponty is trying to avert us from thinking of the opening of this "other side" as either empty space or disembodied. For this would only repeat the same old mistakes: in perception, on depth; and in ontology, on the mind.

Merleau-Ponty's favored depiction of this "side" of his ontology seems to be in terms of folds or hollows, but a folding space or a hollowed-out space sunken or submerged so deeply into density—so 'at one' with it—that it becomes (for me at any rate) almost impossible to think this "other side" apart from the depth of voluminosity.

> The bond between the soul and the body is...to be understood as the bond between the convex and the concave, between the solid vault and the hollow it forms...the soul is the hollow of the body, the body is the distention of the soul. The soul adheres to the body as their signification adheres to the cultural things, whose reverse or other side it is— —
>
> But this (plenum and hollow) does not suffice: for idealism also says that, and we do not say it in the same sense. The soul, the for itself is *a hollow and not a void*, not absolute non-being with respect to a Being that would be plentitude and hard core.[26]

The "other side" of the body is not an empty space because it is percipient. It is hollow only in the sense of being hollowed out of a perceptible density.

To begin to feel your way into what I think Merleau-Ponty meant by these "hollows" or openings of percipience, you might try a body experiment. Try to focus all your sensitive attention on the oval region of your visual field. Try to see the rest of your body as "belonging"— "out there," to visibility—in the field of sensibility, as a "thing among things." This is one mode of what I call "opening up onto from out of perceptibility." If you persist with this exercise, you can begin to experience the percipient or the seeing "side" of your body as a caved-in effacement of a (good) part of your (sensible) face, as a cavity filled with your vision. Now think of your face as a recessed surface, "folded over on itself," and notice how difficult it is to say where, precisely, your seeing starts. This seeing side seem to underlie even the region where you "know" your eyes to be.

Of course your sensible eyes (and sensible face) are still there. Without them, you would not see at all. Merleau-Ponty is obviously not trying to say that you could. He is saying just the opposite—that we see "through" our eyes only because they are visible, because they are "of" or "belong to" visibility. However, I believe that he might also have been trying to call our attention to just how deeply (how imperceptibly) percipience is recessively hidden with*in* the perceptible; and the point I am trying to establish through this example is that even though percipience "belongs to" the perceptible, ontology has still to contend with *this* "opening" of percipience, for there is still this other "side" to the "matter."

This "other side" to the "matter" of our "aestheological body" is, ontologically, the distancing of a divergency that has "overstepped" the obstacle, the en-closure, of its own density by segregating, by folding over upon itself and "hollowing out" some sensitivity. The point appears to be that the perceptible, as a ground or a source in Merleau-Ponty's ontology, must open itself up—to some degree—in percipience. It is difficult, even in exegesis, to think these openings of percipience "apart" from their ground. The openings of perception cannot really be thought apart as a "hole" or as "empty space." They obviously cannot be identified with anatomical cavities—with, say, the pupils of our eyes, the pores of our skin, or the nostrils of our nose. The openings of perception are deeper sorts of openings.

They are circumscribed; they are with*in* the perceptible. They are conceived as openings from which percipience blossoms or bursts forth and within which percipience dwells and conducts its exploratory movements.

These "folds" in the "fabric" of Flesh are also openings to which we, as percipient-perceptibles, ontologically belong. It is because of the percipient side of our flesh—this sensitive "other side of our body" and its distancing from the depth of perceptible flesh—that we are "incomplete," as a riddle, gaping, open.

We do, after all, see through our eyes and feel through our skin; and that is why, even as enfleshed beings, we cannot be reduced to "material." We can still be described as "half-open."[27]

Depth as the Dimension of the Hidden

In the Flesh ontology, Being is more than being-perceived. Some of it is imperceptible.[28]

As a "total voluminosity," Depth—the Depth "behind" the Flesh, is the universal "Hiddenness" of Being. It is a dark space or pure depth that is always already there and with which we are always already occlusively permeated. Some of this depth may surface and partially reveal itself. Some of it may diverge, in openings of perception. But we cannot perceptually penetrate to the "bottom" of this Depth. We cannot perceive all the way "through" it. We cannot perceive all of it directly. Nonetheless it is thought to be "There"—"behind" every surfacing of sensibility and all of our perceptual experiences.

The only working note devoted exclusively to a discussion of depth is the one whose quotation follows. In it, we see that Merleau-Ponty continues to associate depth, temporally, with simultaneity—with the thickness of a present holding a past and a future together—and that he regarded Depth as a hidden "dimension of dimensions"—"behind" everything, including the "Flesh."

Depth and "back" (and "behind")— —it is pre-eminently the dimension of the hidden— —(every dimension is of the hidden)— —

There must be depth since there is a point whence I see— since the world surrounds me— —

Depth is the means the things have to remain distinct, to remain things, while not being what I look at at present. It is pre-eminently the dimension of the simultaneous. Without it, there would not be a world or Being, there would only be a mobile zone of distinctness which could not be brought here without quitting all the rest—and a "synthesis" of these "views." Whereas, by virtue of depth, they coexist in degrees of proximity, they slip into one another and integrate themselves. It is hence because of depth that the things have a flesh: that is, oppose to my inspection obstacles, a resistance which is precisely their reality, their "openness," their *totum simul*. The look does not overcome depth, it goes round it.

Depth is *urstiftet* in what I see in clear vision as the retention is in the present—without "'intentionality'"—

cf. Metzger saying that it arises at the moment when it was going to be impossible to have a distinct vision of 2 points at the same time. Then, the two images that are out of phase and not superposable "take" suddenly as profiles *of* the same thing in depth—This is not an *act* or an intentionality (which would go to an *in itself* and would give only juxtaposed in itselfs)—It is in general, and by virtue of a field property, that this identification of two incompossible views is made, and because depth is open to me, because I have this dimension so as to move my look in it, *this openness— —*[29]

Merleau-Ponty's earlier view of Space as a precession is taken for granted here. Because of the phenomenological logic Merleau-Ponty had previously construed, his phenomenological ontology cannot get "behind" this "dimension of the hidden."[30] Depth is thought as a metaphysical necessity—as a condition for the being of perception. Every dimension is thought to be "of" it.

We can also see by this note that the Depth behind the Flesh is paradoxical. For one thing, Depth is simultaneously the source or origin of openings of percipience *and* its terminus or that which "stops it up." For another, as a generalized field property, Depth is defined as an identification of incompossible views.[31] The "identity of incompossibles" is a new expression for "unity through disparity." As we saw in the demonstration on page 41, this paradoxical unity *is* achieved in depth perception, in the superposition of two incompossible images "taking."

We will return to these important senses of Depth in the next chapter, where, generalizing from them, I show how we can construe Depth as the Reversible Process of Becoming, and in Chapter 7, where this depth is applied to the notion of emotional depth as an alteration in identity.

The Intertwining at the Chiasm

In the Flesh ontology, the intertwining at the chiasm refers to the relation between the two sides of bodily being. Merleau-Ponty's thinking about "chiasms" evinces an underlying thinking about depth, particularly depth as an identity of incompossibles and as a "blind spot."

For Merleau-Ponty (and anyone else who is not anesthetized), it is evident that our bodily flesh has a sentient side ("Yes or no: do we have a body—that is, not a permanent object of thought, but a flesh that suffers when it is wounded, hands that touch?"[32]), a "double belongingness" to the "subjective" and "objective" orders. He also believed that it was evident that our flesh unites these two sides within itself.[33] His problem is to say how—that is, "to determine how the sensible-sentient can also be thought" and specify the relation between them.

Because he specifies this relation as an 'intertwining' at a chiasm (and given his extensive background in the psychology of visual perception), it is reasonable to suppose that Merleau-Ponty thought that the two (different) sides of the (same) body are united in a manner analagous to the way in which our visual system unites the binocular disparities between the two (spatially segregated or different) sides of the (same) visual field; namely, as a relation of mutual superposition: of two laps overlapping—encroaching upon, slipping or crossing over into each other—so that portions of each "wind up" on the other's side. However (and again apparently analagous to the way our two spatially segregated eyes nevertheless work together and "belong to" the same visual system), the two sides of the body are kept together *as two* sides *of* the *same* (unified) body only because they *are* somewhat spatially segregated or distanced from each other.[34]

In the Flesh ontology, the "chiasm" is not only the "bond" between perceiving and perceived; between the two sides of "Flesh"—it is also a "medium of exchange" between the self and others. That is, it also "grounds" Merleau-Ponty's notion of intercorporeality.

> like the chiasm of the eyes, this one is also what makes us belong to the same world—a world which is not projective, but forms its unity across incompossibilities such as that of *my* world and the world of the other— —By reason of this mediation through reversal, this chiasm, there is not simply a for-Oneself for-the-Other antithesis, there is Being as containing all that...
>
> Chiasm, instead of the For the Other; that means that there is not only a me-other rivalry, but a cofunctioning. We function as one unique body
>
> The chiasm is not only a me-other exchange (the messages he receives reach me, the messages I receive reach him), it is also an exchange between me and my world, between the phenomenal body and the 'objective' body, between the perceiving and the perceived: what begins as a thing ends as consciousness of the thing, what begins as a 'state of consciousness' ends as a thing.[35]

Merleau-Ponty's thinking about chiasms *also* evinces an underlying thinking about depth in its sense of a "hidden dimension." For, as we shall see, "chiasms" create "blind spots" in the Flesh ontology. They are related to the ontology's "reversibility" thesis and to the sense in which reversibility is "incomplete." They can also be likened to Gibson's notion of an occluding edge. From this "incompleteness" of reversibility we can—finally—derive the "deepest" sense of depth this ontology has to offer: "this idea of proximity through distance."

Reversibility as Proximity Through Distance

Merleau-Ponty characterizes Flesh as "reversible"[36] and believes reversibility to be "the ultimate truth."[37] The first reversal in the ontology is that of Flesh folding back over upon itself and creating, through openings of percipience, distance from itself—distance requisite to Perception, to Flesh's ability to see, hear, touch, smell, taste its-Self.

From this pro-found "reversal,"[38] Merleau-Ponty develops his reversibility thesis, a thesis that teaches that Perceptibility is diacritical: a two-sided or doubled-up (seeing-being seen, uttering-being heard, touching-being touched) "relation of reciprocity in which neither of the relata is intelligible apart from the other."[39]

> reversibility, is the idea that every perception is doubled with a counter perception . . . , is an act with 2 faces, one no longer knows who speaks and who listens. speaking-listening, seeing-being seen, perceiving-being perceived circularity. (it is because of it that it seems to us that perception forms itself in *the things themselves*)— Activity = Passivity.[40]

We find at least three divergent senses of *reversibility* in *The Visible and the Invisible*. One sense construes reversible flesh on the model of reversible fabric.[41] Another construes reversibility as a "becoming"—as a relation of partial or complementary identification between "sides" of perceptibility. Yet another sense construes reversibility as a translation—as a communication holding between different realms or modes of perceptual experience.

One way in which sides of perceptibility reversibly "become" each other is in the sense of complementing—by doubling up so that "each is only the rejoinder of the other, and which therefore form a couple, a couple more real than either of them."[42] Seeing and visibility, touching and tangibility, tasting and tastability, are reversible in this sense. Another way in which sides of perceptibility can reversibly "become" each other is modeled after the "circle" of touching-tangible hands. Each is "reversible" to the extent that each may become, turn into, change places, or shifts sides with the other. My touching hand can "reverse" or become the hand that is touched and vice versa.

There may also be interperceptual complementary doublings or reversibilities. For example, my seeing and touching may "double up" and "reverse" in the sense that I can see what I touch and touch what I see and experience that these modes of perception complement or "become" each other.

Because Merleau-Ponty does not regard perceptual experiences as "interior, worldless activities," because he founds intersubjectivity on an intercorporeality, and because he has made belonging to the same *Flesh* (rather than to the same "consciousness") his criterion of unified sensibility,[43] reversible relations are not confined to our own "individual" experiences. The circle of touched and touching hands is extended, to incorporate the experience of others.[44] "What happens in me can pass over into the other. Our being is contagious. . . .Our experience is not immanent but transitive. . . .We communicate, since we are all 'perceiving perceptibles,' since the same 'flesh of the world' makes us see, makes us perceive."[45]

No reversible "circle" of perceptibility is entirely self-contained or entirely closed off from any other. They overlap. They are intertwined. They cross over into each other at "chiasms."

The "translation" sense of reversibility applies to exchanges of overlapping communication between differentiated perceptual modes. For example, seeing and touching are reversible in the sense that my seeing can see whether something will be smooth or rough to my touch. In other words, I can see texture. Similarly, I can feel what I see. By the way that it touches my vision, I can feel that the "glaring" sunlight is painful to my sight.[46] Tactility and Visibility overlap and intertwine.

> We must habituate ourselves to think that every visible is cut out in the tangible, every tactile being in some manner promised to visibility, and that there is encroachment, infringement, not only between the touched and the touching, but also between the tangible and the visible, which is encrusted in it, as conversely, the tangible itself is not a nothingness of visibility, is not without visual existence.[47]

Tactility and Visibility can reverse as translations because they share some common space—some medium that allows them to "cross over" into each other and exchange information. However, translations between the two modes are never perfect, for seeing and touching are not strictly identifiable. They do not "become" each other in the sense of "coinciding." "There is double and crossed situating of the visible in the tangible and of the tangible in the visible; the two maps are complete, and yet they do not merge into one. The two parts are total parts and yet are not superposable."[48]

This slight decentering of reversible phases of the "circles" so that they are somewhat distanced from each other and do merge into one or "fuse" is a critical aspect of the Reversibility thesis: its "incompleteness." Reversibility is *always* incomplete, "always imminent and never realized in fact." For although reversibility is a coupling or translation of sides of Flesh, it also involves an "incessent escaping." Something is lost in the translation. The two sides of a reversible relation never completely "become" each other in the sense of a strict identity or in the sense of perfectly coinciding. There is always some experienced interruption, some hiatus, in reversible relations between the "sides." Their coincidence will "eclipse at the moment of realization."[49]

For example, although it is true that my left hand can touch my right and that I can reverse this relation so that my right hand touches my left, as I do so I experience a breech in the hold that one of my hands has on the other—and this despite their remaining "in touch" with each other throughout. I can experience that something is "lost" in the interchange, in the "reversal." A similar sort of "eclipsing" can occur on an interpersonal level when we reverse touching-touched relations while we are shaking or holding hands with someone. For example, the touch of your touch, which I am enjoying through ("passively") experiencing the sensitive tangibility of my hand in yours and through the sensible tactility of yours, will tend to slip away or recede or be "eclipsed" the more I "reverse" the relation and begin, myself, to (more "actively") palpate your hand with my touch.

Because our tangible skin is "open" to touch, both sides of our flesh are intermingled in this tactile experience. However, there is also, and especially as we interchange and "cross over" or reverse "directions" in the circle of this experience, a felt distancing of flesh *between* us, which we palapably and paradoxically do *not* feel. We may be clasping hands or embraced in a caress, but as we reverse "sides" in the circle of these interchanges, we can feel that we are in some sense losing our grips— we do not have a complete, simultaneous "handle" on the experience from both "sides" at precisely the same time. There is this "incessant escaping." The intermingling of "sides" of Flesh at "chiasms" is therefore, in some respect, occlusive. The two sides are incompossible; yet we also experience them as together. Although we can reverse the "sides," the reversal is "incomplete" in that it hides or eclipses something that remains between the sides of the experience.

However, it is precisely this 'incompleteness' of reversibility—the hiatus of this *betweenness* that differentiates and *distances* sides of Flesh from each other—that *unifies* Merleau-Ponty's ontology. For Merleau-Ponty has paradoxically thought the sides of Perceptibility together through their commingling, and he has simultaneously segregated them through a *distance* of *density*—the depth of Flesh—that keeps them apart.

Because percipience belongs to or is "of" the perceptible, there are limits to the logic of percipience: We cannot, directly or immediately, sense sentience, perceive perceiving or its "opening." I cannot touch touching, for example,—my own or yours—without the intervening medium of some *im*-perceptible flesh (depth) holding *between* the "sides" of the experience. Similarly, I cannot see myself seeing or hear myself listening. To the extent that I can and do experience my percipience (or yours) in "reversible" relations, it is only by the means of their "circulation" in and through the depth of the tangible, the visible, the audible.

However, this does *not* mean, in Merleau-Ponty's ontology, that touching or hearing can be entirely or completely identified with (or "become" in the sense of "be reduced to") the tangible or the audible. What it means is only that my hearing can , so to speak, re-sound only by "doubling up" and "re-siding" within a perceptible depth (in this case, of audibility) and that this perceptible depth is its source.

For to say, as the en-être thesis does, that percipience is "of" the perceptible is just to say that hearing is not "itself" anything. That is, it cannot be thought apart from its audible other "side," any more than seeing can be thought apart from the visible or touching can be thought apart from the tangible. Disembodied perception is senseless. A purely "subjective" perceiving—perception "in the air"—does not exist.

The occlusively permeating "spread" of carnality Merleau-Ponty apparently envisioned as holding between "sides" of Flesh and which, at the same time, unifies them and facilitates their reversibilities, is likened to the relation "holding between my two eyes," the relation that "makes of my two eyes the channels of one sole Cyclopean vision."[50] Again, we have a reference to the optic chiasm, so again, I will rely on it to interpret the ontology.

The optic chiasm derives from areas where the optic nerves leave the eyes. Because these nerves are not photosensitive, neither are the areas. Hence these regions create hidden blind spots in the periphery of our field of vision before the chiasm reversibly rejoins the two sides of the visual field in one unified visibility.

To say that there is "nothing there" corresponding to the blind spot is of course false. There is a density of (*non*sentient) sensible flesh there "translating" visual information and literally, at the chiasm, diverging and crossing over itself to maintain the spatial sidedness of the visual field.

Merleau-Ponty appears to have envisioned his "chiasms" analagously; that is, as creating "blind spots" in the Flesh ontology and its laterally styled philosophy of body-mind, by regarding reversibility's incompleteness as a necessary "eclipse." Thus, these areas of "incomplete" reversibility circumscribe the "hidden" or implicit depth in the Flesh ontology (its invisible, intangible dimensions). The regions of the chiasm—the areas where reversibility is *in*complete—are "spreads" where percipience cannot, itself, penetrate because they are the regions from which it unfolds.

In Merleau-Ponty's view, the juncture where percipience and perceptibility reversibly "hinge" on each other (where percipience is thought as "opening") is literally and necessarily an ontological obscurity. These eclipsings also explain why Merleau-Ponty occasionally will, in *The Visible and the Invisible*, say things like "all feeling takes place in and through what is, on principle, unfeelable"; "all seeing takes place in and through what is, on principle, invisible." For it is only by the means or the "medium" of this "eclipsing" or "incompleteness" of reversibility, *this thickness of a distance* interposed between "sides" or dimensions of Flesh that Merleau-Ponty is able to ensure our remaining in ontological "touch" with Depth. That is to say, without making reversibility "incomplete," without his ontological "blind spots," Merleau-Ponty's ontology could not be unified as it is. Moreover, it appears to be unified as it is only because Merleau-Ponty still adheres to the philosophical conviction that, at its earliest or most profound "level," spatial experience is that of "blind adherence" to a "total voluminosity."

From the moment we exist as perceptible bodily beings, we are interwoven in this "tissue." Although we may, from time to time, be re-turned[51] to this Depth, when, for example, we lose our sense of direction or feel ourselves "at one" with it all, we cannot, in any wholly "externalized" sense, be "removed" from it. Nevertheless, something about it is distanced from us, incessantly escaping.

Hence, reversibility's incompleteness is *not* a failure or a shortcoming of Merleau-Ponty's "reversibility" thesis. That there *not* be a "complete" identification or reciprocity between the sides of Flesh, that neither side wholly absorbs its complementary "other," that there *be* "something missing"[52] or "incessantly escaping" our perceptual grasp is essential to the way in which Merleau-Ponty—by blurring or "debordering" the boundaries of body and world—has unified his ontology.

if these experiences never exactly overlap, if they slip away at the very moment they are about to rejoin, if there is always a 'shift,'

a 'spread,' between them, this is precisely because my two hands
are part of the same body, because it moves itself in the world,
because I hear myself both from within and from without. I
experience—and as often as I wish—the transition and the
metamorphosis of the one experience into the other, and it is only
as though the hinge between them, solid, unshakeable, remained
irremediably hidden from me. But this hiatus between my right
hand touched and my right hand touching, between my voice
heard and my voice uttered, between one moment of my tactile
life and the following one, is not an ontological void, a non-being:
it is spanned by the total being of my body, and by that of the
world; it is the zero of pressure between two solids that makes
them adhere to one another.[53]

In his notes, Merleau-Ponty will sometimes identify reversibility
with the chiasm. This is confusing. Reversibility is a relation of doubling-
up that occurs *at* chiasms. Reversibilities can occur between sides of
Flesh only because they are intermingled at chiasms. That is, the chiasm
is a space of crossing-over. It is the space that lies between the
encroaching, and intermingled "sides" of Perceptibility, the space that
holds them together, the space where sides of flesh reverse. The chiasm
itself, however, does not "reverse." The chiasm does not "become" or
"translate" into another side, because *it is not, itself, a side,* but that which
lies, as a bond, a "vinculum" *between* them and that which makes
reversibilities possible.

However, the chiasm *may* be identified with the *incompleteness* of
the reversibility of the Flesh—with the "spread," the "hiatus," the
eclipsed "betweenness" that *distances* "sides" of Flesh from each other.

There is a complex "reversal" that takes place at this phase of
Merleau-Ponty's ontology. For as we begin to construe the chiasm as
the region of reversibility's incompleteness, we find that we "wind up"
or "wind round" (*serpentement*) once more, to the "dense" side of Flesh,
to the "side" or the site of "blind adherence." The incompleteness of
reversibility can be understood as a stopgap of sorts. It represents the
thick, the imperceptible "dark space," the occluded "side" of the
ontology. What is so interesting, however, is that this "stopgap" does
not (simply or one-sidedly) represent a *barrier* to percipience; on the
contrary, for it is also thought as the source or condition of all
percipience—and it is, at the same time, the unifying "element" of the
ontology.

Hence, once reversibility's incompleteness is identified with the
chiasm and the chiasm is identified with the thickness or "pulp" of

Flesh, it appears that Merleau-Ponty has managed, finally, with his thesis of the *incomplete* reversibility of the Flesh, to think proximity and distance together, as "mutually synonymous." The depth of distance and the depth of occlusive permeation are of a piece. Surfaces of sensibility, however "removed" they may be from each other, are nonetheless united within the depth or "folds" of Flesh. Simply put, reversibility's "incompleteness" *just is* "this idea of proximity through distance."

With this idea of proximity through distance, Merleau-Ponty was able to radically unify his ontology of perception, and he was also able to do so in such a way that distance and differentiation (between the perceiving and the perceived and between perceptible phenomena themselves) were nevertheless accommodated.

He was further able, with this idea of distanced contact, to resolve what he called, in his *Phenomenology*, "the paradox of perception." This is the puzzle of how there can be perceptual constancy, "an absolute within the sphere of the relative" or "an in-itself for-us."[54]

> The superficial pellicle of the visible is only for my vision and for my body. But the depth beneath this surface contains my body and hence contains my vision.[55]

> if there is flesh, that is, if the hidden face of the cube radiates forth somewhere as well as does the face I have under my eyes, and coexists with it, and if I who see the cube also belong to the visible, I am visible from elsewhere, and if I and the cube are together caught up in one same 'element' (should we say of the seer, or of the visible?), this cohesion...prevails over every momentary discordance.[56]

> he who sees cannot possess the visible unless he is possessed by it, unless he *is of it*, ...

> We understand then why we see the things themselves, in their places, where they are, according to their being which is indeed more than their being-perceived—and why at the same time we are separated from them by all the thickness of the look and of the body; it is that this distance is not the contrary of this proximity, it is deeply consonant with it, it is synonymous with it...the thickness of flesh between the seer and the thing...is not an obstacle between them, it is their means of communication.[57]

Summary

Merleau-Ponty and James J. Gibson were both severely critical of "empty space" theories of depth perception and their failure to take occlusions and embodied, ecologically niched and mobile, perceivers into account. Rather than continue in the empiricist tradition of construing depth as "distance in the air," they both came to re-vision depth as distance along the Ground of a recessed Surface.

In Gibson's ecological optics, these surface recessions are sited/sighted at "occluding edges." In Merleau-Ponty's ontology of perception, they are depicted as overlapping "folds" of a Fabric in which we are intertwined. This Surface or Ground of Sensibility—a Surface to which we, as embodied beings, always already belong or are "of"— is what Merleau-Ponty came to mean, in its ontological or "elemental" sense, by *Flesh*. I have shown in this chapter that Depth is the 'other side' of this Surface—the "other side" of "Flesh."

Flesh cannot be thought apart from Depth, for any surface of sensibility—any visible or tangible item in our experience—is embedded in this dimension of the hidden. It must be, to be perceived in depth; to be to be perceived at all. Reality is not all "up front."

Depth "as such" or "in itself" is neither completely perceived nor completely perceptible. It is that "dimension of the hidden" which every dimension is thought to be "of" and which is thought to exceed and elude our perceptual grasp. What is perceived in the vision of depth is the e-mergence of something appearing or unfolding from behind something else.

In doubly referential Gibsonian terms, what is also perceived in the vision of depth is the significances of surfaces in relation to our body; that is, their "affordances." Merleau-Ponty's phenomenological focus on "inhabiting" a spectacle aligns him with this aspect of Gibson's "ecological" approach to perception.

In Gibson's and Merleau-Ponty's commensurately "circulatory" or nondichotomous views, the visible and the invisible—like the here and the there, the past and the future, the active and the passive, and the near and the far—are thought to be continuous and complementary ("becoming") "sides" of the same Reality. Both of their theories of perception were intended "to cut across the dichotomy of subjective-objective and help us to understand its inadequacies."

Merleau-Ponty's reversibility thesis—the notion that "sides" of Sensibility "double up" and partially or incompletely "become" each other—evolved from his earlier phenomenology of perceived depth. In *The Visible and the Invisible*, depth as space of copresent implication and as "unity through disparity" is finally rooted in the medium of "pure depth": the "dark space" of occlusive permeation with its identification of incompossibles. This medium, what I have called the Depth "behind" the Flesh, is also related to the impersonal depths of our personal identities. Simultaneously, we are "of" and are not, this "innate Anonymity."

In "Eye and Mind," we saw that Merleau-Ponty had begun to sense that some piece to puzzle of depth was missing; he was perplexed about an enigmatic "bond" between "the near and the far." He reversed his earlier focus on the visibility of depth as a "third" *dimension* and began to formulate a new sense of depth after appreciating how paradoxically depth is a revelation of concealment. Depth "thus understood," he realized, is not, in the usual sense of "dimension," a dimension at all. Depth "thus understood" is the "level of all levels," the "dimension of dimensions," the voluminous and simultaneous "locality" from which all dimensions are abstracted and the experience of their "reversibility."

In *The Visible and the Invisible, this* understanding of Depth evolved into an ontology of 'Flesh': a Flesh that is "adherent to *location* and to the *now*"[58] and is incompletely "reversible."

The *incompleteness* of reversibility—this idea of proximity through distance—is, evidently, that "incessantly escaping" bond between "the near and the far," the missing piece to the puzzle of depth. Simply put, *proximity through distance is a space of copresent implication that has taken occlusions into account*. Situated at "chiasms" and functioning precisely as Gibson's "occluding edges" do in his ecological approach to perception (that is, as uniting and separating "sides" of something), this "bond" is the space where imperceptible "cross-overs" take place and where "sides" of a unified experience can reversibly "become" (copresently implicate, turn into or complement) each other. The "blind spots" created by the "overlapping" of "sides" unifies Merleau-Ponty's "laterally" styled ontology of 'Flesh,' perception.

It is evident that this "bond"—which also connects Merleau-Ponty's en-être thesis to the "incompleteness" of his reversibility thesis—can be traced back to the *Phenomenology*'s discussion of a "pure" or "primordial" depth and its quest for "an absolute within the sphere of the relative"—as a ground for realism, for being to be more than being perceived.

For even in the *Phenomenology*, and although he did not really elaborate on it there, Merleau-Ponty realized that depth—as a "clear" or empty space of distance, as a "third" dimension or "level," and even as a bodily "holding in front of"—could not adequately account for the being of perception. He realized that there had to be "more," so to speak, to Depth than that, that the perceptible also had to have *its* imperceptible "other side" for perception to be: "what we see is always in certain respects not seen: there must be hidden sides of things, and things 'behind us,' if there is to be a 'front' of things and things 'in front of' us, in short, perception."[59]

4

Depth and Reversibility

the present, also, is ungraspable from closeup, in the forceps of attention.

—Merleau-Ponty, *The Visible and the Invisible*

Although we commonly misconstrue it as being so, Depth is not just the "far side" or the "background" or the "past" or the "hidden." These all play a part in the phenomenon; but to identify any one of them with Depth would still be too flat, too "onesided," and too dichotomous a conception of Depth.

The medium of Depth is better thought as a midway: as some "where," some "there," between the background and the foreground, between what is here and what is there, between what is visible and what is invisible. As an "absolute within the sphere of the relative," Depth is "in" Between Space. This Depth is Presence; and this Presence "remains itself" only by remaining at a distance.

Spatially associated with the location of distance, with what "there Is" or what "is There," Depth is also associated, temporally, with Simultaneity and with the "Now"—between what is past and what is future. That is, Depth is also associated with the medium of the Present.

To say that this Depth is paradoxical is to say that it identifies incompossibles and is open ended. To say that this Depth is imperceptible is to say that it is Pre-sense—that it is "there," before that which is sensed.

Depth as a "Break/Brake"

Studies on perceptual depth make substantial use of the notion of breaks/brakes—of occlusive "stoppings" of our sight and of discontinuities that are nevertheless and paradoxically continuous. In Gibson's ecological approach to perception and his revisioning of depth, these "breaks/brakes" are thought as surface recessions, and they are located at "occluding edges." An occluding edge, you may recall from Chapter 2, is an edge taken with reference to a mobile observer (at a distance from here) that causes surfaces to hide one another. They are paradoxical in the sense of simultaneously separating and connecting, uniting and dividing, hidden and unhidden surfaces. In Merleau-Ponty's ontological approach to perception, these "breaks" are depicted as "folds" in the fabric of Flesh; and they are located at "chiasms." Chiasms, as we saw in Chapter 3, are, roughly, spaces where "crossovers" imperceptibly take place so that "incompossible" sides of something are identified (or disparately unified) through their "overlapping."

In our perceptual experience, Depth as a medium is imperceptibly implicated as a break/brake in that site where things can come into view only by eclipsing others and that sight where one *gestalt* can unify or form itself only by coherently de-forming another, which nevertheless remains continuously and latently "behind" it.

This Depth is the "thickness of a medium devoid of any thing" that is always already "there," stabilized and holding between "overlappings" or sur-facings of sensibilities.

To see this Depth "in action" ("overstepping" or as "Ueberstieg"), consider the "reversibilities" of the ambiguous cube drawing in Figure 4.1. Take a moment to note how, and because of an imperceptible "chiasm" holding them together, this drawing can di-verge or "cross over" into one, or an other, of the ways in which it can be seen.

Now, focusing your attention on the "side" of the central square, try to "see" how this side, which is a near one in the first gestalt, can "become" a far side in the second. Try to see how the near and far sides reversibly "become" or turn into each other. Notice how they appear to be turning themselves "inside out." Like "the finger of a glove" or any reversible fabric, as one is folded over, the other is folded under.

This happening of that backgrounding of the foreground and that foregrounding of the background that occurs in the process of any perceptibly ambiguous scene "taking shape" in this manner—reversibly unfolding into one or an other of the ways in which it can be seen—is Depth in the process of Reversibility.

Because of its belonging to the Now, the momentum (the moment-um) of this process cannot be "arrested" as it is happening. This quantum "leap" (or "lap") of Perception is Depth as *Ueberstieg*.

Because of this "overstepping," the two "incompossible views" of this ambiguous drawing can be identified as two "sides" *of* the same drawing. The "break/brake" that is *between* them and simultaneously facilitates both their divergency from each other *and* their "overlapping"

FIGURE 4.1

Ambiguous Cube Drawing

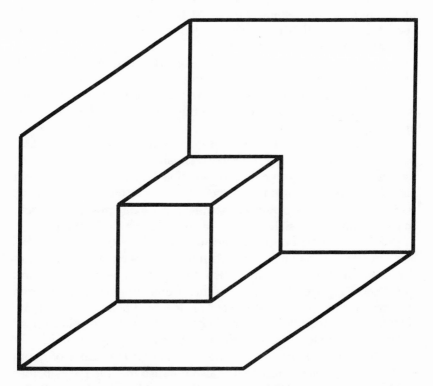

Source: Anthony J. Steinbock, "Merleau-Ponty's Concept of Depth," *Philosophy Today* 31 (Winter 1987): 339. Reprinted with permission.

is an interplay. It is not a *complete* break, one that separates them entirely from each other. They still "complement" or continously "become" each other. Their "breaking" from each other is therefore "incomplete." In other words, this "break" is not the oppositional "break" of polarity, of repulsion, of dichotomy. This "break" can be thought as a stepping–aside, a divergency, an "écart."

One further, and related, perceptual 'brake/brake' is to be noted here. Although two "sides" of an ambiguous reality may reversibly "become" each other, we apprehend, perceptually, that we cannot see them in both of their different configurations simultaneously or coincidentally. Because there is some conflicting distance or tension "between" them (despite their remaining "in touch" with each other throughout), we simply cannot see these two views in their different ways "there" *at once*, at the *same* time.

This is where the medium of depth as the Present, as "between-time" and *its* reversibilities (the past and the future reversibly "becoming" each other[1]) is implicated. In the process of Becoming, Time does not, so to speak, stand "still" enough for this—on either of its "sides." Although they are both drawn from the medium of the Present, we cannot observe, experience, the future and the past at once.

That is, as the hidden side of the future or foregrounding view is coming to the fore or unfolding in the medium of the present, the apparency of the other view must reversibly co-lapse into the background of the past. It must step a-side in time, for this other "side" to appear or emerge. After in-visibly resituating itself "there" "behind" its other "side," it may then take its reversible "turn" in another present slot of time and once again "become" the future or foregrounded view, while the former foregrounded view, its other side, must install itself, must resume its invisible "place," in the background of the past.[2]

What is to be noticed is the ways in which the imperceptible stopping of the one vision opens up onto the perceptible starting of the other and the way in which this process is therefore, and paradoxically, "open ended." Depth is thus not a simple "hidden dimension," not a simple "stopping" or closure of perception—with no relation to its opening or beginning. Because of its "reversibilities," Depth is a complex, and somewhat paradoxical, phenomenon.

Moreover, it is not simply the case that "it is because of depth that the things have a flesh."[3] It is also the case that the reversibilities of Flesh and the reversibilities of Depth cannot be thought apart from each other. For the "flesh" or any surface of sensibility to become apparent or to reverse in this manner, some recession of this surface, some Depth, is always already there or necessitated.

Perceptually, we can experience some continuity between "the visible and the invisible." They are no more dichotomously opposed to each other in Merleau-Ponty's ontology than are distance and proximity, surfaces and depth, or Depth and Flesh.

The sense of Depth as a medium, which I have alluded to in this chapter, aligns with our use of the expression in phrases like "the deep of the night" or "the deep of the winter" or "the depths of despair." Some of these uses connote a middle position; and these uses of the expression *depth* are also suggestive of a reversible turning point—a space of crossing-over, in which the onset of the dawn, or the spring, or hope, can take place.

We will refer back to the notion of Depth as a reversible medium and the considerations in this short chapter in Chapter 7, where we will apply the reversibility thesis to emotional experience and see how our identities and our "deep" emotions can be implicated in this Depth.

II
EMOTION, DEPTH, AND IDENTITY

5

Emotion and Emotional Depth

The depths are on the surface.

—Wittgenstein, *Zettel*

A woman's face can say, "I love you."

—James J. Gibson, *The Ecological Approach to Visual Perception*

We must reject that prejudice which makes 'inner realities' out of love,
hate, or anger, leaving them accessible to one single witness: the person
who feels them. Anger, shame, hate and love are not psychic facts hidden
at the bottom of another's consciousness. They are. . .visible from the
outside. They exist *on* this face or *in* those gestures, not hidden behind
them.

—Merleau-Ponty, "The Film and the New Psychology"

Introduction

Because I am interested in its literally spatial significance, I do not
regard the expression *emotional depth* as "merely" metaphorical, and
neither do I mean by it simply to refer to its dictionary definition:
"intensity of feeling."[1] However, in the use that I do try to make of this
expression, I *also* do *not* mean to refer (or to ex-ile) emotional "depths"
to some "there" that is thought as being some "where" *utterly* below
or behind or inside "surfaces"—which are thought as being *entirely* or
all "up front."

So, I do not mean by this expression to refer the "depths" of
emotions, either to the (un-conscious or sub-conscious) "depths" of
"depth psychology"—that is, to some "where" thought as utterly behind
or below the surface of consciousness[2]—and neither do I mean to refer

them to some "there" that is thought to be "deeply" in or inside (the surface of) our bodies—"deep inside" our hearts, for example, or our viscera.[3]

In keeping with the nondichotomous spirit of Merleau-Ponty's and Gibson's re-visionings of perception and depth, I mean by the expression *emotional depth* to blur traditional, or dichotomous, surface-depth distinctions by trying to interpret the "depths" of emotional experience as doubly referential "affordances" and by trying to bi-locate them—as depths of distanced contact as being some "where" in-between.

I am more interested in the question of "where" an emotion is or "where" emotional depth can be than I am in the question of what an emotion is.[4] (In any case, as we shall see, John Dewey's definition of an *emotion* as "the effort of the organism to adjust its formed habits or co-ordinations of the past to present necessities as made known in perception or idea"[5] will more than suffice for our purposes.) However, because I am also interested in relating emotional to perceptual and corporeal depths and insofar as I am trying to make sense of emotional experience in the context of an ontology of perception that construes the mind as the "other side" of the body, I do assume the position that emotions are neither "purely" mental nor "purely" physical phenomena. I assume the position that they are sensed—that they are phenomena of perception—and that they "belong to" the "expressive space" of Flesh.

In assuming this position, however, I recognize the fact that emotional experience does not exist on a level of abstract generality. There are significant social, linguistic, cultural, historical, racial, class, and gender influences and variations in emotional experience, perception, and expression. Just as there are different "forms of life"—different cultural or linguistic communities—so there are differences in emotional "worlds"—different styles of emotional conduct, gestures, and expressions. The meaning of a particular emotional gesture, like that of a linguistic one, can emerge only in the context of other socially acquired and available meanings and may be fully comprehensible only to those living in a similar emotional "world."

That said, I mean by emotion to refer to experiences such as anger, love, bliss, hatred, fear, sorrow, disappointment, pride, and so forth. I do not claim that my descriptions of these experiences are universally applicable or extendable. I do nevertheless hope that they are recognizable enough to elicit some general, and embodied, understanding of emotion and emotional depth.

Emotional Depth and Place Perception

Emotional experiences involve perceptions of meaningful change—"in" a situation and "in" ourselves in relation to that situation. We experience emotion when we feel ourselves being distanced from or moved out of a prior orientation and dis-placed or dis-"located" with respect to it, as we begin to assume another emotional stance or "position" in adaptive response to the perceived alterations.

This felt phenomenon of being moved or being distanced is, to my mind, a core, prototypical sense of "emotional depth": emotional experience cannot take place without some such dis-"orientation"; some such dis-positioning. This emotional di-"stancing" may be experienced as a fleeting breach or interruption in the continuity or the "sense" of our activities as another begins to emerge; or it may be experienced as losing or acquiring some "ground" of support.

This depth is implicit in John Dewey's depiction of emotion as "the conscious sign of a break"[6] and Janet's description of emotion as "a dis-organizing reaction which comes into play whenever we are stuck."[7] This felt phenomenon of emotional dis-positioning can also be related to Quentin Smith's metaphysics of feeling (particularly, to what he calls "directions" of "feeling flows")[8] and is also key to Glen Mazis's "philosophy of becoming" and its re-visioning of emotion as "e-motion"— insofar as Mazis means to capture by this expression a dis-placement with regard to (*regard* in the sense of "an eye toward") situation.[9]

"Where" are we when we are experiencing this emotional depth, when we are emotionally "moved," is a good question. It appears that we are some where—"in"-between the Surfaces of Flesh, de-bordered and re-bordering.

Places are spaces with meaning. Nothing is "placed" without a border, without bordering on something else.

As we live our body as attitude, our flesh as "expressive space," we do not experience it as being primarily *"in"* space as an extended substance or spatial fragment.[10] As adaptive "breaks," our emotions are set, behaviorally, "in a space which is not "empty" or unrelated to them."[11]

Emotionally speaking, not all of space "matters" or "makes a difference" to us. Where we are emotionally "at" will depend on a spatiality of situation, which is dependent upon goals and desires in a field of personal concerns.[12]

As you may recall from Chapter 2, a lived distance is a space of "personal outlook" to which we "adhere" or are "bound" and which was thought to establish "links"—between the accessible and the inaccessible, "a here and a yonder, a now and a future." It is as we "cross over" these areas of personal concern, through these emotionally lived "bindings" of distance, that we may become "dispositioned" with respect to a prior "placement" or with respect to our physical or "objective" locale: "an environment which is not necessarily that of my life." Through the process of this emotional distancing, as we are being oriented some-place *else*, we can "feel out of touch with" that prior place or that "objective" locale.[13] Through this emotionally lived depth, our emotions can inform us of how and where we are—"placed" (ad-apted or "fit")—in relation to the field of our concerns.

Our perception of these placements and displacements of emotional sense—like the perception of "affordances"—is not to be thought apart from the "ground" or the "surface" of Flesh, our own or that of the world's. We must also keep in mind that we are not emotionally "placed" as butter is placed on bread or as a "side" of aluminum is placed on a house. Emotionally, we are "placed" as a "side" that cannot be thought apart from its other side—the evocative. The emotional and the evocative are "placed" with respect to each other as the right and left sides of our body or the convex and the concave are.

We are now in a position to examine Merleau-Ponty's phenomeno-logical account of emotions as quasi-perceptible "living meanings"—meanings thought to be "blindly apprehended" and communicated via a "reciprocity" that "links body to body"—and to see how continuous these aspects of living meanings are with his later notion of "carnal ideality" and his thesis of the (incomplete) reversibility of "Flesh."

Emotion as a "Living Meaning"

Cezanne used to say of a portrait: "If I paint in all the little blue and brown touches, I make him gaze as he does gaze.... Never mind if they question how, by bringing together a green of various shades and a red, we can sadden a mouth or bring a smile to a cheek."

—Merleau-Ponty, *Phenomenology of Perception*

In the *Phenomenology of Perception*, emotions are thought as quasi-perceptible phenomena of "the body as expression and speech." As "a nexus of living meanings" and in its capacity as an "expressive space," our body is thought to be "comparable to a work of art."[14]

Perceptions of emotional significances were also regarded as latently apparent in, and even partly identifiable with, the corporeal gesticulations (art-iculations) of bodily attitudes. We also find in the *Phenomenology* the contention that communications of emotional significance occur through "blind" apprehensions and "reciprocities" of corporeal intentions and gestures. The following passage is illustrative of Merleau-Ponty's position on emotional perception and apprehension:

> Faced with an angry or threatening gesture, I have no need, in order to understand it, to recall the feelings which I myself experienced when I used these gestures on my own account. I know very little, from inside, of the mime of anger so that a decisive factor is missing for any association by resemblance or reasoning by analogy, and what is more, I do not see anger or a threatening attitude as a psychic fact hidden behind the gesture, I read anger in it. The gesture *does not make me think* of anger, it is anger itself. However, the meaning of the gesture is not perceived as the colour of the carpet, for example, is perceived.... The sense of the gestures is not given, but understood, that is, recaptured by an act on the spectator's part. The whole difficulty is to conceive this act clearly without confusing it with a cognitive operation. The communication or comprehension of gestures comes about through the reciprocity of my intentions and the gestures of others, of my gestures and intentions discernible in the the conduct of other people. It is as if the other person's intention inhabited my body and mine his. The gesture which I witness outlines an intentional object. This object is genuinely present and fully comprehended when the powers of my body adjust themselves to it and overlap it.... I do not understand the gestures of others by some act of intellectual interpretation; ...The act by which I lend myself to the spectacle must be recognized as irreducible to anything else. I join it in a kind of blind recognition which precedes the intellectual working out and clarification of the meaning.... It is through my body that I understand other people.... The meaning of a gesture thus "understood" is not behind it, it is intermingled with the structure of the world outlined by the gesture, and which I take up on my own account. It is arrayed all over the gesture itself..[15]

As a model for Merleau-Ponty's phenomenological position on emotion, we may think of occasions when it seems appropriate to say that we "see guilt written all over" someone's face. Merleau-Ponty would, similarly, hold[16] that I can hear the sorrow in your weeping, the regret in your apology, or the delight in your laughter, just as he might hold that I can see the confidence in your stance, the gaity in your step, the embarrassment in your fumblings, or feel the love in your caress.

Although he does not deny that feeling may be integral to the phenomena of emotional experience, Merleau-Ponty is clearly not identifying emotions with (introspectible) "feelings" or "inner realities."[17] They are neither (purely) psychic nor (purely) physiological "facts." They are some "where" in between—"in" the perceptibility of its gestures. By the same token, these gestures are not themselves regarded as "outward signs" of an entirely hidden or "inner" emotion (for that would be too far back for our perceptual grasp); but neither are the emotions regarded as entirely or perceptibly "given" as the observable features of the gestures themselves (for that would ignore the incarnated depth of their quasi- or virtually perceptible presence).

So (and the import of behavior in his earlier philosophy notwithstanding), neither is Merleau-Ponty depicting in this text a classically "behavioral" approach to emotions.[18] For the gesturing, itself, is not the emotion—because the emotion is thought to lie "in" the gesture *as* its expression.[19]

So anger, for instance, would be only partially identifiable with "furious" bodily gesturing. The anger (proper) is to be read "in" the perceptible gestures of (in our culture): the reddening of faces, the glaring of eyes, the volume of voices, or the clenching, shaking, or pounding of fists.

In the course of his phenomenological investigations, Merleau-Ponty remarked that he had discovered "a new meaning of the word, "meaning": a meaning "not conceived as an act of thought, as the work of a pure I," but "a meaning which clings to certain contents" which "is not the work of a universal constituting consciousness" but which the mobility of our bodily experiences "forces us to recognize."[20] He calls these meanings *living meanings. Living meanings* are "open" meanings, and they are related to meaning found in artwork, to poetic or musical meaning.

As living meanings, emotional meanings are thought to be "secreted" in bodily gestures in the same way that the musical meaning of a sonata's phrase (interpreted as an intermingling of joy and sorrow—"the essence of love")[21] is thought to be "secreted"—as an "idea veiled in shadows," presenting a "clouded surface" to the "mind's eye."[22] What are we to make of these "secretions"—these "leakages" or "clouded surfaces" of meaning? What are we to make of Merleau-Ponty's claim that emotional significances are "blindly" apprehensible?

As we shall see, Merleau-Ponty will "flesh out" this obscure dimension of his own phenomenological thought with *The Visible and the Invisible* notion of "carnal ideality." We may, however, say something here about these "blind" conveyances of emotional apprehension. For one thing, this "blind" apprehension is not to be confused with cognition or with "some act of intellectual interpretation." This, according to Merleau-Ponty, is the "whole difficulty." (This "whole difficulty" will become, by the way, the "most difficult point" of the Flesh ontology—the "bond" between the Flesh and the idea.) The apprehension of which he speaks is a prethematic, obscure "understanding" of "living meanings." We are thought to "catch on" to these meanings beneath "the intelligence...as a categorical process."[23]

In the conveyance of emotional meaning, it is, he says "as if the other person's intention inhabited my body and mine his"; and the meaning of an emotional gesture is thought to be fully comprehended when I "lend myself" to a spectacle and "the powers of my body adjust themselves to it and overlap it."

That is, to "blindly apprehend" an emotional significance is to "understand" it by way of its opening onto the conformatively expressive possibilities of one's own bodily powers. For example, says Merleau-Ponty, "A sight has a sexual significance for me...when it exists for my body" as a power available for adapting sexual conduct to it. He continues: "There is an erotic 'comprehension' not of the order of understanding, since understanding subsumes an experience, once perceived, under some idea, while desire comprehends blindly by linking body to body."[24] We may call to mind here Dewey's definition of an emotion as a bodily "adjustment." We may also recall some of our examples to illustrate "blind apprehension."

Think back to Meursault in *The Stranger* and to how, by lending himself to the spectacle of the courtroom's loathing and indignation of him, he experiences a (bodily) desire "to burst into tears." The sight of their loathing has emotional significance to him insofar as he can adapt emotional conduct (crying) to it. By the same token, his impulse to kiss the man with "moist eyes" and "trembling lips," who has tried his best to help him by "standing up" for him on the witness stand is also an instance of his "blindly" apprehending an emotional gesture by the conformatively expressive or "overlapping" powers of a bodily adaptation. That is, Meursault "fully comprehends" the apologetic kindness in this man's gestures through his bodily desire to embrace him in a loving demonstration of gratitude—just as he "fully comprehends" the loathing and indignation of "all those people" in the courtroom through his desire to burst into tears in a conformatively "overlapping" demonstration of distress.

One aspect of what is "blind" about this process of apprehension is the way in which we do not (and, if the Flesh ontology emphasis on chiasmic "blind spots" is correct, cannot) experience the "border" that "sides" aspects of these experiences *as* they are being "fully comprehended." This is because the chiasmic space—the space where the evocative and the emotional "cross over"—is "secreted" or "occluded" as a recessive edge or "fold" which is holding these "sides" simultaneously together and apart from each other. So (and because of this depth in between the flesh of the world and our own) we are prevented from the experiencing of where, precisely, someone's kindness may, so to speak, be "crossing over" into an overlapping demonstration of gratitude on, as we say, "our part"—or prevented from experiencing "where," precisely, the loathing and indignation of a number of a people may be "bordering" with our adaptive distress of it.

As another illustration of "blind apprehension," we might also recall our discussion of Oedipus in *Oedipus Rex* and the way in which he "fully" comprehends himself—by lending himself to (or "inhabiting") the spectacle of himself as Jocasta's son: "all. . . sealed with the womb that bore" him. The "blind" apprehension to be noted here is not simply Oedipus' emotionally motivated and isolated "act" of blinding himself, but his doing so in an embodied relation to Jocasta as his mother. The focus is on his body in relation to hers. He is adaptively "displaced" out of the "position" of being her husband and is replaced into a fetal "position"—into a "position" in relation to her where he can no longer see himself as her husband or see her as his wife. Blinding himself is his way of rectifying their incestual situation: symbolically sealed in her womb, no longer "in a position" for sexual intercourse with her; he resumes his identity as her son.

Gibson's ecological approach to visual perception with its theory of affordances is also based on the notion of "inhabiting" a spectacle. Although Gibson did not explicitly extend his theory of affordances into the emotional realm, I do not see why it cannot be; and I wonder if it is not already implicitly operating behind his theory of affordances.[25] In any case, we may also relate Gibson's theory of affordances to Merleau-Ponty's notion of emotionally "blind" apprehension.

To take Gibson's example of cliffs; at the site/sight of a cliff, we are thought to directly perceive it visually as a "falling off" place because "one's body in relation to the ground is what's getting attention." But Gibson does not pay sufficient attention to what one's body may be *doing* or emotionally *feeling* in relation to that "ground." Gibson's example tends to ignore the fact that at the sight/site of a cliff, we are simultaneously placed thereby (there bi-placed) evocatively "in" danger and emotionally "in" fear. It is not simply the case that we passionlessly *see* cliffs as "falling off places"; it is also the case that we sense that cliffs are dangerous and that we are afraid of falling off them.[26]

When I lend myself to the spectacle of a cliff I am walking toward, my body conformatively "overlaps" and "blindly apprehends" it as a *dangerous* falling-off place by walking on it as though it is, as though the ground beneath my feet might give way at any moment. As I approach a cliff, my sense of the danger and my fear of falling off are evident in the curtailing of my stride and in my taking of small, deliberate, and tentative steps as I proceed toward the edge. In fact, I walk as I walk when I am descending a slope. Thus, in an attitude of caution, my body "blindly apprehends" the danger of falling off a cliff—sensing it by conformatively "overlapping" with it in the style of its movements. Thus I "join" the spectacle of a cliff "in a kind of blind recognition which precedes the intellectual working-out and clarification of the meaning": "falling-off place."

Apart from the perceptible imperceptibility of emotional significance and their "blind" or secretive apprehension, perhaps the most interesting claim Merleau-Ponty makes with regard to emotion in the *Phenomenology* is that "Feelings and passional conduct are invented like words." According to Merleau-Ponty, emotion has "the same power of giving shape to stimuli and situations which is at its most striking at the level of language."[27]

Merleau-Ponty regards both speech and gesture as uses we make of our bodies, uses that endow them with a transcendent (relative to the body as a biological entity) *"figurative significance which is conveyed outside us."* By a certain way of bringing itself into play, the body as speech may suddenly "put up a new sense," doing so no less "miraculously"—as he puts it—than the way, for example, that love emerges from desire.[28] He argues that this power of the body[29] to open itself to some new kind of conduct—"this open and indefinite power of giving significance—that is, both of apprehending and conveying a meaning—by which man transcends himself toward a new form of behavior, or towards other people, or towards his own thought, through his body and his speech—"must be recognized as an "ultimate fact."[30]

He also considered the bodily power of creating and conveying emotional meanings to be "irrational," since "Behavior creates meanings which are transcendent in relation to the anatomical apparatus, and yet immanent to the behavior as such, since it communicates itself and is understood."[31]

If Merleau-Ponty had more explictly "thought together" his chapter on space with his chapter on the body as an expressive space, this bodily potential (which he simply relegated to the domain of the "miraculous" and thought to be a paradox of humanity's "genius for ambiguity") might have appeared less "irrational" to him.

For one thing, he might have connected his work on depth perception with his work on the perception of emotional gestures. He might have related the emotional body's "genius for ambiguity" to his sense of depth as space of copresent implication—and called some more explicit attention to the lived binding of a distancing copresently "holding" between the here and the there so that they are unified through their disparities.

For another thing, in claiming that it is "the body which points out, and which speaks,"[32] he might also have called some more specific attention to the indicative[33] nature of emotional gestures—relating it to something like Cassirir's remarks on "the indicative gesture" and his account of the formation of a primitive and "pecular" twofold "bond" in speech.

According to Cassirir:

> what characterizes the very first spatial terms that we find in language is their embracing of a definite 'deictic' function. We have seen that a fundamental form of all speech goes back to the form of showing—that language can only come into being and thrive where consciousness has developed this form. The indicative gesture is already a milestone in this development—a crucial stage on the way to objective intuition and objective formation. But what is embedded in this gesture comes to clear and complete unfolding only when language takes up this tendency and guides it into its own channels. With its deictic particles language creates the first means of expression for near and far and for certain fundamental differences of direction...with this distinction of the I from the "thou" and from objective being which it confronts, man has broken through to a new phase of his world view. Between the I and the world *a bond is now formed which, while binding them closer together, at the same time keeps them separate* [my emphasis]. The intuition of space that is elaborated in language is the plainest indication of this peculiar twofold relationship. Here distance is posited, but by this very positing it is in a sense surpassed.[34]

As forms of speech, emotions are also indicative gestures, related to forms of showing and participating in a "peculiar twofold relationship" of a distance, which in its "positing" is surpassed.

To realize the extent to which emotional experience is indicative, we have only to think back to *Nineteen Eighty-Four* and consider how horrifyingly oppressive it would be to have our facial expressions continuously monitored by a "Big Brother." Along with this novel's protagonist, Winston Smith, we realize that, emotionally *speaking*, the smallest "improper" facial expression can sometimes "give us away." Indeed, we sometimes even deliberately avoid contact with those who have learned to "read" our emotional gestures well, precisely because we know that they can and might "catch on" to some emotion or other we would rather they not detect. Even in masking them from others or in suppressing our own, we try not to let them show—to "cover them up." These efforts, which are frequently a struggle, are a tacit admission of the extent to which emotional gesture and feeling are "indicative" or demonstrative "showings"—how *telling*, as speech, they can be.

As an expressive space or form of speech, the body appears to distance a-side of itself, stand back, so to speak, from the thickness of its own anatomical corporeality so that its emotional expressions[35] can "stand out" from it "like the darkness in the theatre needed to show up the performance."

Philosophically, it is customary to regard emotional and aesthetic meanings as kindred. However, in Merleau-Ponty's philosophy and because of its emphasis on the body as expressive space, attention is diverted away from emotions as introspectible "inner" realities, and we are led to pay some significant attention to the fact that, as speech, these "living meanings" are, after all, creations and conveyances of perceptibly living bodies and to notice the multifaceted ways in which they are, so to speak, corporeally "exhibited."[36]

What we can say from a phenomenological perspective is that without the "vital" content of these "living meanings," art and emotion—as "speech"—can both be reduced to "sentimentality" and both be said to lack a certain "depth." Just consider, for example, how discernably hollow is the sound of "forced" or "polite" laughter or think of those times when someone is saying something without an emotional conviction in the inflections of their speech—those times when someone is not "saying it ('I love you,' 'I'm sorry,' or 'Thank you') like they (really) mean it." Just as unconvincing dramatic performances can be said to fall "flat" on their "faces," so can we, when our "heart" is not "in" something that we have to do or say. At these times, we just, as we say, "go through the motions," and whatever emotional "speech" we do manage to muster *appears* to be "put *on*" (like that aluminum side of a house or that butter on the bread). During these charades, the emotion appears as though we *are* "making it *up*"—as a facade or a "front."

We may conclude our discussion of Merleau-Ponty's position on emotions in the *Phenomenology* by saying that he thought Emotion to be the creation and (secreted) conveyance of "living" meanings,[37] which emerge "in" the expressive space of a body's purposive movements.

The quasi-perceptibility of an emergent emotional significance that appears in or on bodily gestures is one sense of "emotional depth." The "secretion" or "leakage" of this living meaning "outside" of itself and so as to be "blindly" apprehended by those living in the same emotional world is another. Beside its "secretion," this "blind apprehension" has also apparently to do with our bodies' "catching on" to emotional meanings by conformatively overlapping or "lending itself to" a spectacle.

A third sense of emotional depth has also suggested itself. This one concerns the body's ability, as an expressive space, to somehow distance features of its emotionally significant physiognomic expressions from the enveloping proximity of its physiological features. Emotional significance appears to surface as a relief, standing out or distanced from our biological or anatomical corporeality, at the very same time that it appears to be intimately hidden or embedded "in" it.

This peculiar twofold relation of lived distancing can also be thought situationally and intercorporeally: the latter as a reciprocal "overlapping" of gestures and intentions or as a "linking" of body to body; and the former as a body "stepping a-side" from a situation so as to respond, emotionally, to some perceptible change in it.[38]

The necessity for some such distancing in an ontology of perception was discussed in Part I. The necessity for some such dis-positioning taking place in emotional experience I addressed at the start of this chapter. (We may, however, wish to recall here that it is precisely Meursault's *absorption* in his surroundings which is responsible for the "flatness" and the "strangeness" of his emotional character). So let us move on to what (little) Merleau-Ponty had to say about emotions in *The Visible and the Invisible* before we try, in following chapters, to interpret emotional experience—and its "depths"—in the context of the Flesh ontology.

Emotion as a Carnal Idea

There is only one reference to "the passions" in the manuscript of *The Visible and the Invisible*, a reference that categorizes them as "carnal" or "sensible" ideas: "an idea that is not the contrary of the sensible, that is its lining and its depth."[39]

Merleau-Ponty appreciated the philosophical "strangeness" of "an ideality that is not alien to the flesh, that gives it its axes, its depth, its dimensions"[40] in the course of his addressing the transition from a mute to a speaking world, through the openings or re-conversions of silence into speech. Indeed, Merleau-Ponty regarded the most difficult point of his Flesh ontology precisely to be "the bond between the flesh and the idea, between the visible and the interior armature which it manifests and which it conceals."[41]

In *The Visible and the Invisible*, Language is considered to be this "bond between the flesh and the idea." Language is thought to mediate (as a distanced contact) between mute perceptibility and invisible essence; and Meaning is regarded as an expresion or articulation of ideas and "not on the phrase like the butter on the bread, like a second layer of 'psychic reality' spread over the sound: it is the totality of what is said, . . . it is given with the words for those who have ears to hear."[42]

According to Merleau-Ponty, all forms of knowledge involve "the exploration of an invisible and the disclosure of a universe of ideas."[43] He does, however, differentiate between the "invisibles" (ideas or essences) of science and the "invisibles" of "the passions" and the arts. He believed that the latter, unlike the former, "cannot be detached from their sensible appearances and be erected into a second positivity." They

> have their logic, their coherence, their points of intersection, their concordances, and here also the appearances are the disguise of unknown 'forces' and 'laws.' But it is as though the secrecy wherein they lie. . .were their proper mode of existence. For these truths are not only hidden like a physical reality which we have not been able to discover, invisible in fact but which we will one day be able to see facing us, which others, better situated, could already see, provided that the screen that masks it is lifted. Here, on the contrary, there is no vision without the screen: The ideas we are speaking of would not be better known to us if we had no body and no sensibility; it is then that they would be inaccessible to us. . .they owe their authority, their fascinating, indestructible power, precisely to the fact that they are in transparency behind the sensible, or in its heart. Each time we want to get at it immediately, or lay hands on it, or circumscribe it, or see it unveiled, we do in fact feel that the attempt is misconceived, that it retreats in the measure that we approach. . . . Thus it is essential to this sort of ideas that they be "veiled with shadows," appear 'under a disguise.'. . .We do not see, do not hear the ideas, and not even with the mind's eye or with the third ear: and yet they

are there, behind the sounds or between them, behind the lights or between them, recognizable through their always special, always unique manner of entrenching themselves behind them,...[44]

Carnal ideas are thought as an extremity or a limit of perceptibility. They do not appear without "sensible screens"; and they cannot "be given to us as ideas except in a carnal experience." With his notion of carnal essences, Merleau-Ponty provided some coherently philosophical background for the quasi-perceptible way in which emotions, as "living meanings" appear. So we may still continue to construe their perceptibly imperceptible presence as one sense of "emotional depth."

We may also continue to construe emotional significances as "living meanings" and as belonging to the expressive space of Flesh—as embodiments of Speech, of Language. Emotional significances, as living meanings (incompletely) expressive of sensible essences, will differ from others in being (necessarily or by definition) more apparently or perceptibly veiled. However, we must be careful of how we interpret these "living meanings" in the context of the Flesh ontology, because the Flesh ontology (completely) "reverses" our understanding of Language.

According to it, we do not speak of Being; Being speaks itself through us. In the Flesh ontology, "language is everything"[45] and "the voice of no one, since it is the very voice of the things, the waves, and the forests."[46]

Given this view of Language and no reason to believe that Merleau-Ponty had altered his view of emotions as living meanings or speech, what we must notice, if we still intend to construe emotions as "living meanings" is that the *power* or *source* of generating these emotional significances is no longer attributed solely to *humanity* (or to its 'genius for ambiguity'). They too, belong to or are 'of' the Flesh.

It might also be wise to differentiate the process of the generation of these living meanings, as Speech, from the generation of "another flesh"; viz., a "flesh of language" that is (relatively) transparent and "detachable" and that is thought to become further subliminated, transparent, and "detachable" in reflection or thought. For, unless we do this, we ignore their "solidity" and the basis for their distinction from other sorts of ideas—which is precisely that they can*not* "be detached from their sensible appearance and erected into a second positivity."

In *The Visible and the Invisible* and because of their relation to carnal ideality, it appears that Merleau-Ponty is continuing to affirm that the apprehension of emotional significance is not wholly identifiable with thought. (Remember, in the *Phenomenology*, this was "the whole difficulty.") He says that in the experience of carnal ideas,

> what I live is as 'substantial,' as 'explicit,' as a positive thought could be—even more so: a positive thought is what it is, but precisely, is only what it is and accordingly cannot hold us. Already the mind's volubility takes it elsewhere. We do not possess the...sensible ideas, precisely because they are negativity or absence circumscribed; they possess us.[47]

With respect to the living of emotional meanings and especially with respect to those we would describe as being "deep," this contrast between the lucidity of having relatively transparent and fluent thoughts and the arresting, relatively obscured and stabilized sense of being possessed by an emotional significance seems, to me, phenomenologically credible. As Merleau-Ponty remarks, in a different context, "the thought, precisely as thought, can no longer flatter itself that it conveys all the lived experience: it retains everything, save its density and its weight. The lived experience can no longer recognize itself in the idealizations we draw from it."[48]

The silent speech or language of thought is comparatively abstract, rarified. Because emotional significances are muted into the language of our own living Flesh, our experiences of living emotional meanings are more "substantial." There is a felt bodily depth to the living of emotional meanings that seems to be lacking in our experience of having thoughts.

For instance, consider how "flat" or how "rationalized" or "abstracted" a view that grief is "essentially" a "thought" of loss appears compared with the following depiction of living through a meaning of grief in which felt bodily depths of this significance *are* taken into account: "the loss pressed down on her chest and came up into her throat.... It was a fine cry—loud and long—but it had no bottom and it had no top, just circles and circles of sorrow."[49]

The carnal dimensions of the experience "flesh out" the essence of grievously mourning the loss of a loved one: the (otherwise) inaudible depths of sorrow are heard through the audibly "fine cry"; the bodily sense of being suffocated suggests not only deprivation, but also the felt weight of the demise of someone close. In living through this significance, the mourner appears to be palpably *feeling*—in touch with—her loss; and her sorrowful grief is articulated through her *body*.

This artistic rendering is obviously not the only way for grief to be expressed or articulated. However, a comparison of it with what William James had to say on the topic of emotions as carnal experiences provides an interesting complement to Merleau-Ponty's view and to the "whole difficulty" of confusing emotions with cognition or intellection: "what would [grief] be without its tears, its sobs, its suffocation of the heart, its pang in the breast-bone? A feelingless cognition that certain circumstances are deplorable, and nothing more. Every passion in turn tells the same story. A purely disembodied human emotion is a nonentity."[50] Perhaps it will suffice here to say that in the context of the Flesh ontology, emotional significances can be described as belonging, in a strict sense, to a Language of Living Flesh.

Such a depiction emphasizes both their belonging to perceptible Flesh and their belonging to a body of Speech, of expressive space. At the same time that this depiction differentiates them from the discursive, less dense, and more detachable "flesh of language," it prevents their further theoretical sublimation into the reflective transparencies of thematic "cognition" or "thought." Moreover, by regarding emotional meanings as belonging to a Language of Living Flesh, their affinities to the significances of Touch, to the communications of Tactility, to the percipient (and more or less obscurely informative) "feeling" side of an emotional experience can also be implicated. Because the logic of touch also belongs to the order of carnal ideality,[51] emotions can theoretically be placed back "in touch" with feeling—not as "inner realities" but in their tangible dimensions. (I explore a textural approach to emotional feeling in the following chapter). Because they are quite obviously nonvisual, emotional feelings elicit another sense in which emotional apprehension may be "blind."

The thesis of sensible ideas offers still another philosophical accounting for the "blindness" of emotional apprehension. To "blindly" apprehend an emotional significance may involve being in a distanced contact with its in-visible essence.

For example, the agitated feeling that I am "burning up" or losing my patience, the utterance of a particular gutteral sound, the gesture of spreading and tautening my fingers and hands and then shaking them back and forth (as though they are around some imaginary object), the thoughts that "I've had just about enough of this" and that "something must be done," together with a willingness to confront and the desire or the behavior of striking out physically or lashing out verbally—articulate ways in which I have experienced or lived through the meaning of anger. I apprehend my anger through experiencing this cluster of feelings, gestures, thoughts and behaviors. I apprehend that

I am, through them, in touch, if you will, with the "essence" of anger rather than with the essence of joy or of shame.

However, the essence of anger (of anger itself or even the essence as the "style" of my own anger) is obviously not *exhausted* by these particular articulations of its meaning. Sometimes instead, I cry in frustration rather than lose my patience, and at other times I express anger through a solid, stony silence. From what I understand, anger is expressed in Japanese culture through a gesture of smiling. Nevertheless it remains apparent that I have no way of *directly* apprehending the "idea" of anger without the intervention of their articulated mediation. For without them, the essence would not be articulated, as it is, into meanings of anger to begin with, and I would therefore not apprehand myself as angry. This is simply an extension of the view that for a carnal idea to make an "appearance" is for it to appear as a circumscribed absence, "behind" a sensible screen. However, because of that sensible screen, my apprehension of the essence or the in-visible depth of anger, itself, is substantially obscured.

This latter consideration is important, for it is the sense in which, in the context of the Flesh ontology's view of carnal ideality, the apprehension of emotional significance is both "blind" and depthful. The living of emotional significances circumscribes or articulates an essence (its "depth"); but the essence of the emotion is only blindly and partially apprehended—for as an *essence* or a circumscribed absence, it is thought to be inexhaustible, imperceptible, and to have hidden "sides" in other emotional and nonemotional essences, and as a *sensible* essence, it is thought to be embedded in the thickness of Flesh. In any case, Merleau-Ponty believed that we are held and possessed by these "circumscribed absences"—that we are "at their service."

The feeling of being possessed or "held" by an emotional essence is familiar to us in the sense we have, while we are undergoing an emotional experience or appreciating a fine work of art, that we are being "swept" into *its* grasp. It is the felt sense of the "passivity" of emotional experience; the sense of having *been* moved, emotionally. It is akin to the experience I described earlier as being emotionally "dispositioned" and is related to the experience I will later describe as "apprehending that you are being apprehended."[52]

However, although it is true that, compared to the earlier phenomenology, the Flesh ontology generally places much more philosophical stock in "the passivity of our activity" (a passivity about which Merleau-Ponty believed philosophy had "never spoken" and is exemplified in his claim that Being speaks through us—it is not we who speak of Being) and that his depiction of the way in which we experience carnal ideas (these "open vortices" "possess" us, we do not "have" them) is certainly suggestive of the stance, Merleau-Ponty does not say enough, specifically, about emotions in *The Visible and the Invisible* for us to say that he thought of emotions as "passions"—as forces beyond our control that simply happen to us. For one thing, "the passivity of our activity," relates more to his thesis of reversibility than it does to his thesis of carnal ideality. For another, although passivity is emphasized in the ontology, it does seek, as the expression *the passivity of our activity* itself suggests, to reinterpret, through reversibility, the active-passive dichotomy as a complementary relation, into an "active-passive circularity" or a "being as a winding."

However, without saddling Merleau-Ponty with a dichotomy he himself has rejected and one according to which philosophy has tried, unsuccessfully, to comprehend emotions, we may say, at least, that his remarks about the way in which carnal ideas are experienced suggest that emotions, as carnal ideas, are experienced passively and that the thesis of carnal ideality might provide some accounting not only for their "blind" apprehension, but also for the felt experience of emotional "passivity."

Admittedly, this reliance on the thesis of carnal ideality to account for the experience of emotional passivity is only half the story of the "depths" of emotional apprehension—one "sided." It accounts only for the side of how we, as emotional experiencers, feel ourselves to be grasped or held by emotional significances. It coincides with the senses in which we might say that we have fallen into love, are gripped with fear or seized by terror, burdened with remorse, overcome by shame, filled with joy, cast into despair, and so forth. It coincides, that is, with a view of emotions as "passions."

In any case, I do not think that the relation between emotional depth and emotional passivity should be ignored. It does appear to be true of our deeper emotional experiences to say that "the emotions have us; it is not 'we' who have the emotions."

However, it still remains for us to relate these "openings" of emotional meanings to the other or evocative side of flesh—the flesh of the world. Although Merleau-Ponty said nothing about how his reversibility thesis might apply to emotional experience, it seems like the most promising way to go in this regard. So we will focus on it in the next chapter.

Summary

None of Merleau-Ponty's works is exclusively devoted to a discussion of the emotions. His stance on emotion appears as an outgrowth of his interest in aesthetics, his work on perception, his theory of embodiment, and his later Flesh ontology. It reflects their novelty. His approach to the emotions is neither cognitive nor behavioral. Although he is critical of a "subjectivist" view of emotion as entirely hidden "inner realities," he consistently takes their occlusions, their "invisible" dimensions, into account.

Emotional significance is thought to be perceived "in" or "on" bodily gestures—neither entirely visible nor entirely invisible. They are also thought to be "blindly recognized" in bodily attitudes and "fully comprehended" when bodily powers "adjust themselves to it and overlap it." His view of emotions as "open, living meanings" that "secrete" their sense evolved into a later view of them as carnal or sensible ideas, ideas that are essentially "veiled in shadows" and cannot appear without the aid of a "sensible screen."

One of the more interesting extensions of Merleau-Ponty's thought on depth and Flesh that can be applied in the emotional realm is the notion of lateral "sides." The notion of "sides" with a requisite "blind spot" in between allows us to begin to think of the evocative and the emotional as disparate "sides" of a unified affective experience. Once we do so, we can start deconstructing the evocative-emotional dichotomy and offer some accounting of their "reversibilities."

The Flesh ontology reverses our understanding of language and emphasizes the "passivity of our activity." Accordingly, it contends that in our vision Being sees itself and in our language Being understands itself. It appears to be in keeping with the spirit of this ontology to say that in our emotional experiences, Flesh is emotionally sensitive to itself, is adapting to itself, in harmony or in conflict with itself, apprehending its interest in safeguarding and enjoying itself, its own animation—its Life(!).

This could he, so to speak, the "big picture" of emotional apprehension, generally, in the Flesh ontology. It is not the only one. The evocative and the emotional can themselves be thought together as a "side" and thought of as overlapping with other "sides" of experience such as cognition, memory, tactility, audition, imagination, and so on.

Merleau-Ponty's metaphysics is fundamentally grand, but his ontology of 'Flesh' is remarkably postmodern in its accommodation of a multiplicity of meanings, its permission of "overlaps," and its attention to "blind spots."

6

Emotions "in the Flesh"

Introduction

In this chapter, I show in detail how the reversibility thesis can be applied to emotional experience. In recounting some personal experiences, I also depict a "decentered" view of the "subject" of emotions, in the context of interpreting Merleau-Ponty's expression: *being as a winding*.

For some reason, Merleau-Ponty never connected his view of emotionally "blind" apprehension with tactile perception or emotional feeling. I make these connections as I explore some of the overlaps between touch and emotional feelings. In the final section of this chapter, I extend the discussion on touch and emotional feelings into the area of "embodied politics" and assess some of the social implications of thinking in terms of 'Flesh.'

Emotion and the Reversibility Thesis

As you may recall from Chapter 3, Merleau-Ponty described reversibility as

> the idea that every perception is doubled with a counter-perception..., is an act with two faces, one no longer knows who speaks and who listens. Speaking-listening, seeing-being seen, perceiving-being perceived circularity (it is because of it that it seems to us that perception forms itself *in the things themselves—Activity = Passivity*.[1]

You may also recall that "chiasms" function in the Flesh ontology to ensure that reversibilities are always "incomplete"; that is, although they allow for the occlusively permeated "sides" of perceptibility to reversibly 'cross over" into each other, they simultaneously distance them from each other and preclude a total coincidence.

It is worth emphasizing at the outset of our attempt to apply the reversibility thesis to emotional experience—particularly as so much contemporary literature on emotion adopts a kind of "doubling" thesis with the view that emotions are "intentional" (intentionality is the view that a "subjective" emotion is "directed" toward a frontally perceived, "external" object or the view that an emotional, like any "mental," state is "about" something), that *the doublings of reversibility are* not *the doublings of "intentionality."* Reversibility of the Flesh is *not* a relation of unilateral "directedness" toward frontally perceived objects.

Also—and despite the fact that the notion of 'Flesh' "deborders" the body-world boundary—the "chiasms" thought to effect "reversibilities" are nevertheless *not* to be thought as a subject-object correlative "fusion," unless this "in-mergion"[2] that "holds" between the percipient and perceptible "sides" of a reversible relation is thought together with a "break."[3]

To avoid lapsing into the domain of the subject-object language in the realm of emotional experience, it will help us to think of the doublings of reversibility as a twofoldedness and of reversible flesh on the model of reversible fabric. Merleau-Ponty apparently had something of this sort in mind when he said:

> Reversibility: the finger of the glove that is turned inside out—
> —There is no need of a spectator who would be *on each side*. It suffices that from one side I see the wrong side of the glove that is applied to the right side, that I touch the one *through* the other (double 'representation' of a point or plane of the field) the chiasm is that: the reversibility—[4]

This view of "reversibility" is related to the idea that "once a body-world relationship is recognized, there is a ramification of my body and a ramification of the world and a correspondence between its inside and my outside, between my inside and its outside."[5] As one commentator remarks,

> The *reversibility* of the flesh can be grasped by borrowing images from topology. . . . From a Cartesian point of view, concepts such as 'inside' and 'outside' are fundamental determinations. The 'subject' attempts to get 'outside' to the 'objective' world, or he attempts to return the 'objectivity' of the world to its 'subjective' conditions. . . . But with topological entities such as the Mobius

strip and the Klein bottle, these concepts lose their sense. To follow the contours of a Mobius strip or a Klein bottle is to move from 'inside' to 'outside' and 'outside' to 'inside' in one continuous motion. Insides turn into outsides and vice versa. At best these discriminations are provisional, relative. For Merleau-Ponty this perplexing mobility comes not from some inattention or trick: it is the norm. It is, to steal a phrase, the way of all flesh....

...Subject and object are not two opposed domains to be somehow united, they are both aspects of the same flesh: the flesh seeing itself, turned upon itself, overlapping itself, folded upon itself, reversible.[6]

It seems to me that any application of the reversibility thesis in the emotional realm must at least make some sense of Flesh folding over upon itself to create "openings" of emotional percipience. It must also make some sense of perceptible-percipient "doublings." It must show how there are at least two "sides" to every affective experience, that neither of these "sides" is intelligible apart from the other,[7] and that they "become" each other, by overlapping or crossing over into each other, but never completely. In short, it must show that these sides are in distanced contact with each other or in a relation of proximity through distance.

One approach to the project of applying the reversibility thesis to emotional apprehension is simply to highlight reversible "doublings" in emotional experience, show how they relate to "the passivity of our activity" and show the respect in which this active-passive "circularity" is "incomplete."

We may fill this bill simply by acknowledging that—as we are living through them—emotions have both active and passive or reversible "sides" and that, in the course of an emotional experience, we can chiasmically "wind up" on either—and to the extent that "one no longer knows who" is perceiving and "who" is being perceived.

Fearing and being endangered or loving and being enamored are two such two-sided and "reversible" emotional experiences. For example, "actively" fearing some danger—a car speeding or veering toward our own on the road, say—is, simultaneously an experience of being "passively" frightened or endangered by it. The perspective is also reversible, for I may also say that the speeding vehicle is "itself" frightening and endangering me. (By the way, there is that "in" or "en" locution again.[8]) "In" actively fearing or "in" passively being frightened *by* such a danger, our emotionally lived bodies are prospectively and reversibly dis-positioned—reversibly *bi/by* placed on their "other side" through some "overlapping" with it so that, to return to our example of a speeding vehicle veering toward us on the road, it is as though this vehicle has already *had* its "impact" on us. As we live through these awful moments, we cannot even tell what is evocative and what is emotional, what is active and what it passive. They blur, as we jam on our brakes and jam up our body—which is retracting itself—in fearful response to the impending crash. Clenching the steering wheel, no longer "in control" of the road, and anticipating the car's inscription on our bodies through some overlapping with it, we "fully" or emotionally and somewhat "blindly" apprehend. Again, or as Gibson would say, our attention is focused on the significance of surfaces in relation to our body.

Because emotional experiences have both active and passive dimensions and because these "sides" can sometimes blur, we cannot very intelligibly call emotions, strictly speaking, either "actions" or "passions." But because they are both at once, neither can we eliminate this distinction altogether. That is, we do not want, entirely, to collapse—we want only to confuse, the "boundaries" *between* the evocative and the emotional. We want to confuse them just enough so that they can *incompletely* "become" (complement) each other and "reverse."

For if we were to regard fear just in its "passive" aspect as an experience of being frightened by a danger, we lose the important sense of its being an active response *to* the danger, a way of dealing with it, addressing it, on its "other side." Similarly and to take another example, although actively to love someone involves being passively enamored of that person (and being bi/by placed intimately "close" to them—physically or even to the extent of partially sharing our identity with them), we are never *so* en-amored "of," or so physically en-grossed "in" another person, that we are *completely* identified with—or actually do become (coincide with)—them. This is impossible; if this were to happen, we could no longer be enamored "of" them at all. At best, we coin-"side."[9] Moreover, without simultaneously responding to this enamourment by actively loving back in response or in return (or in "reverse"), we do not "fully" comprehend the depth of the experience; we do not capture the whole *sens*—the whole direction or the whole "meaning"—of the experience of being "in" love.

Either way or on either side, if we entirely collapse the passively evocative and actively emotional (or the actively evocative and the passively emotional) distinction we lose the important sense of an emotion as a response, as speech, as expressive space with a "side," so to speak, of its "own."

Once we do acknowledge the "passive" dimensions of emotional experiences (without making our emotions "passions"), however, we are already open onto reversibilities between evocative and emotional significances—reversibilities between the Flesh of the world and our own and begin to see how it is true, even of emotional percipience, that they are perceptions "formed in the things"—so that they cannot take place or be apprehended without the perceptible.

We come at this point to two perplexities in emotional apprehension. One—that of its being "action at a distance"—I hope to have already abetted with the foregoing discussion of activity vs. passivity and with the conception of depth I have been developing all along—that of a living distance, a distanced contact, or the idea of "proximity through distance." The other perplexity concerns the perceptibility (or the imperceptibility we should say, because they too are on the order of carnal ideality) of evocative significances. One might object, for instance, that I can perceive the color, the speed, the sound of the car rushing toward me, but how can I, in what "sense" do I, perceive the danger?

My answer to this is through my emotional sense—"through my fear of it." We sense the danger through or as our fear of it. That is, we cannot, in some disembodied or intellectualized fashion, directly or "fully" apprehend the significance of danger or what it is to be endangered, without appealing to our emotional flesh, without apprehending, emotionally, the significance of fear. Any more than we can "fully" apprehend the significance of something being "precious" or "worthy" without emotionally responding or adapting to it as being cherishable, or worthy of respect in our bodily attitude or adaptation to it. A precious vase and a cherished person are both "handled with care"—not, instrumentally, as "objects."

Like Merleau-Ponty's model of reversible fabric—and his example of "the finger of the glove that is turned inside out": "There is no need of a spectator who would be *on each side*. It suffices that from one side I see the wrong side...that is applied to the right side, that I touch the one *through* the other..."

Through the openings of emotional percipience, evocative significances "in" the perceptible are grasped. Through curiosity, the significance of the odd or the novel is apprehended. Through serenity, the significance of peace or tranquility is grasped. Through grief, I perceive, emotionally, the significance of loss; just as through boredom, I apprehend the significance of monotony. And so forth.

And it is worth mentioning or repeating here that neither can we "fully" apprehend emotional significance or percipience without appealing to or recoursing to some other perceptible "side." If my logic of percipience—my claim that we cannot sense sentience (see seeing, touch touching, hear listening, and so forth)—is correct,[10] then this same logic must be applied to emotional percipience. That is, we *cannot* just, directly or immediately and "all by itself," emotionally perceive or feel our emotional feelings. To the extent that we do or can emotionally perceive, we must do so, our emotional feelings must be felt, through an evocative "other side"—"in" the perceptible. For percipience "all by itself" is nothing at all. This is the (very) important point *of* the Flesh ontology and its twofold conception of "percipient perceptibility."

Overlappings of evocative and emotional significance are characteristic of emotional experiences "fully" comprehended. We must notice how intimately worldly Flesh is intermingled or occlusively permeated with our own. In the "circle" of these experiences, the evocative ("voice of no one") and the emotional (flesh "responding" to it) "copresently implicate" each other, are "compresent" as "sides"—"sides" that cannot, intelligibly, be thought apart from each other, any more than the touching and the tangible or the hearing and the audible "sides" of Tactility or Audition can be. In the embodied language of expressive space, as "in" perceptible Flesh, they are "mutually synonymous."

If this twofold model of "overlapping" percipient perceptibity is right, then emotions can*not be* purely "subjective experiences," purely "inner realities." And if we think the evocative and the emotional "sides" together, as a "side" of, if you will, "Emotionality" and apply the thesis of reversibility to it, then there is no reason why this "side" of Emotionality cannot "overlap" with other perceptual or psychological "sides"—with the imaginative, the mneumonic, the sexual, the cognitive, the behavioral, the motivational, etc. Indeed, this is the beauty of Merleau-Ponty's "laterally styled" philosophy of mind as the "other side" of the body: that there *be* "overlapping" and "encroachment" *between* "sides" of 'Flesh,' enough to facilitate their 'crossing over' into each other so that there is a "double" or a "cross situating" of the one in the other, so that these "maps" are superposable—but are never entirely so. Because "reversibility" is always "incomplete"—effected as they are, through "chiasms"—the thesis is not vulnerable to the objection that it collapses these distinctions altogether.

One further point. Because of these overlappings, we sometimes say things like "I sensed the danger" or "I felt his anger" or "She felt the loss." This is not simply a matter of careless speaking—if, as Merleau-Ponty contended: "'What happens in me can pass over into the other." That is, if our "experience is not immanent but transitive,"[11] then we *can* sense his anger by reversibly going *through* our fears of them; just as she *can* feel the loss, by going *through* her grief over it.

For just as we may extend the circle of touched and touching hands (in shaking or holding hands with another), so our body can "annex" or "incorporate" the emotional body of another "in that 'sort of reflection' it is paradoxically the seat of"—so that we and they compresently coexist "like organs of one single intercorporeality." This is because the same "flesh of the world" makes us perceive and because the "chiasm," "like the chiasm of the eyes...means that there is not only a me-other rivalry, but a co-functioning"—a co-functioning "as one body."

Phenomenologically, as we are being emotionally dis-positioned or dis-placed (de-bordered and re-bordering), we feel the danger as well as the fear, the loss together with our grief; the intermingling of his anger with our fear "of" it. My earlier point was that we cannot feel the emotional and the evocative with-out or apart from each other. The present point is slightly different. It is that, because there is no strict body-world boundary in the Flesh ontology and because percipience is "itself" conceived on the model of "openings," we *can* be said, through the "openings" of fear and grief, to *sense the* danger, *the* loss, *his* anger. What we cannot experience or sense is where, precisely, these "cross overs" take place—"where" the loss "becomes" my grief, for instance, or "where" his anger has intermingled and crossed over into my feelings of fear toward it. But this is just the "occluding edge" of the chiasm, the "blind spot" at work. There is still the Flesh of the world between us. All feeling takes place in and through what is, on principle, unfeelable. There must be some imperceptible non-sensing for the sense of the perceptible to be "in."

I believe that the "deeper" the emotional experience, the more blurred or de-bordered the world-body border becomes, the more we experience ourselves as belonging to or caught up in the Flesh of the world. This is the experience I call, in the next section, *apprehending that you are being apprehended*. (Please keep in mind that the Flesh ontology's reversals and emphasis on the "passivity of our activity" would inflect this as "apprehending that *you* are being apprehen*ded*." For "we" do not have the emotions, remember, the emotions have us.)

Some sense of "being apprehended" is visible in our language about emotional experience. That is, the deeper the emotional experience is, the more we tend to emphasize the passive voice. For example, to experience a deep joy is to be over-jo*yed*, ec-static, "beside oneself"; to experience deep anger is to be en-rag*ed*, temporarily "out" of "self"-control; to be deeply fearful is to be "seized" with terror or terror-*ized*, frozen still or "petrified." Deeper emotional experiences expand, if you will, our "personal" horizons beyond that of our own body, our own living flesh. We tend in these experiences to lose or to expand our sense of "self" or "subjectivity." We do not experience ourselves as active "agents"—choosing to respond to a certain situation at some isolated remove. We experience ourselves as "winding up" through them on the (perceptible) other side of our body—identified with the flesh of the world. In deep emotional experiences, we experience ourselves "being as a winding."

Emotional Depth and "Being as a Winding"

The maniac is centered wherever he is.

—Merleau-Ponty, *Phenomenology of Perception*

beyond the 'point of view of the object' and the 'point of view of the subject,' a common nucleus which is the 'winding' (serpentement), being as a winding. . . . It is necessary to make understood how that (or any *gestalt*) is a perception 'being formed in the things.'

—Merleau-Ponty, *The Visible and the Invisible*

When I am being emotionally dis-positioned—that is, when I begin to apprehend that I am being apprehended and that, in being apprehended, I am emotionally apprehending—then I enter, affectively, into that spiraling current of experience Merleau-Ponty calls *active-passive circularity* and into an experience of myself as "being as a winding." That is to say, in being moved or disposed toward a significance in which I have just been, am, or am about to be emotionally "caught up," I tangibly and kinesthetically experience the living of my emotionally responsive flesh as de-bordered and re-bordering.

This experience of being emotionally de-bordered or dis-placed is an experience of emotional depth. This depth, which is a depth of distanced contact, is an experience in which our usual, or visual, perceptual experience of the here and the there, as well as the before and the behind, and the inside and the outside, reversibly alternate.

These reversibilities of emotional depth can take several forms: the form of feeling that it is only through the significance of what is there, that I, here, am, emotionally as I am (that it is only through its being caught up "there" that my flesh is "catching on" emotionally "here"); or these reversibilities of emotional depth may take the forms of the feeling that *I am not all here*, the feeling that I am *there*, simultaneously, as well *and* the feeling that what is there is also and simultaneously here.

During these reversibilities of emotional depth, "I" experience my "self" dispersively—as alternating "back and forth"—caught up somewhere in between these heres and theres. "I" am in no one particular "place" and on neither "side" exactly, but am somehow on both at once. For example, here, I may be, beginning to fall in love with you, but there, as we say, goes my heart; there, my heart might also go, out to you or for you, while here, I am sympathetic to your troubles. While here, I am feeling disappointed, I might simultaneously realize that "there" go all my hopes; although I have been hoping "here," my hopes are always shattered, there, where they must have been, in some sense, all along.

Not only am I "not all here" when I experience emotionally, I also do not experience my emotions as static mental "states," as "still life." Life is not still, and my emotional life—the way I experience myself as living through these evocative-emotional circlings of experience—is intrinsically dynamic, is apprehended kinesthetically through my living body.

That I am no longer where, a moment ago I was; that a breach or shift in the continuity of my prior activities has occurred and my sense for "where," just a moment ago, I "was" has receded to the extent that *now* I sense that I *am* some *place else*; that I have been and am being de-situ-ated and am re-situ-ating in adaptive "response" to a change in my world due to a new sighting of significance—these I take to be integral to any adequately described or phenomenological account of emotional experience. As I mentioned in the last chapter, I also take this emotional dis-positioning to be a core or prototypical sense of "emotional depth."

"Here-there" relations in the space of affectivity are, to use an expression of Merleau-Ponty's, "coherently deformed." Because this deformation also coherently deforms the philosophical sense of self as a private and "inner" subjectivity, the reversibilities of the heres and the theres in affective space wreak havoc with the philosophical notion that emotional experience belongs, primarily, to "inner realities" in the exclusive domain of the "subjective." During an emotional experience, I do not spatially experience my enfleshed being as a "centered" "subject"—as centrally and completely and absolutely "here." Neither do I experience *my living, moving, feeling body as an emotionally* expressive space as a *source* of space, as that source who is "laying down that first coordinate" (*Phenomenology*) or whose interests, "reach," goals, or "grasp" is determining, in advance, what is "there"—for one to do or to manipulate or before one, to see or to use.

These models of the relation between the here and the there are characteristic of visual experience or of "instrumentalist" space—the "instrumentalist" space of Gibson's ecologically "affordant" approach to visual perception or the Heideggerian space of readiness to hand, for instance.[12] It is precisely these visual and instrumentalist "here-there" models (where the "here" is determining the "there") that "reverse" or undergo a coherent deformation in emotional experience (where the "there" is determining the "here"). In its incompletely reversible alternations between what is here and what is there, through its kinesthetic apprehensibility of being both here and there at once and yet not specifically situated in either "place," in taking place "before us"; in being simultaneously active and passive, in involving simultaneously a being grasped and a grasping back, *the space of affectivity resembles the space of tactility* much more than it does either the space of visibility or the space of instrumentality. Probably this is because there is more of an "overlapping" between the "sides" of tactility and affectivity—because they share, between them, the space of feelings.[13]

The achievement of tactility is its establishment of a certain optimal *proximity* between the here that is feeling and the there that is felt. This tactile proximity is not just a proximity of spatially static contiguity. It is proximity established through the body's exploratory movements.

In the *Phenomenology*, Merleau-Ponty paradoxically contended both that the "knowing touch projects us outside our body through movement" *and* that "Tactile experience...adheres to the surface of our body; we cannot unfold it before us, and it never quite becomes an object." He also recognized that "tactile experience occurs 'ahead' of me, and is not centred in me."[14]

In tactile experience and because it seeks to establish a proximity through movement, the boundary between what is touching "here" and what is touched "there" is not only vague but is also experienced as continuously shifting. In the cross-overs of tactile experience, we experience first hand the dynamics of occurrent deborderings and "reversibilities" between the feeling here and the felt there. Here, if anywhere, the here and the there, the touching and the touched, the active and the passive, are experienced as intimately and ambiguously encroaching on and usurping each other's "domains"—enveloping and folding over on each other, crossing over to each other's "sides," shifting back and forth; in short, "being as a winding"—winding round and chiasmically winding up, to some extent, each, on each other's "side."

These windings or shiftings occur and we experience them as occurring, I believe, because the two sides of tactility are immediately and directly *experienced* as occupying or as sharing *between* them, the *same* common space—the same Flesh. Tactile experience is corporeal experience, and in tactile experience, we cannot deceive ourselves about the extent to which our bodily flesh is embedded and engrossed in the flesh of the world or about the extent to which the flesh of the world is engrossed and embedded in us.

As Merleau-Ponty came, more and more, to appreciate the "passivity of our activity" and as he came to believe that bodily movement must be meshed with the tangible, he began to see that "touching" is not a wholly "active" experience. It, too, has a passive, perceptible "side": "The touch = movement that touches and movement that is touched."[15]

As I hope to show, the heres and the theres of emotional experiences enjoy an analogous sort of spatial and tangibly felt proximity—a certain proximity that unifies, as depth does, through disparities and through which reversibilities occur. I will also try to show how, when we occupy space affectively, the "heres" of emotionally lived significances and the "theres" of evocatively emergent significances enjoy a certain *felt* proximity, have a certain way of mutually implying while mutually excluding each other, how there is in emotional experience a certain reversibility of sense, and a certain way of communicatively intertwining the bodily flesh that we live with the flesh of the world that we also are, which "de-centers" or dis-positions us. As we consider how these intertwined significances wind round and wind up each, to some extent, on the other's "side," we come to realize just how false is a subjectivist account of emotions—an account in which "I" am either the source or the center of these experiences or an account which would "center" emotional significances in some closed-off and privately experienced space of "subjectivity." Finally, I also hope to show, through examples of how I have inhabited space affectively, how caught up our "own" bodily flesh can be, in the flesh of the world and in the intercorporeal flesh of humanity.

For example, I am awed by the imposingly expansive and radiantly enfleshed beauty that emerges in the colored brilliance of a sunset— the golden glows; the luminously muted warmth of pinks, the firey, blazing oranges; the tangibly rich hue of a deepening blueing that thickens the sky and brings it closer; the starkened silhouetting of trees; the criss crossings of their blackened branches. . .

When I am moved into feeling in awe of a sunset's beauty, I am simultaneously being grasped, being felt by its beauty and grasping-feeling this beauty back through feeling in awe of it. I apprehend that I am being apprehended (by the "breathtakingly" beautiful sunset) and that, in being apprehended, I am apprehending emotionally (becoming awe inspired)—as I feel myself becoming more and more *en-grossed* in the beauty of its colors, more and more appreciative of its evocatively "secreting" (or "leaking") its significance "there" through me "here," and more and more aware that an emotional significance, that of awe, is unfolding "here" and that through the unfolding of this emotional significance I am more "open" to the beauty of the sunset.

We may even say that the sunset's beauty, initially perceived as visually "in front of" me—that is, at some distance, there—reversibly "winds up" being felt/experienced/blindly apprehended here, through the density of my own living flesh, and "behind" the opening of my sense or feeling of awe.

The sunset feels itself through me. . .touches me, touches off this sense of awe in me (the sense through which, in the language of my own living flesh, I am open to it or am touching or feeling it back), when Flesh (to which the beauty of the sunset "there" and my own living flesh "here" belongs) "reverses"—folds over on itself—through its own/my own living flesh, "here," where some of this beauty is also experienced as being and where it is opening up, doubling up with, and crossing over into a living of its meaning. In the radical and reversible terms of the Flesh ontology, we would say that Flesh is awed by the beauty of its own being.

This flesh I am living, this flesh I also am, is touched by this radiant beauty and not only do I apprehend—kinesthetically, tactually—that the beautiful sunset "there" is also and simultaneously appreciating itself here, through me, through my emotionally experiencing awe "in response" to its imposingly beautiful presence. No. I also apprehend that the beauty of this "worldly" flesh or the flesh of this "worldly" beauty is encroaching on, intermingling with my own flesh, as eventually I come to the "de-bordered" realization that I *am enlivened and involved*—all *caught up* in this beauty—that my flesh *belongs to* it, is *"of it,"* and I begin to feel privileged to be intermingled and inter-mingling with this beautiful flesh—this flesh of the world that has folded over and touched *me, here,* into feeling, not only awed "in response" to it, but also so beautifully enlivened. I might then begin to experience awe not only toward the beauty of the sunset, but toward my own life, toward life itself.

As I emotionally experience it, the beauty of the sunset is not all "there" and the awe I am experiencing is not all "here." As I become further engrossed in the "windings" and reversals of this experience, as some of these significances "wind up" on both "sides" of Flesh, it becomes progressingly more difficult to tell the awe-inspiring "there" from the awe-inspired "here." For now I do not have, as initially I did, the sense that I am here, feeling in awe of its beauty there, as I have the sense that the sunset, there, itself, is not just beautiful, but awesome or awesomely so. Another reversal has apparently taken place. The awe I was experiencing is now felt—to be there, more there than here. The significance of awe seems to have folded back into/onto the sunset itself and now I may be grasped by the awesome significance of the sunset, and its awesomeness might feel itself through me by unfolding or doubling up with another emotional significance; that of a reverent humility, say. But even this emotional meaning, once it emerges through my emotionally living body "here" may also reversibly wind up "there"—for I may then be to prone to appreciate, as I do, that certain lack of ostentation, that certain humility one finds in all natural beauty; and this may be felt through me by opening up another emotional significance, that of serenity, for example, or that of a respectful love; but then of course the sunset itself may appear to be serene or lovely— and these meanings "there" may unfold through me "here" emotionally, "opening" as contentment or admiration and so on.

Which emotional significances unfold is not the point. That they do unfold and that their unfolding is an opening, by and onto the "flesh of the world" so that these sorts of "cross overs" or reversibilities can take place even to the extent that "one no longer knows who" is perceiving and "who" is being perceived, is.

When we construe emotional depth as a sort of dis-positioning, and being as a winding, what Marcel observed about "deep" or "profound" thought seem to hold true of our "deep" or "profound" emotional experiences. In the reversibilities of evocative and emotional meanings, we see that there *are* times when "we have to transcend the spatial and merely pragmatic distinction between what is here and what is somewhere else."

In the context of my larger project, which is not simply to show how the reversibility thesis is applicable to emotional experience but also to develop meanings of emotional depth through the Flesh ontology's understanding(s) of Depth, what is especially noteworthy here is that awe is a deep emotion. What sense, from the ontology, might we make of its "depth"? Two, at least, and already; and the first by noticing how en-grossing the experience of awe is.

Engrossing is of course suggestive of voluminosity, and as I mentioned earlier, awe is an experience we describe ourselves as standing *in*. This *in* is not the *in* of a "container" view of space.[16] It is an *in* of (what I shall call, for lack of a better word) "in-mergion." Note also that we would not say, "I am awed *about* the sunset's beauty."[17] What we do say is that we are in awe *of* it. This *of* is not the *of* of intentionality. It is better thought in terms of the *of* of the "en-être" relation—an *of* of "belonging to." The meaning of the *en* in its sense of *of* in "en-être" seems to be close to the sense in which we might say that we are "of" a particular generation or "of" a particular ethnic descent. So, when I say that "I feel myself to be en-grossed by or in awe of a sunset's beauty," what I am meaning is something like this: "I experience myself as in-merged with and as belonging to or as being of the same sensible voluminosity as it." I am saying that we are in-merged in the depth of the same 'Flesh.'

We might compare this "en-grossing" sense of awe to its less "depthful" cousin—admiration. For we say that we are "in admiration of" someone, too. What is the difference in the "depths" of these two emotions? As mentioned earlier, in admiration, we seem to stand apart or stand back from the object of admiration. We can, for example, admire someone "from afar"; but when we are standing "in awe of," we do not have this same "from afar" sense. We cannot be en-grossed "from afar." The experience of standing "in awe of" something or someone is an experience of "proximity through distance." The differences in "depth" between awe and admiration seem to have to do with a felt difference in "distance." That is, in admiration, we appear to be more aware of a distance or a difference between ourselves and the objects of our admiration; we do not experience ourselves as being so in-merged, so "caught up" in them. In addition, the *of* in "in admiration of" can be an intentional *of*—directed toward or about some "object." Even though we might say that we are "standing in admiration of" someone too, what we mean to say here most of the time, I think, is that we are taking a certain position with respect to that person— "looking up" or wishing we were more like the one we admire. We are not so aware, in admiration, of being in-merged with or en-grossed in them. (Can there be such a thing as "deep" admiration for someone? Yes, but this involves us in a different sense or sort of depth—the depth of identity. And this I discuss in the next chapter.)

To return to my experience of awe and to the second sense of depth we can appropriate from the Flesh ontology, we might note that the en-grossing depth of this emotional experience is one with the ability to generate other emotions and the process of reversibilities I depict. The process of this generation (or the generation of this process) is Flesh in its "elemental" or "inaugural" sense—Flesh as a source—which is

"external." Through our flesh and thanks to Tactility, we are always already out-"side" of our-"selves." As perceptible bodily beings, we are always already ex-posed. As percipient bodily beings, we are always already open.

The tactile is meaningfully sensed through the density of our skin, the thickness of our flesh. Although it may "cross over" into the visual or the audible, as it does when we see a smooth surface or hear the scrape of a sound, the tactile is originally "blindly" apprehensible.

Emotional Feeling and Cognition

In contemporary theorizing on emotion, the trend has been to adopt a view of them as having "two components": one physiological and the other "cognitive." An emotion is thought to be not just a physiological reaction, but "also the cognitive activity of 'labeling', that is, identifying the emotion as an emotion of a certain sort, which involves 'appropriate' knowledge of circumstances."[22] According to "cognitivist" theorists, emotions are, resemble, or logically presuppose unspoken value judgments, beliefs, or concepts. So, for example, anger involves the belief that I have been harmed; fear is the judgment that I am endangered; and gloom "is a belief that nothing is worthwhile."[23]

Cognitivist theories have helped us to think of emotions as rational and epistemologically important phenomena. Nevertheless, in paying more attention to their "cognitive" side, the significance of emotional feeling is downplayed. A suspicion persists, at least on my part, that philosophy's endorsement of "cognitive components" that supposedly interpret or identify "brute feels," might be an excessively rationalized—maybe even a somatophobic—approach to the emotions.[24] By assigning higher priority to the intellectual and dismissively regarding the feeling component of emotional experience as "dumb" or idiosyncratic sensation, a traditional privileging of mind over body is reinforced, a "one-sided" view of the body as a physical object is upheld, and a (false) feeling-cognition dichotomy is perpetuated.

In "Love and Knowledge," Alison Jagger has exposed a serious difficulty with the postulation of separate "feeling" and "cognitive" components in these theories. They "end up replicating within the structure of emotion the very problem they are trying to solve—namely, an artificial split between emotion and thought."[25]

One way to mend that split and restore some cognitive dignity to the phenomena of emotional feelings may be to extend the overlapping import of tactility to them. The sense of our skin as an organ of perception and the sense of our body as expression and speech, with a "mind," so to speak, of its own, is completely ignored in the "two components" approach to emotions.

Through its interest in justifying the rationality of emotions by ascribing "cognitive" components to them and pointing to the fact that emotions, like other mental events, are "intentional," contemporary Anglo-American philosophy has tended to depict emotional feeling as "dumb" or non-cognitive "internal" sensations—as essentially simple or "raw" feels that cannot be directed toward "objects" and lack a requisite "aboutness" to establish themselves as "mental" phenomena.[26] Considered apart from their intentional objects, causal nexus or situational context, emotional feelings are presumed not to be "deep," interesting, or "substantial" enough for analysis.[27]

Flattened into a sensationalistic mosaic of simple "qualia" or immobilized into static "states" of a physiological body-object, the "Dumb View" of emotional feeling has conceived of them either on the a-rational bodily order of itches, quirks, pangs, and the like, or on a "disturbance" model of disease symptomatology[28]—emotional feeling reduced to heart palpitations, throat discomfort, intestinal spasms, cold sweats, hot flashes, dizziness, and so forth.

I do not wish to deny that emotions have physiological "components." I do, however, wish to affirm that emotional feeling involves felt or tactile feeling as well as internal/physiological feeling. For that reason and because tactility is "intentional" or "reversible," I doubt that emotional feelings are adequately described or that their whole "sense" is captured by the view of them as idiosyncratic and inarticulate "internal" sensation—a view that presupposes that all we can be "in touch" with, when we are emotionally in touch, is a mindless, noncognitive, or afflicted physiological body. I contend that what may be felt when we are feeling emotionally may be extended to the surface of our body as an organ of perception and to its interminglings with other surfaces and the surfaces of others.

In the "two component" approach to the emotions, affectivity is underappreciated because there is widespread adherence to the "dumb view" of emotional feelings.[29] However, emotional feelings are not dumb, because emotional feelings are both like touch and intertwined with touch; and touch is not dumb[30]—senselessly speechless, inarticulate. In fact, the "cognitive" component of emotions may be, or may be based on, the felt or tactile dimensions of emotional feelings.

Touch and Emotionally Felt Feeling

Tactile and emotionally felt feelings overlap. They are reversible. They cross over in ordinary language. There are tactile dimensions to emotional feelings and emotional dimensions to tactile ones. To say that we have been "touched" or that an situation was "touching" is synonymous with saying that we have been emotionally affected.[31]

We already have an informal tendency to think of emotions as "coloring" our perceptions; that is, as "crossed over" into the visual. We say that we "see red" in anger, for example, or feel "blue" when we are sad. I can think of no good reason why emotions cannot be theorized as partially translatable into the tactile. Given that they already are "crossed over" in ordinary language and that we use the expression *feeling* in connection with both, it would be surprising if emotion and touch did not share some overlapping, psychological space; if they were not each, and *inextricably*, informed by the other.[32]

But if they are and because tactile feelings, felt feelings, are sensibly embodied phenomena, that is, neither disembodied cognitions nor meaningless "feels," then incorporating tactility into our discussions of emotional feeling may be a way to avoid the twin mistakes of excessively "rationalizing" them—away—or dismissing them as unduly "dumb."

Manford Kleins's work on emotion in music is an example of an effort to theorize emotions in terms of their tactile dimensions. Kleins, a neuroscientist, has experimented with gesture, in the form of simple pressure signals converted into shapes and sounds:

> Subjects were asked to use finger pressure to express different emotions. For many subjects, the gesture and the emotion apparently reinforced each other. Soon a set of gestures similar for many subjects emerged.
>
> ...New subjects were taught a series of seven different gestures [expressions of joy, anger, love, grief, reverence, sex, and hate]....Once the subject has memorized all seven gestures, he's asked to match them up. It's the first time he's seen the list. Several hundred subjects in Australia and America have no difficulty matching gestures to the emotions which it first generated.[33]

Kleins concluded from his series of experiments that the shape and forms of these gestures compose "a kind of emotional language." Crossed over into the audible and translated into sound, Kleins believes these gestures are "to be found everywhere in music." I quote Kleins: "Music is par excellence a language of emotions. The more precisely you perform it, the more precisely it conforms to a biological form, the more convincing, the more eloquent, the more contagious it is to convince others to change the state of feeling in their person."[34]

Before exploring some more of the felt dimensions of emotional feeling, we need to situate them some where in lived experience.[35] Let us call the space through which we emotionally apprehend or grasp how we are feeling, *affective space.*

Affective space is the space in which emotional percipience is *felt* to be "there" somehow: hesitantly advancing (working up courage) or obtrusively loitering about (a lingering depression), gently blossoming (in love) or suddenly bursting forth (outrage). It is the space in which we are, emotionally in touch—open to the world and aware of its "affect" on us. Emotionally felt feelings are a way we have of being in touch with the sense of our situational surroundings.

Affective space is not, so to speak, "free floating" and neither is it necessarily a wholly private or "mental" space of intro-*spec*tive "subjectivity.' It is not modeled on the specular, but on the tactual, hence it is not so detached from the body. But it cannot be "reduced" or confined to the "objective"—the anatomical or physiological—body; and it intermingles with situational space.

For example, we could not, in affective space, feel those apprehensive "butterflies" fluttering in our stomach without an anatomical[ly objective stomach and unless some appropriately alarming situation is "setting them off." But it certainly does not follow from this that "all we feel" is "nothing but" our own spastic stomach, apart from its bearing on our situation. Indeed, if that physical "sensation" *were* "all we felt," we would seek medical attention; and we do not.

The fact that we do not may be offered as a reason for not identifying the emotion of apprehension with the "raw feel" of a spastic stomach. However, if those 'raw' physical sensations are *not* "all that is felt," then we are *not* sufficiently justified in concluding on their basis that emotions cannot be "feelings," that they are necessarily "inner sensations," or that feelings are essentially dumb.

If we do allow for "cross overs" between emotional and tactile perception and remember that what is unique about touch is that "in contact, things 'outside' us are felt inside us—inside our bodies," then we may be more apt to notice that we do not even *say*, when we are feeling apprehension, that "all we feel" is our own spastic stomach. We say instead that we are feeling "butterflies" fluttering inside (in touch or in contact with) it.[36] The feeling that is felt is a distinguishably embodied ("butterflied") and kinesthetically styled ("fluttering") expression of an emotion, apprehension.

This felt feeling of apprehension is tactually informed. The fluttering of butterfly wings must first be sensed or imagined as intermingling with our skin for this feeling to be apprehended "inside our stomaches." We may then "reverse" this feeling—turn it "inside out," so that what is "outside" becomes "inner" and what is inner becomes outer. Because of their reliance on the tactile, felt feelings are not *simply* or *completely* "internal" sensations.

Neither are they dumb or non-"cognitive." Can we honestly pretend that apart from some physiological distress, this feeling of apprehension is senseless, that it makes no sense to say that the feeling of apprehension is like fluttering, trapped butterflies? This perfectly ordinary albeit metaphorical depiction seems perfectly coherent, "fitting" to me; it captures the situational *sense* of how our body "lives" its apprehension—the sense of how our motivational energy just starts building up, and up, and up. . .and goes nowhere; the sense of how we are propelled, but are not quite able, to "go ahead," to go forward, to proceed. . .in the face of our fear, which is holding us "back."

Might not the "cognition" that "This is scary" *be* this felt feeling? Does the *body* not *know* that "This is scary" through it? Does this feeling, which "identifies" itself with the flutter of butterfly wings trapped behind a "wall," not serve to "identify the emotion as an emotion of a certain sort" through an "appropriate" knowledge of circumstances? Is there anything, except a tradition of conceiving the body as mindless matter, that prevents us from calling this felt feeling of apprehension a *cognition*? I think not.

I grant that to say "I felt apprehension" does not mean the same thing as saying "I felt my stomach convulse"—anymore than to say, "I felt love toward her" means the same thing as saying "I felt a pang, or a heartthrob, toward her." I also agree that emotions are not these "dumb" sensations. What I doubt is that this goes to show that emotions cannot be feelings or that emotional feelings are necessarily "dumb," because "internal" sensations are not exhaustive of feeling phenomena and because they do not even scratch the surface of Surface knowledge.

Let us take another example of a "cross over" between touch and emotional feeling. We might feel suspicion toward persons we perceive as being "slick"—a "smooth"-talking politician or salesperson, for example. Again, our sense of touch helps to explain why we might feel this way and why this feeling is coherent. We have difficulty "holding on" to slick surfaces. They slip away from us. We are liable to slip on them.

What is felt in this feeling of suspicion is that "slick" or smooth-talking people may not be trustworthy of our support. In feeling suspicious of them, we sense that they might not be dependable, that they might let us "down," that we may not be able to "hold" them to their words. They try to "sway" us with words, they may "butter us up" with flattery, but their speech is glib—too smooth to be convincing. Through a felt feeling of suspicion, we are placed on guard against "falling" for an unreliable "spiel."

The cognitive element of the emotion might be based on this felt feeling, which is evidently based on the tactile—the "slickness" of an appearance and the "smoothness" of talk. But we can't just *think* of slickness or smoothness. Our skin, as an organ of perception, must be implicated.

It appears to me as Merleau-Ponty observed:

> We know: hands do not suffice for touch—but to decide for this reason alone that our hands do not touch, and to relegate them to the world of objects or of instruments, would be, in acquiescing to the bifurcation of subject and object, to forego in advance the understanding of the sensible and to deprive ourselves of its lights.[37]

In the next section, I catalogue a number of ways in which our talk about emotional feeling is intertwined with the tactile as I explore some of their "textural consistencies." My hope is that it will eventually prove to be some improvement over the Dumb View to incorporate the tactile into our descriptions of emotional feeling. There is some indication that it may be. For example, to say "I felt soft and tenderly toward her" is *not*, after all, so very different from saying "I felt love toward her"; and it strikes me as a marked improvement over the physiological, "inner," "sensational" rendering, "I felt a pang."

Textural Consistencies of Emotionally Felt Feelings

In affective space, emotional feelings are palpably felt—and felt to have divergent textures. To have a texture means to have a surface that can be felt. Whatever is perceived as having texture is always already experienced as having depth, a certain thickness. That there are felt variations in emotional feelings necessarily implies that they have a certain depth—depth enough for at least some texturally descriptive analysis and through which we may identify an emotion as an emotion of a certain sort.

The language of emotional experience pays attention to felt experience, but we in philosophy, do not. In literary art and ordinary speech, descriptions of emotionally felt feelings are already cast in tactile, skin-depthful terms. Where would we be, descriptively speaking, without them?

In affective space, we feel ourselves to *be* (apparently this is why we say that we are[38]) frozen solid in terror or petrified with fear, laden with a cold and leaden misery, radiating with love or basking in pride, drowning in sorrow or effervescently bubbling over in happiness, blissfully walking on air or cautiously treading on pins and needles (or on thin ice or shaky ground), wallowing in self-pity or ebulliently brimming over with joy.

These descriptions characterize some textural consistencies in affective space. The grating abrasiveness of irritation—the felt feeling of being rubbed the wrong way—is another.

Lust is steamy—hot, moist. Boredom is dry—stale and stifling. Serenity is smooth. Gratification has a plush, or a lavish felt feeling to it. Anger is felt to be a "wearing thin" of patience. In fatigue, we are simply "worn out."

We can detect and do respond emotionally to that icy or frosty edge in someone's voice or that cold shoulder that puts us off, just as we can detect and do respond emotionally to the warmth of an affectionate smile or the inhospitable glare of a glance—in eye contact. These felt perceptions are all skin deep. And distinguishable. And have affective tones to them.

Extremes in temperature are generally unpleasant; and affectively feeling-speaking, we can "tell" the difference. We feel a scathing remark when we hear one; just as we can affectively sense "the third degree" when we are exposed to it. Consider how scorchingly and affectively apt the metaphor of scalded flesh is in Sharon Olds' poem, "Burn Center":

When my mother talks about the Burn Center
she's given to the local hospital
my hair lifts and wavers like smoke
in the air around my head. She speaks of the
beds in her name, the suspension baths and
square miles of lint, and I think of the
years with her, as her child, as if
without skin, walking around scalded
raw, first degree burns over ninety
percent of my body. I would stick to doorways I
tried to walk through, stick to chairs as I
tried to rise, pieces of my flesh
tearing off easily as
well-done pork, and no one gave me

a strip of gauze, or a pat of butter to
melt on my crackling side,. . .*

Less dramatically of course, situations are themselves often
depicted as being "sticky." We try to refrain from "getting into" contact with them. Else they may be perceived as delicate—requiring a
gentle touch, special hand-ling.

We may feel affectively stuck, stuck not in a "tacky" sense, like
glue, the way in which we perceive companions or couples "sticking"
together or contiguously by each other, but stuck in the sense of being
in a pinch or in a jamb. In "hard-pressed" situations, such as those
of distress, we can hardly tell ourselves and our situations apart from
each other. When my car breaks down, for example, I do not feel that
my car is stuck; in distressed frustration, I feel as though I am—even
as I am pacing around outside of it.

The felt fabric of affection between people is tactile, depthful. In
personal relations, we strive to "iron out" the rough spots, patch or
smooth over our differences. The felt feeling of friendship is that of
being woven in tight, "closely knit" or "in thick" with another. While
cooperatively engaged in social causes, what we feel is solid-arity. We
call those who cross picket lines *scabs*.

In relation to others, we might also perceive ourselves as "going
soft"—or as being an "easy touch"—malleable, or elastic. The feeling
of being manipulated is of being "putty" in someone else's hands or
"wrapped around their little finger."

Adolescents "view" love as "mushy" or "fuzzy." We tend to
perceive love as being soft or tender. Applied to difficult teenagers,
however, it may become "tough" or "toughlove." Love is sometimes
"hard" to us; and we acknowledge this alteration by altering its textural
"sense."

The felt sense of an extremely emotionally reserved person is that
of a "stuffed shirt"—starchy, rigid, fixed in place, a stick in the mud,
a "stiff." One who does not exhibit any vital signs of life.

Cruelty is more skin-depthful. The calloused, cold-blooded,
"hardened" criminal is depicted as emotionally scarred on the other
side of his body.

Some persons are assumed to be emotionally "tougher," more
"thick skinned" than others. Nevertheless, in affective space, we all have
our "sore" spots—and these are skin-depthful—like bruises. We try to

---

*From *The Dead and the Living* by Sharon Olds. Copyright © 1983 by Sharon
Olds. Reprinted by permission of Alfred A. Knopf, Inc.

avoid touching on them. By the same token, we also have an affectively felt sense of privacy—a sense for which of our thoughts and feelings we want or need to guard, to keep, to ourselves; and we can tell, in this region of affective space, when someone is intrusively trying to pry or probe their way into it.

A harsh word can, emotionally, upset us; and we may wince, affectively, from that biting sarcasm. In affective space, we can be stung by snide remarks or cut to the quick by caustic ones. Other sorts of comments may tickle us or strike us funny. Some others may come as a shock or a blow—hitting us hard. They are not absorbed, they do not "sink in"—right "off the bat." We may be numb until they do. These felt feelings are all distingishable by virtue of our skin.

We learn about obstacles through our flesh by colliding into things. Affectively, we seem able to feel when something (like a wall) has "come between us"; just as we seem able to affectively discern—in futility or in frustration—when we "cannot get through" to someone: if our ideas or our overtures are being met with some resistance or if we are otherwise being "brushed off."

Time barriers can also be affectively felt. When we long, nostalgically, for what once was or we ponder, regretfully, what might have been, we are in touch with the depth of time—sensing that we cannot turn "the clock" back; that the thickness of the present separates us from our past.

Guilt is felt to pick or gnaw away at us. In humiliation, what is felt is that we are being effaced or erased—"rubbed" out, be-littled. We experience a felt diminution of our being, which we express in a bodily gesture between our thumb and forefinger and verbally as "feeling *this* small."[39] In addition, we may feel de-faced—"like an ass"—as the flush of embarassment rises to our cheeks.

Laziness is felt to be flabby, baggy, whereas the "fabric" of sternness is firm, taut: it does not not want to "give."

Felt feelings of awkwardness are lumberous, stilted. They have a wooden quality to them. When I am feeling awkward, my limbs are loglike, my movements are not dextrous, they do not flow. I am "all thumbs," and they are dis-jointed, unnaturally stiffened, inflexible— "as a board."

Felt feelings of disillusionment are like bubbles bursting; and when, in disappointment, we realize that they will not be realized, our hopes shatter or evaporate. Because they hinge on possibility, they are felt to have the texture of something that is fragile or ephemeral— something that might, at any moment, vanish into thin air or splinter into pieces.

Then there are those felt feelings of expectancy—that vague sense that something (you do not know what) is about to happen, is bound to begin. Sometimes what is felt is felt simply to be "in the air"—pervading the atmosphere—like an escalation of friction heating between people or the sense that something "funny" is "going on." Moods typically have this sort of atmospheric quality to them, and they, too, might be sensed through our skin.[40]

Those whom we loathe or hold in contempt are perceived texturally, felt by us, to be "bad apples," sleaze or grease balls, scum or slime bags, "shitheads." Their textural consistency is that of things we excrete and do not want to touch or things we cannot "stomach" or ingest. We may recoil from them, in disgust or in disdain. (As I discuss in the following section, these felt feelings can be related to the aversions of prejudice and the complex of our identities as they are expressed in the phenomena of racist and homophobic fears and repulsions.)

It is sometimes claimed that we cannot identify our emotions or tell our emotions apart from each other on the basis of feeling alone.[41] Although I think that there is no such thing as feeling, alone, I nevertheless believe that some attention to these textural consistencies calls these claims into question. "I felt love toward her" does not translate into "I felt hard and calloused toward her."

In ascribing a "consistency" to them, however, I do not claim that all humans experience emotional feeling in these ways. I only mean by this expression to invoke some tactility, some depth, some "thickness" in the depiction of emotional feeling and to suggest that there is a certain logic, a certain sense that can be made of the inter-twining of touch and emotional feeling.

These descriptions of emotionally felt feelings are not fully fledged. They only begin to scratch the surface of Surface knowledge. They need to be thought together with others I have tried to elaborate—"freezing" in terror, for instance. The focus on the tactile or embodied dimensions of emotions needs also to be thought in the wider context of the notion of "blind apprehension," the mobility, behavioral, and expressive capacity of the body, and the theory of affordances—in a socioecological approach to tactile perception. How anger or confidence "feels" to us may not be specifiable unless we extend our descriptions into these areas. We do not all "fit" into mainstream behavior; we do not all occupy the same "place" in society. But even in its social, behavioral, gestural, or physionomic modes of expression, an emotion may inscribe or exhibit a style of touch—as it does when we clench, shake or plummel our fists in a gesture of anger or spread and tense our fingers around an imaginary object in a clutch of strangulation. This is how our *bodies* may cognitively *"grasp"* that we are violently angry.[42] By the same token, unless we extend the feeling of confidence to the sure-footed stability of our step and contrast this felt feeling with that of nervously treading on pins and needles or anxiously "walking on eggs"—which may resound as marbles in the mouth or stuttering in speech—we may be unable to fully "grasp" the felt, the sensible significance of confidence or the ways in which it is undermined.

Focus on embodied dimensions of emotional feelings must also be placed in the context of social, political, and economic oppression. Unless we understand the extent to which emotions are socially constructed, we ignore the ways in which they can be put to political purposes and manipulated to serve economic and imperialistic ends in a predominantly white, capitalist, and patriarchal culture.[43]

Embodied Politics and Border Anxiety

> All around me the white man, . . .and there is a white song, a white song. All that whiteness that burns me. . .
>
> —Frantz Fanon, *Black Skin, White Masks*

In her description of bourgeois respectability, Iris Marion Young has provided an excellent example of how the behavioral can normatively intertwine with the bodily in a devaluation of flesh.

> Respectability consists in conforming to norms that repress sexuality, bodily functions, and emotional expression. It is linked to an idea of order; . . .The orderliness of respectability means things are under control, everything in its place, not crossing the borders. . . .
>
> The body should be clean in all respects, and cleaned of its aspects that betoken its fleshiness—fluids, dirt, smells. The environment in which respectable people dwell must also be clean, purified: no dirt, no dust, no garbage, and all signs of bodily function—eating, excreting, sex, birthing—should be hidden behind closed doors.[44]

Clearly, Young's delineation of the rules of respectability have implications for the homeless; our emotional feelings toward them; a

morality based on the notion of respect for persons; and public policy—
or lack thereof. Through it, we can analyze the appall we, as sheltered
members of society, may experience in our encounters with "street
people" who "offend" our middle-class sensibilities by "breaking" these
rules of decency.

As a consequence of their being dis-lodged and according to this
embodied, white, middle-class understanding of "respectability," most
homeless people do not count as respectable persons. "Respect for
persons" is fleshed out into respect for "respectable" persons and the
continuance of the plight and the oppression of the homeless is
seemingly justified—at the emotional level of attitude and through a
"reversal" that mis-places the appall and the apparent "offense." Instead
of being appalled and offended by the fact that an affluent society fails
to provide adequate housing for millions of its members, we blame the
victim—for crossing the border of "respectability" as we understand
it and for evoking feelings of revulsion in us. Attention, and emotions,
are thereby deflected away from conditions of exploitation that may
drive people out onto the street in the first place. Emotions are in part
motivational, and covertly, at the level of attitude, this "reversal" may
then operate as a justification for dis-regarding their interests, divesting
them of their rights, and oppressing them further at the level of law
and public policy. "Respectable" society expels them. Our political
"representatives" can afford to ignore them. The public does not really
seem to care about the homeless after all. Their own emotions tell
them so.

Societies have their "untouchable" classes; American society is
no exception. Those who beg know that "respectable" people are averse
to touching them. That is why they "pan-handle"—with their cups or
their containers—on "our" streets.

We may spot the homeless rummaging through trash bins. As
"marginal" members of society, they eat what is "left-over." They wash
in "our" public bathrooms, a place we go only to defecate, urinate, and
wash our hands—if anyone is looking. They wear what we "hand
down," what we discard: second-hand clothes for second-class citizens.
They beg for change, any that we can "spare." They may work at this
in subway cars—vehicles we use only as a means for transportation to
our "legitimate" labors, our privileged places of employment. Nevertheless, we trouble over those nickels and dimes as we consider
handing them out—how concerned we are that *they* may be "exploiting"
us (are they *really* homeless? what are they going to do with our money?
buy liquor? drugs?). Once more, we "reverse" the situation and deflect
attention and emotion away from the situation of homelessness—and

are all ready to blame victims by focusing on the possibility of *their* wrongdoing. If we do extend some thought to their situation, we may call it "hard luck," from the comfort of our fortunate position and as though their situation is a product of chance, or divine (*divine???*) will. Maybe we lend them some sympathy—mumbling something like "There but for the grace of God go I"—but this is a false sense of identification and compassion. Because we don't go "there"—do we? They move on, and we go home.

The homeless are "left out"—like garbage. We call them "bag ladies" and we treat them like trash. In averting our eyes and turning our backs, we render them invisible and we only reinforce that wall between the housed and the homeless.

As we try to understand the ways in which an ecological approach to the tactile intermingles with the visual and affects us emotionally, we might also consider some of the social implications of Merleau-Ponty's remark that

> the visible spectacle belongs to the touch neither more nor less than do the 'tactile qualities.' We must habituate ourselves to think that every visible is cut out in the tangible, every tactile being in some manner promised to visibility, and that there is encroachment, infringement, not only between the touched and the touching, but also between the tangible and the visible, which is encrusted in it...[45]

First of all, we must keep in mind that seeing can be thought as "a form of touching at a distance," as is exemplified in eye *contact*.[46] Next, we must appreciate that touch is our first medium of communication. "In the evolution of the senses the sense of touch was undoubtedly the first to come into being....It is the sense which became differentiated into the others..."[47] Finally, we need to remember that our skin is not just an organ of perception; it has its other perceptible side.

This perceptible other side of our body is not simply "objective" or biological; it intermingles with its "place" and it is signified, inscribed in a number of ways: as lame or abled, female or male, black or white, fat or thin, sick or healthy, beautiful or ugly, as clean or dirty. A host of connotations, and consequences, attach to each of these inscriptions. It may be true, as Merleau-Ponty says, that "we perceive because we're perceptible." But we are not all perceptible in all the same ways and our perceptions diverge accordingly. The claim that women are all "sisters under the skin" has been hotly contested in feminism, for example.[48]

The significations of our skin and our skin colors matter to us, and matter deeply—in the ways we are perceived by others and in our emotional responses to those perceptions. They make a difference in terms of the groups with which we identify, and they affect our emotional responses to those with which we do not. They influence our self-esteem and our status in society's eyes. To a large extent, they govern the degree of our visibility and invisibility, determining the extent to which we can mask our values and perspectives as normative and universal, determining whether we will be simply overlooked or stared at as "exotic," whether we will be oppressively harrassed or mercilessly beaten up.

The body can itself be viewed as an object of coercion[49] and an instrument of oppression. Some of us are more closely identified with our bodies than others. Some of us are more closely identified with "disrespectable" places than others. Some of us, more than others, perceive ourselves in a sort of double vision—through the duress of externally imposed stereotypes, as we struggle to distance ourselves from the imposition of their roles and meanings. As a surface of human sensibility, there is no "flesh" that is not of a particular color, size, or shape; and there is no body that has not incorporated the results of its own enculturation.

"Flesh" cannot speak for all of us, although it appears to occupy a universal position—"the" human condition of embodiment. For the expression *flesh* is not a neutral term: when it is translated into the visual—even in French ("la chair")—it refers to the color of a white person's skin.[50]

"Blackness embodies the ostracized."[51] To a person of color, the world is already given, felt to be a racist world. In this aspect, one's experience of oneself can be marked by a "double consciousness," an experience that arises when one refuses to coincide with devalued, stereotyped visions of oneself in the dominant culture.[52]

In his discussion of the phenomena of double consciousness, Thomas F. Slaughter observes:

> The multiplexity occasioned by double-consciousness is not an existential dimension distinct from a unity constituted by my lived-body. In fact the stubborn primacy of my lived-body is the precondition of double-consciousness. It poses the impossibility of my succumbing totally to that thorough denigration (!) of Blackness, apparently intended by the society. Consequently, double-consciousness is precisely the expression of the contradiction posed by this immovable immediacy of my lived-body on

the one hand, and the society's apparently irresistible compulsion, on the other, to fashion my physiognomic degradation.[53]

There exists a familiar, vicious process of "internalizing inferiority." Slaughter points out: "It is thus probable that in my routine state, I carry White hatred of me within me."[54] He then discloses a basic mode of being Black—" 'epidermalizing' the world";[55] and he figures the crucial role of language in oppression based on skin color and in the struggle for liberation.

In my rage, I scour my environment for resources. . . . Key among my findings is "the language," the very tool so instrumental in the previous process of my devaluation. Thus in order to appropriate it for my own needs, I "brutalize" the language. I jar the syntax and shuffle its semantics. Through my violence to the language, I mediate the being I was to the world through my body. "Black is Beautiful."[56]

In my thrust toward personal reevaluation, in the absence of real revolution, my skin becomes the very seed of my wrought salvation. Whereas Blackness was my condemnation; Blackness, subjectively revised, is my vindication.[57]

Redefinitions of identities and reemphases on particular cultural histories are not simply reactive, defensive postures, however. In seeing them as such, as only a response to racism, we deny groups their own reality and we assume "that entire societies can be de-cultured; . . . that the oppressed group automatically internalizes the culture of its oppressor. . ."[58]

Certainly racism wounds—it can often mutilate individual self-respect, but this is not the same thing as saying that it conditions an entire community's perception of itself. Moreover, what is left out of this image is the group's actual history. This history is not one in which passivity was the name of the game.[59]

Iris Marion Young argues "that racist and sexist exclusions from the public have a source in the structure of modern reason and its self-made opposition to desire, body, and affectivity. Modern philosophy and science established unifying, controlling reason in opposition to and mastery over the body, and then identified some groups with reason and others with the body."[60]

When the dominant culture defines some groups as different, as the Other, the members of those groups are imprisoned in their bodies. Dominant discourse defines them in terms of bodily characteristics, and constructs those bodies as ugly, dirty, defiled, impure, contaminated, or sick. Those who experience such an "epidermalizing" of their world...discover their status by means of the embodied behavior of others, in their gestures, a certain nervousness that they exhibit, their avoidance of eye contact, the distance they keep.[61]

As she points out, women, as well as old people, "gay men and lesbians, disabled people and fat people also occupy as groups the position of ugly, fearful, or loathsome bodies."[62] In her analyses of the deep structures of racism, sexism, homophobia, ageism, and ableism in our culture, Young points out that as explicit and discursive forms of prejudice have lost legitimacy, they have "gone underground"— "dwelling in everyday habits and cultural meanings."[63] She believes that in their covert forms, racism, sexism, ableism, ageism, and homophobia also take place on the level of a basic security system—at the level of a subject's ontological integrity.[64] They are an attempt to preserve one's identity. Because one's self-identity is caught up in one's group identity, it strives to border itself from other groups.

Young uses Julia Kristeva's conception of the "abject"[65] and the notion of an ambiguous "border anxiety" to account for "a particular and crucially important aspect" of oppression: "the group-connected experience of being regarded by others with aversion"[66] and its "other side"—group-based fear or loathing.

Kristeva figured abjection in a manner similar to the way Merleau-Ponty figured 'Flesh'; that is, as prior to the emergence of an opposed subject and object and as making possible that distinction.[67] As a peculiar experience of ambiguity, the abject, "as distinct from the object,...is other than the subject, but is only just the other side of the border...next to it, too close for comfort..."[68]

Abjection is expressed in disgusted aversion to expelled or excreted bodily matter and fluid: "matter expelled from the body's insides; blood, pus, sweat, excrement, urine, vomit, menstrual fluid, and the smells associated with each of these."[69] The process of abjection is an expulsion followed by a repulsion. It is a process in which the inner effectively becomes outer and thus confounds the distinction between a body's inside and its outside.[70]

Kristeva claims that abjection arises from the primal repression in which the infant struggles to separate from the mother's body...

For the subject to enter language, to become a self, it must separate from its joyful continuity with the mother's body and acquire a sense of border between itself and the other...the border of separation can be established only by expelling, rejecting, the mother, which is only then distinguished from the infant itself; the explusion that creates the border between inside and outside is an expulsion of itself....

The expelled self turns into a loathsome menace because it threatens to reenter, to obliterate the border established between it and the separated self...I react to the expelled with disgust because the border of myself must be kept in place. The abject must not touch me, for fear that it will ooze through, obliterating the border....The abject provokes fear and loathing because it exposes the border between self and other as constituted and fragile, and threatens to dissolve the subject by dissolving the border. Phobia is the name of this fear..[71]

Today the Other is not so different from me as to be an object; discursive consciousness asserts that Blacks, women, homosexuals, and disabled people are like me. But...they are affectively marked as different....The face-to-face presence of these others...threatens aspects of my basic security system, my basic sense of identity, and I must turn away with disgust and revulsion.

Homophobia is the paradigm of such border anxiety. The construction of the idea of race, its connection with physical attributes and lineage, still makes it possible for a white person to know that she is not Black or Asian....Homophobia is one of the deepest fears of difference precisely because the border between gay and straight is constructed as the most permeable; anyone at all can become gay, especially me, so the only way to defend my identity is to turn away with irrational disgust. Thus we can understand why people who have fairly successfully eliminated the symptoms of racism and sexism nevertheless often exhibit deep homophobia.[72]

Person's bodies are not just objectified and "epidermalized." As a means of acquiring a sense of border between ourselves and others who have been marked as different through affective and symbolic associations with "dirty," "ugly," "sick," or "smelly" bodily surfaces, they are also "abjectified."

When we regard and treat others "like shit"—when we expel them, exclude them, find the thought of marrying them repulsive and so on—

we are not simply responding to pre-established "barriers" between us. In a movement of abjection, we *create* those barriers, in an attempt to perpetuate our self-group identities, so that "we"—purged or "cleansed" of "them"—can be "different."

Many emotional gestures can be related to the dynamics of abjection. We "poo poo" ideas; we feign vomiting; we spit in disgust. If Young's analysis is correct, these gestures are all self-defeating, all forms of "spitting in the wind." For we succeed only in expelling ourselves.

Young's analysis of aversive reactions to Others suggests that at our deepest levels, at the level of our identity, we do not experience others—even those whom we hate, loathe, or are repulsed by and strive to distance ourselves from—as entirely separated from ourselves. It would appear that there is something like intercorporeality and something like a "reversal" of Merleau-Ponty's notion of depth as proximity through distance—namely, distancing through proximity—operating behind the scenes, even here, where we might least expect it. It is just because of their insinuation and encroachment on our identities that we so violently reject despised or "loathsome" Others.

In any case, it does seem to me that, unless we revert to something like a surface theory of emotional perception, and acknowledge our disinclination to mingle with "abject" surfaces, we cannot makes sense of certain, but deplorably common, expressions of group-based fears and repulsions.

Abjection is not the only way in which we may strive to distance ourselves from others. Our flesh may also become desensitized, in a number of ways and in differing degrees of severity—from taboos against crying, to constant exposure to battering or molestation.

For example, some incest survivors experience themselves as not coinciding with their bodies. They live their bodies and perceive themselves at some remove, "behind" them. They appear to have survived their abuse by carving out a "safe space." As children, trapped by the circumstances of physical, sexual, and emotional abuse in the home, there is nothing else that they can do but "back up"—to shield themselves from abusive others and to try to escape. There *is* no where else for them to go except "inside themselves"; there *is* no other place in which they might seek shelter, refuge, protection, safety. When they begin to inhabit their bodies differently in the process of recovery as adults, they may be startled to discover themselves becoming more tactually sensitive—the water in the bath may hurt, for example, its usual temperature may be experienced as too hot.[73]

Just as skin is an ambiguous, shifting border between ourselves and the world, between percipience and perceptibility, so too our skin paradoxically protects us from others and exposes us to them. How we touch and how we are touched affects us. As any woman who has felt the patronizing hand of a boss trying to "put her in her place" knows, there is a politics to touch.[74]

> when we say the personal is political, we are suggesting that the body is also politicized. It is the sphere in which consequences of oppression are most readily felt. How an individual experiences his or her body will depend, to a large degree, on the "others" in the immediate environment, who continuously monitor and interpret his or her bodily processes. To an extent, the body is society's creature. It will live through the image of those who watch, nurture, punish and reward it.[75]

There is also a politics of emotion. In society's eyes, because we are not all identified with our bodies to the same extent, we are not all regarded as equally emotional.[76] Relations of dominance and subordination can be based on this inequality. As Elizabeth Spelman points out,

> there have been special stakes involved in the question of how the emotions are related to reason, . . . In western cultures there has long been an association of reason with members of groups that are dominant politically, socially, and culturally, and of emotion with members of subordinate groups. It has been argued again and again, in one form or another, that just in virtue of this association, rational types ought to dominate emotional types.[77]

Spelman also discloses an anomaly in this association. That is, "while members of subordinate groups are expected to be emotional, . . . their anger will not be tolerated: the possibility of their being angry will be excluded by the dominant group's profile of them." For example, anger in women "is likely to be redescribed as hysteria or rage" or trivialized as being "cute."[78]

In Spelman's view, this intolerance of anger and its appropriation by and for dominant groups is an attempt to undermine the moral and political agencies of subordinated groups. "If we recognize that judgments about wrong-doing are in some sense constitutive of anger, then we can begin to see that the censorship of anger is a way of short-circuiting, of censoring, judgments about wrong-doing. . .to silence anger may be to repress political speech."[79]

Women are thought to be more emotionally perceptive and tactually sensitive than men;[80] but even this is turned against us. "Emotional types" are "touchy"—they do not "know best" because they do not "see clearly."

In the use of visual metaphors to describe knowledge, Western culture clearly associates reason with vision. Through this association, the reality of tactility, as well as its cognitive dimensions and epistemic import, is eclipsed: "only what is seen clearly is real, and to see it clearly makes it real. One sees not with the fallible senses but with the mind's eye. . . . In the visual metaphor the subject stands in the immediate presence of reality without any involvement with it."

"The knowing subject is a gazer"[81]—not a toucher—an observer who stands apart from the object of knowledge, who is not touched, "disturbed," affected by it. The perceiver and perceived are thought as separated, as sight is opposed to touch.

It seems to me that the opposition of sight to touch and the relegation of touch to an epistemically "inferior" position is just dichotomous and hierarchical, business as usual. It also seems to me that a way to block this move and "ground" an affective understanding of knowledge might be to recall that "every visible is cut out in the tangible," that "Touch is the parent of our eyes, ears, nose and mouth."[82]

In their awareness of discourse as a site of women's oppression, French feminists since the time of Simone de Beauvoir have stressed the import of touch[83] in their attempts to linguistically re-figure women's bodies and female sexuality.[84] Luce Irigaray in particular is extremely critical of "oculocentrism" and the historical role it has played in the oppression of women.[85]

Several of Irigaray's theses were fashioned to redress the relegation of women to a position of silence and the status of invisibility: her sense for how woman's desire is submerged by a predominantly visual logic, her understanding of how the opposed categories of dichotomous thought have been imposed upon the female body, and her complex metaphor of the "incomplete" form of "two lips"—speaking in and of plurality.[86] Irigaray's philosophy has a special relevance to our study, because it appears to be both based on and critical of Merleau-Ponty's.[87] That is, at times, Irigaray may be read as both critiquing and elaborating Merleau-Ponty's notions of "proximity through distance," his thesis of the "reversibility" of 'Flesh,' and his conception of Depth as a voluminosity.

For example, Merleau-Ponty's reversibility thesis was apparently modeled on the circle of touched and touching hands. Irigaray seems to be countering the manual, and relatively distanced, import of this imagery, as she brings the structure of "proximity through distance" closer in, to focus more specifically on women's pronounced pleasures in nearness—the pleasures of blurring and blending, which are enjoyed in tactile experience and in the experience of female sexuality. Irigaray accomplishes this by concentrating on "that contact of *at least two* (lips) which keeps woman in touch with herself, but without any possibility of distinguishing what is touching from what is touched."[88]

In part, Irigaray's vulval imagery of "two lips" was intended to disturb the sense of female genitalia as only a "lodging," a substitute "when the forbidden hand has to find a replacement for pleasure-giving. . .a hole envelope that serves to sheathe and massage the penis in intercourse: a nonsex, or a masculine organ turned back upon itself, self-embracing."[89]

However, in the light of this passage, we can also see how, when it is applied to sexual difference, the "doubling" of reversibility, as "the finger of the glove that is turned inside out" becomes an oppressive structure; another version of what Irigaray calls *homm(o)sexuality*—a recurrence of the same[90] masculine project of conceptualizing female sexuality along its own parameters. For "her sexual organ, which is not *one* organ, is counted as *none*. The negative, the underside, the reverse of the only visible and morphologically designatable organ (even if the passage from erection to detumescence does pose some problems): the penis."[91]

And yet, Irigaray's imagery of "two lips" as a model for female identity does appropriate the "incomplete" form of chiasmic inter-twinings from Merleau-Ponty's Flesh ontology. (The "chiasm," you may recall from Chapter 3, is the notion Merleau-Ponty uses to think percipience and perceptibility, and sight and touch as simultaneously together and apart. As pointed out in Chapter 3, the chiasm is identifiable with the incompleteness of reversibility.) Irigaray's meta-physics does not "remain coincidence"; it too is based on "this idea of proximity through distance"; and she is as intent as Merleau-Ponty was on thinking through the body to think beyond dichotomy. According to Irigaray, woman, "rigorously speaking," is *"neither one nor two."*[92]

Another area of comparative contrast between Irigaray and Merleau-Ponty is their respective views of Depth. On the one hand, Irigaray appears to agree with Merleau-Ponty about the import of embodiment to an understanding of depth. For instance, she says: "Our depth is the thickness of our body. . . .Where top and bottom, inside and outside, in front and behind, above and below are not separated, remote, out of touch."[93] However, in the same breath, she appears to be differing from Merleau-Ponty in her assertion that "Depth for us is not a chasm. Without a solid crust, there is no precipice."[94]

Merleau-Ponty's ontological view of depth as a "voluminosity" is based on a "solid" economy.[95] In leaving "fluidity" out, the 'Flesh' ontology leaves much to be thought out.[96] For it may be, as Irigaray observes, that Western cultures have tended to identify solidity, as well as visuality, with rationality.[97]

Whereas, in sight, we remain "at the service of perception from a distance" and privilege what is "well-formed,"[98] in an epistemology based on "solid mechanics," we privilege what is "hard" and well-"founded." Irigaray believes that in letting ourselves be *touched* differently, we might "escape from a dominant *scopic* economy" and "be to a greater extent in an economy of *flow*."[99]

The project of "women's writing," with its strategy of thinking through the body and incorporating its fluidity to achieve a certain fluency, is controversial and incomplete. Nevertheless, the endeavor has called important attention to discourse on the body and the liberatory potential in "letting ourselves be touched differently." In this regard, as both an instance and a commentary on this project, Chantal Chawaf, another French feminist, observes:

> Linguistic flesh has been puritanically repressed. Abstraction has starved language, . . .when I write. . .I move in close. . .I magnify the word. . .I examine it at close range: it has its own way of being granulated, ruffled, wrinkled, gnarled, iridescent, sticky. I try to respect its variations in elevation, its sheen its seeds, and like an artisan I offer them so that they may be touched and eaten. The word must comfort the body. . . .
>
> I feel that feminine writing is social, vital. I feel the political fecundity of mucus, milk, sperm, secretions which gush out to liberate energies and give them back to the world.[100]

Summary

We have seen in this chapter how Merleau-Ponty's reversibility thesis and his conception of being as a winding may be applied to emotions "in the Flesh." We have distinguished this *in* as an *in* of "inmergion" and related it to Merleau-Ponty's "en-être" thesis. We have also sketched some account of "cross overs" between emotion and tactility.

We have shown that if the reversibility thesis is correct, then a "subjectivist" account of emotions—one that regards emotions as wholly private or "inner realities"—cannot be. We have also demonstrated, insofar as felt feelings can be shown to have divergent textures, that the claim that emotional feelings lack depth enough for analysis is, simply, false.

We have argued for the need for an ecological approach to tactile perception and a surface theory of emotional perception. We have also argued against the view that emotional feelings are necessarily "dumb," "inner" sensations and have tried to elaborate some instances where the "cognitive" component of emotions may be, or may be based on, felt or tactile feeling. Finally, some of the social implications of an ontology based on 'Flesh'[101] and the interminglings of sight and touch were also addressed.

A "primacy of tactile perception" strand seems to run through some of Merleau-Ponty's later thoughts. This is because all percipience is cut from the same "cloth"—the fabric of Flesh—which, as a Surface, is itself "carved out" of a "total voluminosity" (the Depth "behind" or "between" it) to which we also (always already) "blindly adhere" and through which we remain in Touch, in Con-tact,—and sensitively open, or insensitively closed, to Others.

Whether or not it is explicitly acknowledged, the popular philosophical thesis that emotional feelings are "incorrigible" (if you seem to be feeling, then you are feeling) is probably based on its overlapping with tactile experience. This thesis appears implicitly to subscribe to the wisdom of the adage that "Seeing is believing; but touching is the truth."

We may recall from Chapter 1 that it appeared to be characteristic of some "deep" emotional experiences to be feeling so much, that one "winds up" not feeling anything at all—as happens when we faint or are "in shock." This is another application of the reversibility thesis in the area of emotions: in "extreme" situations, we realize the limits of perception; we appear to "wind up" on or "cross over" to its imperceptible "other side."

In another of its "deepest" senses, "emotional depth" is also, so to speak, "beyond" the circle of feelings-being felt. It involves our identities in the reversible Process of Becoming. We now turn to that sense of "emotional depth."

7

Emotional Depth and Alterations in Identity

Introduction

This chapter is best read in conjunction with the discussion of Depth and Reversibility in Chapter 4. For in this chapter I use the same sense of "reversibility" that applied in the earlier chapter to the "reversibilities" of the ambiguous cube drawing to make some literal sense of emotional depth as an alteration in identity.

Our deepest emotional experiences intervolve changes in our identities and changes in the patterns of our perceptions. They are usually accompanied by realizations that we are perceiving the world or our selves in a new or different "light." Any emotional experience about which it seems appropriate to say that the emotional experiencer is "not [entirely] the same [person]" afterward is a deep emotional experience.

That we use the phrase *deep emotional experience* or *deeply emotionally affected* to connote some perceptible and relatively longstanding transformation in identity seems fairly clear. This sense of "emotional depth" applies, for example, to Sophie and her "choice," to Winston Smith and his betrayals, and to the Stranger during the course of his incarceration. This is also the sense in which we may say that Oedipus was "deeply emotionally affected" by the knowledge that he is Jocasta's son, or we may say that the Buddha in his youth was "deeply" emotionally affected by the "dark" spectacle of worldly suffering—to the extent of emotionally dis-positioning himself away from it, in a complementary process of becoming "enlightened." It is the sense in which we might say that a recovered alcoholic, after the "deep" emotional experience of "hitting bottom," is no longer ("there"-after) "the same person." What we mean, when we use these expressions, is to say that the "sense" or the "course" of lives—their meaning, bearing, direction, relevance or orientation[1]— was there-by altered.

As I shall show, this sense of "emotional depth" is also related to the sense of "deep" we apply to particular emotions—to the sense we might use to refer to Romeo and Juliet's "deep" love for each other or to Hitler's deep hatred of Jews. I shall also illustrate, more concretely during the course of this chapter, how the dynamics of depth, as a reversible "break/brake" in the process of becoming are implicated in this sense of "emotional depth."

Because this sense of "emotional depth" is related to the depths of our "selves," to our identities—and therefore to the depths of time and memory—we need some clarification of the relation between emotion, identity, and time before we can show how personal, perceptual, and emotional depths are intermingled. We shall do this in the interests of placing ourselves in a better position to observe that the same sorts of "reversibilities" take place emotionally as take place perceptually in our experience of ambiguous drawings.

We have already identified emotional depth with signs of "breaks/brakes" and "dis-positionings" and acknowledged the value of John Dewey's definition of emotion as a bodily adaptation for the purposes of our project—this one in particular. As we shall see, Dewey's discussion of the "deepening" of emotional dispositions is an elucidating place to continue with our understanding of emotional depth, this time as an alteration in identity.

Emotion, Identity, and Time

As persons, we have emotional characters as well as emotional feelings—and, to the extent that they are formative of our character and are affecting us perceptually, we can say that emotions are "deep." In a section of his 1887 *Psychology*, John Dewey discussed progressive stages of the "deepening" of emotional feelings.[2] What is noteworthy in Dewey's account is that "deepened" feelings or dispositions eventually deepen into something beyond feelings or dispositions. Although the deepening process is one of repetitious familiarity with a certain emotion or with correlative groups of them, the "depth" of a deepen*ed* feeling does not refer to its intensity, maturity or stability, or even to the process of its "settling" into an emotional disposition. As an organization of emotional life, congealing over time and habit into a constitution or formation of character, the "depth" of a deepened feeling refers to the depth of a person.

Take, for example, the "deepened" anger of the "angry young man." He is not (necessarily or constantly) *feeling* angry. The angry young man *is* angry. He is identified with his anger. It has become a person-ality trait—to the extent that he can be said to *be* angry (or to be regarded as anger person-ified). Anger is emotionally character-istic of who he temporarily or ontologically is—as a "person." This is one instance and interpretation of a "deep" emotion.

(Santa Claus's jolliness is another; as is Hitler's hatred of Jews. Deep emotions tell us how someone emotionally is or can be, hateful or jolly for instance, and show us, by their intermingling with our ways of perceiving, how we are or can be emotionally viewed, as persons.)

Another instance and interpretation of this deep emotion, and to extrapolate from Dewey's discussion, might be to say that the angry young man's "deepened" anger has become, through time and exercise, so "in"-grained that it is no longer an emotional disposition, but a *pre*-disposition. The angry young man "gets" angry, to be sure; but in the "deepened" sense, he always, already is. That is, it is not so much the case that he is emotionally dis-posed toward anger as it is that he is always already "oriented" in its direction. We construe his angry orientation as "stemming," if you will, more from him—from who he is (we say things like: "Don't mind him. That's just the way he is"), and we interpret his angry outbursts as having less and less to do with his actual surroundings. That is, it is not simply the case that he is relatively frequently and predictably dis-posed *by* (bi-placed along-"side" of) selectively perceived injustices in this or that situation so as to belligerently respond to them with his marked hostility and his attitude of righteous indignation. Because his anger has "deepen*ed*," he is always all-ready, all "set"—*pre*-disposed and *pre*-"determined"—to do so.

Moreover (or because), this emotional predisposition "affects" his perceptual stance. Because he is already predisposed, to be irate and contentious, he is always already *looking*, as we say, to "pick a fight." His predisposed anger provides the back-ground for the way he will tend to view the world and his role or place within it—the world perceived as "against" him and so that its injustices are fore-grounded, magnified, or exaggerated to the extent that they provide him with (yet) another opportunity to rail against the "fact" that "life" is unfair.

Not that life isn't unfair. It is. But it is not always so, and because of his emotional predisposition and the way it has altered his perception (it is not simply that less provocation is sufficient to "stimulate" the emotional response; it is that he will tend, actively, to seek and find and to bring out something "offensive" in every situation), the angry young man is not, himself, "in a position" to see that or to see that *he* is (also) a contributing source of so much of his anger. For he is standing in his own way, so to speak, blocking his own view and restricting his own emotional possibilities by his own stance of animosity.

It is interesting to note the reversibilities that can take place here. For often, the angry young man *himself*—because his anger has deepened to the extent that he is no longer perceiving it (as a feeling or an emotional dis-positioning)—"winds up" being perceiv*ed* as unjust or unfair. That is, in so rigidly "adhering" to this emotional *pre*-distancing, he himself "becomes" its evocative other side—a side to which we, in turn, may respond emotionally.

Nevertheless, it need *not* be the case that the injuries and inequities he tends to perceive where others do not, do not "really" exist. They might. That is, he is not, necessarily and because of his deepened anger, "overreacting" to them or "projecting" them onto the situation. Indeed, his deepened emotion might equip him, perceptually, with a sharpened sensitivity to their attendant subtleties and subterfuges and afford him a better, clearer view than others, not so emotionally predisposed, are able to attain.[3] For that very reason however, that is, because his deepened anger *has* so facilitated his focus, it simultaneously eclipses or obstructs his view of other aspects of the situation in question and prevents him from being emotionally responsive to (or emotionally disposed or bi-placed along-side) *them,* that is, in a different emotional mode.

This type of perceptual hiddenness—these "blind spots" in our perceptual fields (and the corresponding "faults" in our personalities)—is also related to the "depth" of a "deepened" emotion.[4] (As you may recall, Gibson's advice was that any discussion of depth "must take occlusions into account." So here we are.)

Also, it is true that emotional habits or predispositions are not easily transformed and that they afford us—as persons—a certain stability or constancy. But, however "fixed" we are as persons, we are *also*, as persons, in process—in the process of becoming; and we cannot talk about the "depths" of our identities without implicating the depths of lived temporality—and with it the felt distances/differences we can experience or perceive as being between past and present versions of our "selves." It may be true, for example, that some angry young men "grow" to be angry, embittered old men. Most don't though. They become "someone else" as they become temporally distanc*ed* from their youth and this characteristic emotional predisposition that belonged to it.

Once we acknowledge, then, the ways in which emotional predispositions affect us perceptually (by preserving certain constancies in our "ways" of perceiving the world and by creating "blind spots" in the field of our emotional vision) and we allow that they need not remain permanently or uni-formly "fixed," we can begin to see that the "depth" of deep emotions does not refer (uni-laterally or in some subjectivist fashion) to a person or a "self" *simpliciter*. It also refers to a person's emotionally induced or focalized "insights"; to what, because of what these reveal, will tend to get simultaneously covered over or concealed (and which may, at some future space and time, come to the fore or unfold); and to the distance/differences (when or as they are doing so) between former and later "selves"—that is, to changes or "alterations" or "breaks" in the continuities of our identities.

Dewey's discussion of the "deepening" of emotional feeling—especially Dewey's notion that emotions are deep insofar as they "return into the self or subject"—can be complemented by Glen Mazis's recent work on the "ongoing originariness" of "e-motional re-turns." Mazis's work on e-motion, which is Flesh ontologically based, is also particularly useful in "fleshing out" the sense of emotional depth as an alternation in identity through the "reversibilities" of time.

Continuously and typically our past is automatically reappropriated and rewoven into a future-directed present. Mazis distinguishes two ways in which this re-weaving of the past within the present can occur. One corresponds to his sense of the time of constricted or pathological emotional returns;[5] the other to his sense of the time of e-motional re-turn—as a time of "coming back to things ever anew" or in their "ongoing originariness," "in the ongoing becoming of the past."[6]

From this latter conception, I think, we can begin to make some sense of "deep emotional experience" as an alteration (or an "alternation") in identity. In Mazis's language of "re-turning," the depth would involve a turning away from or a being distanced from who one once "was" in the past and a turning toward or the becoming of a new "self" in the present. The greater the distance between the present (between who one is now or presently becoming) and the past (who one was), the greater the depth.

In Mazis's "philosophy of becoming," the time of e-motional re-turn is

> a return to what has always been there as something which is new, which is springing up at this particular moment. What is revealed is that the past as the heavy call of what has been in my emotional apprehension can never return simpliciter, but can only re-turn: in emotion one comes back to the old as always altered but still there as somehow turned around, and with this revolution I too am turned around as moved, moved again to where I've been, but moved to a new place in returning. The way I love, hate, fear, am angry, am excited, am sad, am mourning, etc., is always

recreated, in the wake of what I have felt in the past, but always within "the particular turn that things are taking" at that moment, as we say.

> . . . if this aspect of what I call the *originariness* of emotion is taken up and expressed wholeheartedly and affirmingly, it has the power. . .to alter the sense of one's emotional life. . .[7]

The circularity of returning to oneself from the world in e-motion also means a circularity of time which is not foreclosed [as it is in] constricted emotional returns.[8]

One can aim at the depth of the past to open up a present, and assume that emotions follow from preceding emotions, and need to be freed from a prior paralysis in order to gain free play. Alternatively, one can see that the opening up of the present field of perceptual experience. . .allows a wider realm of manifestness and exploration, thereby freeing e-motion to give rise to a *new past of greater possibility.*[9]

The "deepest" sense of re-turning that Mazis develops is that of re-turning to found a new self, a new *past*—in the "becoming of becoming." "Even when we deign to think of becoming, we tend to make it a trivialized becoming, as if the present could be the result of flux, but the past could be and retain a core of identity. However, to really think of becoming, the realm of e-motion and the flesh, is to embrace that becoming itself is always becoming."[10] To embrace that "becoming itself is always becoming," Mazis would have us focus on "the richness of the present to institute a new past, a past in the process of becoming"[11]

The present is rich in the sense of its being a medium of possibility, of changes. The e-motional founding of a *new* past within the density of this "living present"; the re-creation of or the return to a *new* "sens" of self through a *change* in the way in which the past is re-woven in the thickness of a present can be a "deep emotional experience" in its sense as an alteration in identity. In such experiences, one does not simply return, over and over, to the "same old things" and the "same old self" in the same old ways. This is not, in Mazis's progressive sense of the word, a re-*turning* at all. When we are, in his sense, re-turned e-motionally, different "sides" of one's self and the world are revealed.

Mazis's conception of e-motional re-turning and its power of "ongoing originariness"—the founding of a new self, a new past—is compatible with what we call *turning points* or *transition periods* of our life.[12] Such experiences typify emotional depth as an alteration in identity.

What we now need to examine in more detail is how our identities are related to our characteristic "ways" of perceiving; and how, abruptly and simultaneously, these and the sense of our emotional life and our emotional characters, may be altered.

Emotional Habits and Leaps of Perception

> When, for example, a woman first consciously says of her Self, "I am a radical feminist," there is a Shift in the shape of her soul.
>
> —Mary Daly, *Pure Lust*

"Falling" into a "rut" or "fixation" of emotional habits is not just a channeling of our behaviors along certain well-worn paths or "grooves." It also entails a falling into a specific ecological niche and a "fitting" of significance between our attitudes and our situations. Emotional habits or "deep" emotions are correlated with perceptual habits—with practiced perceptions and fixations of meaning. As Gibson's theory of affordances might help to explain, our habits refer as well and as much to the way we are accustomed to in-habiting our world and to the perceptions of meaning with-"in" it.

Both of these are liable to change over time. For there are layers and levels to perceived meanings; and, the "fixed" meanings we are accustomed to perceiving in any of our "given" situations can collapse or di-verge and give "way" to others. This experience is familiar to us as that visual analogue of the "double entendre" we call having to "look twice." *Having* to look twice, that is, as we "catch sight" of these alterations or divergencies of meanings (when the sense of something we thought we knew quite well is perceived in a new or different way[13]) and needing, emotionally, to come "to terms" or "to grips" with this new or different sense, we may be "slipped" or wrenched *"out"* of our "deep" emotional habits and be motivated to form others in "response." That is, our emotional habits are as liable to change, as we, and the "objects" of our perceptions and affections, change—and are changed by—each other, over time.

As I noted in Chapter 5, emotions involve perceptions of change—in a situation and in our selves in relation to our situation. Deep emotional experiences appear to contrast in that they *also* involve a change in the perception *of* our selves and a change in the perception of what our situation or our situational context *is* (not just a change happening in the context of a situation, a change, that is, in one of its multifaceted aspects). Because our "selves" and our situations (or our habits and habitats) ontologically (or ecologically) con-form to each other, these changes will tend to coin-side. That is, breaks or divergencies in the *patterns* of ("ingrained") emotional habits (which are constitutive of our selves) will tend to coincide with breaks in the *patterns* of our practiced perceptions (which they have been "affecting").

So, if I have been "deeply emotionally affected," my world will not appear "the same" to me. In other words (Merleau-Ponty's words), the perceptible "other side of my body" (the Flesh of the world) will also be affected. And I will be aware that a breach or break has already occurred or is presently taking place between the surfaces of my earlier and later sensibilities, between my former and later selves as they are in the process of becoming.

Falling into and falling out of love are both deep emotional experience that *affect* our ways of perceiving. In both cases, we *see* (there) how we feel (here).[14] Let us consider the ways in which we are perceptually affected, and affected by perceptions of depth, in the course of "breaking up."

During the process of estrangement, when lovers are physically or "objectively" close to each other (in the same room or bed, let us say) but experience themselves, emotionally, as "drifting apart"—their visual (and tactile) perceptions of each other are affected as much as their emotional feelings and "selves" are. As the bonds of intimacy, of familiarity, between us start to slacken and we begin to lose our emotional "hold" on each other, we become more tensed, more strained— unable to take the same sort of comfort in each other's presence or secure the same sort of pleasure in each other's flesh. I may stiffen and recoil, for example, when you draw me near, just as you may begin to feel, and look, more remote, removed, more "distant," to me. We may appear less inviting or appealing to each other. As we "drift" emotionally further and further apart and become "stranger[s]" to each other, our recognitions of each other are affected; we appear to *"dense* up." Indeed, without that love "light" conditioning our seeing, what we *now* see (or were "used" or "ac-customed" to seeing) in each other may become gradually and staggeringly more obscure. We might even begin to question ourselves about this—about "what we ever saw" in him, or her, "in the first place." Whatever it was, it is apparently not "there" anymore. Or perhaps what we do (now) see in its place repels or repulses us; and e-motionally, we are re-moved even further "away" from each other—and from our former "selves."[15]

In either case, although we might implicitly have "seen" it coming "all along" and even though we do *not explicitly* "see" it happening—these depths surfacing—at any particular or given moment during this process, we *are* aware when/that this "break"/"brake"—this stopping of our former sight and its re-placement with another—*has* occurred; and we "real-eyes"[16] that it coincides with a breach or termination of our prior (deep) affection toward each other.

These interplayed perceptions of depth—between emotional distancing and visual density—may fleetingly or intermittently "come and go" of course, to some degree, during the course of any intimate relationship, including those of long duration. However, at that indiscernably discernable "point" (or "turning point") when they seem to come and do not go—that is, when you apprehend that you can no longer *see* a lover *as* someone you can continue to love, when there is, so to speak, a formidable barrier "blocking out" that former view so that it has become *perceptibly* irretrievable, "along-side," so to speak, the current one—then, I think, it is *time* to say that you have fallen "out" of love. The "depth" of this emotional experience has as much to do with a change in perception as it has to do with a change in affection—and with their "crossing over" into memory.

The perceptual persistence of a new "way" of seeing *over* or *through* the old is characteristic of, or occasions, "deep" emotional experience. We "see through" the old perceptions because these former presents/presences have (e)lapsed into the past and have "faded" into memory; and although we retain them there, the new, super-posed perceptions, the future presents/presences that are taking their place, are more perspicuously vivid.

However, and to return to my example, because of our history together and even if I have fallen (completely) out of love and am seeing my ex-lover in a new and different way, I am never quite able to see him as a "brand new" person, or as a "total," "complete," or "perfect" stranger. That is because, for the new perceptions to be experienced *as* new perceptions (viz., distanced from the old), the older perceptions, however vaguely they are retained or held alive in memory, must be overlapping on (or intermingling with or "behind") the new.

These "overlappings," this "intertwining" at "chiasms" *between* our affections, perceptions, and memories, this "common nucleus which is the winding" and which is not—"itself"—perceived, remembered, or affectively felt is what gives the emotional experience its depth. The depth is there as that which is imperceptibly holding—as a break/brake—*between* what was there then and what is here now, holding *between* the identity of incompossible earlier and later appearances, so that they are still connected but nevertheless "distances" them from each other so that they never (completely) coincide. This is just the depth of distanced contact.

We should recall here our earlier illustration of this same "reversible" phenomena as it takes place in, for example, ambiguous drawings. We should also note here that it is our characteristic "ways" of seeing and not, if you will, just "what" we see, which is interwoven with our sense of self or who we are. Hence, the experience of seeing in a different "way" or in a different "light" can alter our sense of "self" (and vice versa). This experience, of seeing in a different "way" or in a different "light," is an experience of the incomplete reversibilities of depth.

The experience is that of a certain draping of perception being drawn back and exposing what was previously "hidden," out from under, behind it. Looking "back" on it, it ex-cites "hind"-sight realizations that we were "in the dark." As these "scales" fall from our eyes; as these blind-folds are unfolding and the "stopping" (braking) of a former sight "crosses over," "all at once," into the launching of another "way" of seeing, we are making, what has been called by Mary Daly, *a transformative* leap *of perception*[17]—an expression that suggests a sudden, perceptual surmounting or prevailing over (the pre-veiling of) past obstacles, a surgence in the growth of an understanding, and a critical shift in the growth of an identity. To see in this depthful manner is, for Daly, to "real-eyes."[18]

Although we must be careful of being misled by it, we also must appreciate what we are saying with this metaphor of "light"—just how apt or fitting a metaphor this is for the phenomenon under discussion. For although we cannot see without it, the light itself, is not seen. The light is that according to which we see. The light, *itself*, is a "mediating element" that leads or directs our gaze and acts on its behalf as a "discreet intermediary" between us and the "coloring" of our perceptual world. So that when we exclaim, for example, that, "Ah, *now*, we 'see the light'," we do *not* mean that we *see* the *light*. What we mean is that we are beginning to see (something else) in a different "way"; that a certain 'path' has been discerned/dis-covered; that a certain "way" has been sufficiently cleared or clarified for a new "stage" of our seeing-our understanding to take place in, to seep or settle into.

Merleau-Ponty discussed the phenomenon of these quantum leaps of perception (as stoppings and startings/obstacles and openings in our ways of seeing) in his texts. In the *Phenomenology of Perception* (and its analysis of orientation experiments that show the necessity for "an absolute [space] within the sphere of the relative"), this leap is described as a "first perception"—one drawn from the source of a "primordial depth," a depth to which we "blindly adhere" and which represents the event of our birth and "a communication with the world more ancient than thought."[19] In *The Visible and the Invisible*, this establishment of a new way of seeing (over or through the old) is Depth as *urstiftet*—a "first" or original founding.

A related notion in *The Visible and the Invisible* is the percipient "side" of 'Flesh' viewed as an "opening"—and this "opening" understood "in the sense of *Ueberstieg* of the body toward a depth." This "Ueberstieg" is the process by which (perceptible) Flesh is conceived as folding over (and over) upon itself—over-stepping/steppe-ing its own Voluminous bounds and sur-mounting the obstacle of its own or Self-Occlusion to find itself within some clear (percipient) space.

Another Flesh-ontological notion applicable to leaps of perception is, of course, Depth as the "identity of incompossibles"—when, as in ambiguous cube drawings, the transformations of one unified perception depend on the coherent deformation of the other perception and on the maintenance of a certain strife between them. Despite their being inextricably intermeshed, one can only "assert itself by obliging the other to retreat into *hidden* horizons."[20] This latter sense of depth and its peculiar type of "open-endedness" is particularly relevant to the examples of "deep emotional experience" and the attendant "reversibilities" analyzed later.

As I see it, transformative leaps of perception are related to emotional depth as an alteration in identity in at least the following way. However or whenever these perceptible shifts in the *order*-ing of our perceptual world occur (or when a fold in the fabric of Flesh suddenly unfolds and reveals what lay hidden there), they tend to require or demand, from us, a similarly "whole" adaptation "in response." They require that *we* (our "selves") break/brake and change—somehow—that our identity critically shifts itself "in order" to adapt[21] to the changes on this other, perceptible "side" of our Flesh, because we, our "selves" are, or were, also "blind"-folded into the same "fabric" of Flesh as its "reverse" or "other 'side."

As we shall see, Dewey's definition of an emotion as an effort of adapting "formed habits or co-ordinations of the past to present necessities as made known in perception or idea" is particularly suited to this discussion of emotional depth as an alteration in identity. These adaptations, these "fittings" of perceptual and personal significances, are accomplished through the intervening medium of "deep" emotions or emotional experiences. These changes or adaptive mediations *are* our "deep" emotions and emotional experiences. Before we reconsider, in the light of this process of Depth, the tragedy of *Oedipus Rex* and Winston Smith's ordeal with the rats in *Nineteen Eighty-Four*, let us briefly review my example of Sheer Terror.

Freezing in Sheer Terror

As you may recall from Chapter 1, what I felt through the skewerlike opening of terror that simply and suddenly tore through my body when I was assaulted and stopped or sheared its movements short was that I was "stayed still" and "standing on end." In my description of this experience, I noted that the same sense of "sheer" as is applied to cliffs or (l)edges can be applied to the "deep" feeling of terror and that this "depth" could be related to the sense of terror as a "freezing."

We can now interpret this experience as emotionally "blind apprehension," as a bodily adaptation to a present necessity, as an "affordance," and as a "deep emotional experience" in its sense of an alteration in identity. My transformative leap of perception was my discerning, through the blow that he delivered to my head, the mugger's intention to kill me—if need be. My body "blindly" apprehended his intention and—"caught on" to the gravity of her situation, "fully comprehending" that my life life was "at stake"—by "freezing" in that moment, in that opening of experienced terror.

In so doing and on some primal level, the ability of that man to reduce me to a corpse was experienced as having already happened. That is, my "freezing" in terror was *as if I was already dead*, as if he already had. Through that opening of terror, my percipient flesh was *identifying* itself with perceptible flesh, as the body of a corpse.

It is, as Merleau-Ponty observed about emotionally "blind apprehension" generally, as if the other's intention (to kill me) was inhabiting my body; and we may notice, also, how adaptive this embodied alteration in my identity was. For if I was "already dead," still, as a corpse, how could he kill me? There would be "no need" to.

We can now relate the "sens" (the "direction") of my (l)edgelike apprehensions of terror to the sense of terror as a "freezing" and to Gibson's claim that "one's body in relation to the ground" is what we perceive when we are perceiving "affordances." In terror, what our flesh "grasps" is that one false move, one false step, *might* cost it its life. In "shear"/sheer terror we *are* "cut off" from our usual "ground" of support and from our mobility. And what we *are* adaptively and sensibly apprehending, in terror, *is* that we might *drop*—dead. By *freezing* "in" terror and staying *so* still, our flesh paradoxically *stops itself short of that plunge* to the "ground"—by going through it, by "fully comprehending it," by momentarily "becoming" the body of a corpse.

Oedipus Rex

Oedipus' transformative leap of perception is, of course, his seeing (or "real-eyes-ing") that Jocasta, his wife and the mother of their children, is also his own mother. As the story goes, he adapts himself to the knowledge that he is her son and to the "shifting" of the context of their situation, from a marital to an incestual one, by blinding himself.

We have already made some sense of this in Chapters 1 and 5, but let us make some more, noticing in particular that by the end of the play *Oedipus Rex* the (formerly) proud and happy king is wretched, remorseful, and (deeply) ashamed of himself—no longer, emotionally speaking, the person or character he once was.

Part of what Oedipus realizes in blinding himself is that he is *already*, through this transformative leap of perception, incapable of seeing his life in the "same [old] way"; for example, that sights which formerly caused him pleasure could now cause him only pain. This realization and the telltale sign of a "break/brake" in the *order*ing of Oedipus' perceptual world is apparent in the following passage.

> Oh yes, I pierced my eyes—
> My useless eyes—why not?
> When *all* that's sweet
> Had *parted from* my vision....[my emphasis]
>
> It was a good design....
> My best design! What kind of eyes should I need
>   to gaze upon my father's face
>   in Hades Halls, or my unhappy mother's?
> Or eyes that could be eyes that saw
>   my children's faces? Joy? No, no—a sight of pain
>   engendered from these loins....[22]

When Oedipus begins to see himself as Jocasta's son, he is not superficially embarrassed—he is deeply ashamed, ashamed of himself in, as he says, "full view," "the sower and the seed."

Imagine, if you will, an insufferable tension existing for Oedipus between these two "incompossible" views of himself. Imagine further that Oedipus cannot, simultaneously, sustain both views at once. (In other words, they are not simultaneously compossible *as* two distinct or foregrounded views. If one is to come to the fore, the other must fall by the way.) Imagine finally that Oedipus, incapable of tolerating the tension between these two views, is driven either to relieve himself of it or needs to adapt himself to it somehow.

We might then say that in blinding himself, Oedipus is identifying these "incompossible" views of himself, chooses to identify or to reunite, himself, *in shame and in remorse,* with Jocasta, *as* her son *and* punitively, as her partner, in crime. Through the mediation of these deep emotions, he is adapting himself to the view of himself *as* "the seed" who *is* "all incest sealed with the womb that bore" him.

Thus re-solving the crisis in identity provoked by the leap of perception, he is also identified with the obscurity of his own hidden dimensions, his own "depth." And in the process of this depth, his former prides and joys (his children, for example) reversibly "become" his present shames and sorrows, just as Oedipus himself reversibly "becomes," emotionally speaking, a different character.

Becoming a "Rat" in *Nineteen Eighty-Four*

Through the "rat scene" in *Nineteen Eighty-Four,* we can see a reversal of the process analyzed in *Oedipus Rex.* That is, we can see how a critical shift in identity requires making emotionally adaptive leaps of perception. Recall how different Winston Smith's perceptual world looks to him and how, differently, "reversibly," he responds emotionally to that altered perceptual world after the integrity of his character has been broken down and after he has identified himself with the "rats" (through his betrayals and his fear and hatred of them)—by incorporating their vision as his own and "winding up" on their "side."

The rat scene in this text and the text itself with its theme of the "double-speak" of a totalitarian society's political slogans (e.g., "Freedom Is Slavery") can be read as an study of depth as the "identity of incompossibles"—"incompossibles" that are reversibly applied in the area of rationality,[23] in the field of perception, in the ranges of morality (where distances between what is right and what is wrong are also and subversively "broken down"), and of course, in the realm of the emotions (hatred becomes love, betrayal becomes loyalty, loyalty becomes betrayal, and so forth).

Although the rat scene is, so to speak, at the very "heart" of Winston's "deep emotional experience" as an alteration in identity, to apprehend its magnitude, to "fully" comprehend it—and its "incompossibilities"—we must look at Winston, before and after. In a scene preceding the rat scene and in which he realizes that he is being "tortured to the edge of lunacy" and has not yet "crossed over" (his torturer is trying to electroshock him into seeing four fingers as five), Winston can almost (but not quite) "see" things in their 'way'; and he has a fore-glimpse of his own future "self."

O'Brien held up the fingers of his left hand, with the thumb concealed.

"There are five fingers there. Do you see five fingers?" "Yes."

And he did see them, for a fleeting instant, before the *scenery* of his mind changed. He saw five fingers, and there was no deformity. Then everything was normal again, and the old fear, the hatred, and the bewilderment came crowding back again. But there had been a moment—he did not know how long, thirty seconds, perhaps—of luminous certainty, when each new suggestion of O'Brien's had filled up a patch of emptiness and become absolute truth, and when two and two could have been three as easily as five, if that were *what was needed*. It had faded out before O'Brien had dropped his hand; but though he could not recapture it, he could remember it, as one remembers a vivid experience at some remote period of one's life when one was *in effect a different person*. [My emphases.][24]

The rat scene marks the time when Winston's former fear and hatred of Big Brother begins reversibly to become a loyalty and a love (and his former love and loyalty toward Julia reversibly becomes a repulsion and a betrayal); and we know that Winston has (already) become "in effect a different person" after his experience with the rats when he obviously *does* begin to see and emotionally respond to "his" world in *their* "way."

When, for example, Winston says that it is "impossible" for him to "feel the same way" toward Julia after he betrays her; or when, in gazing up at the poster face of Big Brother at the end of the novel, he sees him in a new and different "light" and realizes that he loved him "all along"—we are led to notice that there are "reversibilities" and identifiable "incompossibilities" here. He cannot love Big Brother and feel the same way toward Julia *at the same time*. As his love for Julia collapses into the background of the past and "becomes" the former repulsion he felt toward Big Brother, his present love for Big Brother (what "became" of his earlier love for Julia), can come to the fore or unfold.

Like Oedipus, but in a reversal of the process of emotional depth as an alteration in identity, Winston must adapt, to the changes in himself, to the changes in his character. And this he does, in retro-spect (by looking back on his "world" in a new "light" and through a "reversal" of his deep emotions), by making the transformative leaps of perception he does—and that are *now* required of him and his own emotionally de-formed "character."

Summary

In perceptual experience, depth is "there" at that site where things can come into view only by eclipsing others; and that "sight" (think of ambiguous figures, leaps of perception, and the emotional reversi-bilities we have noted) where one gestalt can unify itself only by coherently deforming another, which nevertheless remains latently and continuously "behind" it.

In Merleau-Ponty's Flesh ontology, the Source of this happening of that back-grounding of the foreground and that fore-grounding of the background that occurs in the process of any perceptibly ambiguous scene, any perceptually ambiguous reality "taking shape"—unfolding into one, or another, but not both, of the ways in which it can be seen—is Depth. This Depth—which "identifies incompossibles"—is an Open-Ended Process. What I have tried to show through the examples in this chapter is that and how, through leaps and "bounds" of perception, our identities and our "deep" emotions can be implicated in this Process.

Feeling Deeply About Depth

How can you love this piece of flesh when you do not love the whole man?

—Simone de Beauvoir, *The Mandarins*

As John Dewey observed: "not all objects excite feelings equally"; although we are relatively indifferent to some, others affect us "to the depths of our being."[1] Correlated with this observation of Dewey's is Max Scheler's demonstration that "feelings are not only of different qualities but also of different levels of depth."[2]

To regard emotions theoretically as being all on the same level is to distort the lived experience of variations in the depths of affective phenomena, to flatten the depths of affectively lived space, and to ignore the configurations of divergencies in their depths as they appear to have been cast, implicitly or explicitly, by the expressions of ordinary language. This leveling of emotional phenomena—this flattening of affective experience—also over-looks and under-appreciates the extent of our own belonging to perceptible depths on the other side of our body and the normative extent to which these depths are implicated in the depths of our own emotions.

That a proper object of love is not, as deBeauvoir so succinctly states, a "piece of flesh" but a whole person; that I may dislike your tie, but will hate your "guts" or you—are two instances of the same general circumstance; viz., we do not experience deep emotions over the manifestly superficial. That is to say, we do not experience deep emotions over peripheral matters in the range of our concerns (over things perceived as having little or nothing to do with us); and neither do we experience them over proximally or frontally perceived "objects" or in response to the overtly "frontal" aspects of an evocative situation (again, as "detached" or apart from us). If we are responding, or adapting, to "something" with a measure of emotional depth, we are responding, or ad-apting to "it" in its horizonal, hidden, or lateral ("edge-wise" or embedded) dimensions.

Generally speaking, the "deeper" the emotion, the more the "self" is affected and the more one perceives oneself as belonging to the scene, as being intervolved—catching onto and "all caught up" in some perceptible or quasi-perceptible surfacing of a depth. The deeper the emotion, the more we are adaptively responding, in our depths or as a whole ("whole-heartedly") to some perceived "gestalt" that appears to be unfolding and in-corporating us in *its* depth or as a whole.

I do not believe that this intermingling of depth with depth—this evocative harkening of perceptible depth to emotional depth—is a haphazardly fortuituous coincidence. I believe that the accepted notion of emotional appropriateness or "fit" (the idea that certain emotions are appropriate in certain given situations and others are not) is also advanceable in terms of a rationale of their depths.

That is to say, perceptions of emotional depth are (also) percep-tions formed "in the (depths of the) things themselves." Perceptions of emotional depth cannot be thought apart from the depths of their evocative "other side." It appears that a sufficient condition for feeling emotions deeply, or for feeling a deep emotion, is a perception of depth; that is, a perception of depth as I have been construing it, as a surfacing or a coming to the fore of something which was "blind-folded" behind something else and is presently being seen *as* unfolding *from* "behind" it (I am still trying to avoid a too facile dualism here); or is presently being sighted in the process of near and far "sides" reversibly crossing over into and "becoming" each other—seen in depth as that "incom-pletely" reversible process of the backgrounding of the foreground and that foregrounding of the background discussed in Chapters 4 and 7.

I will fictively vary a few examples in support of this thesis before addressing the issue of which emotions are traditionally regarded as being the "deepest" and before concluding with a discussion of how this consensus on emotional depth may be related to the Flesh ontology.

In *The Emotions: Outline of a Theory,* Jean Paul Sartre gives an example of a circumstance under which he would feel passively invaded by terror (that is, deeply frightened or fearful) as a counterexample to his own theory of emotion, as a purposely chosen and goal-directed behavior or "activity": "This theory of emotion does not explain certain abrupt reactions of horror. . .which appear suddenly. For example, suddenly a grinning face appears flattened against the window pane. I feel invaded by terror. Here, evidently, there is no behavior to take hold of; it seems that the emotion has no finality at all. . ."[3]

Although it is tempting, initially, to say that the "object" or perceived "target" of Sartre's terror is "a grinning face suddenly appearing flattened against his window pane," this dualistically "intentional" manner of accounting for Sartre's terror is implausible, inadequate, and a theoretical abstraction out of the lived and perceptual depths of the experience. For a "face"—*just* a face, and especially one that is grinning, is no cause for alarm, let alone terror, because faces "all by themselves" can do us no harm.[4]

It appears that a necessary ingredient to the evocation of the deep emotion of terror in this example is that Sartre perceive the face pressed against his window as a surfacing or surface of a depth. Sartre is invaded by terror not just because he has visually perceived "a grinning face at his window," but also because he has perceived that a real human body is hidden beneath that face—and a real malicious intent hidden behind that "grin." In addition, because he himself belongs to the same perceptible depth as that face does (to the depth of perceptibility—of visibility; tangibility, etc.) he must perceive that he is—as a percipient-perceptible, as a bodily being—vulnerable and open to the possibility that something terrible may be about to happen to him.

The depth that Sartre must perceive to feel "invaded by terror" is the doubly referential significance (or the negative affordance of his body in relation to the ground or his situation as a whole as): "life threatening." A frontally perceived and isolated face—by itself—can never be that "depthful."

As I pointed out in analyzing my own experience of it, terror is a deep emotion because it is the felt perception, or "blind apprehension," that the continuity of our lives is "at stake" and that we are hanging, suspended (by a "thread" or by the "skin of our teeth") somewhere in the balance *between* life (percipient-perceptibility) and death (perceptibility). Terror invokes the stark, the "hair-raising" realization that there actually *is* an "indivision" of the perceptible flesh of the world and our own percipient flesh. What we are terrified *of* "in" the grip of terror is "winding up" dead.

When we are overcome by seizures of terror, we are "scared out of our minds." We are frightened to death. That is to say that we realize, in terror, that our own sensitive flesh, our live body, needs to "adhere" but dreads "crossing over" entirely—as a "coincidence" or "fusion"—to its other, sensible "side," as the flesh of a corpse.

As I discussed in the last chapter, precisely this crossing-over is augured in the experience of terror itself, when our body's first and instinctual response to the life threatening is, so to speak, to "flash forward" and to "play dead." In terror, our flesh freezes, immediately, so that it is immobilized—in-mobilized—"bracing" itself for 'the worst' it may "become," a corpse. The behavior it "takes hold of" is the behavior of dying. Our heart slows down; and the blood drains from our face.[5] Terror is also skin depthful. For terror is also a "chilling" experience. We freeze in it. Even afterwards, we may shudder or tremble—even to think of it. This makes sense. The emotion has a "finality." Corpses are, after all, cold.

The purpose of this momentary suspension of animation, this invasion of terror, is to make us aware of the importance of preserving our existence as it "adheres" to the perceptible side of our body, inasmuch as this "side" of our body is the "ground" of our percipient life. By making us so aware of the perceptible side of our body—by momentarily "becoming" it through the stillness of its "freezing," terror purposefully reminds us that we must "save our skin" if we are to remain alive.

To vary Sartre's example, let us suppose that instead of a real human face, the "face" Sartre perceives is a flat, two-dimensional representation of a grinning face pressed against his window pane. Although he may, upon noticing it, be "spooked" by it, it is improbable that he would be seized with terror at the sight. This is because this target, deprived of its real, human, and life-threatening depth, *is just* a "face" in way that real human faces can never be and so cannot evoke a deep emotion, like terror.

Indeed, consider how peculiar it would appear for Sartre to respond with *any* deep emotion to the appearance of just a flat, representational face at his window. We might imagine him as being momentarily surprised or even annoyed by it. He might wonder where it came from or who put it there. But prolonged astonishment or anger *at* the representational face *itself* would appear inappropriate; and if Sartre *were* to respond to this face with any deep emotion, we would say that he was "overreacting" or "making a mountain out of a molehill" (or that he was emotionally disturbed . . .).

Here is a second, fictively varied example. As a female, I am deeply emotionally affected by perceptions of misogyny through a number of deeply felt emotions. I hate (exhibitions of) this deep emotion (back). It enrages me. It causes me sorrow. I am deeply frightened of being harmed by it and deeply sympathetic to women who are. I am also deeply resentful of the subversive way in which misogyny undermines my liberties and restricts or excludes my interests. I can also be thrown into despair over it in the realization that I shall not live long enough to see this worldwide, deeply engrained attitude toward women substantially altered. In short, I feel (very) deeply about misogyny.

I am convinced that my deep emotional responses to perceptions of misogyny are not unique or idiosyncratic—at least among women.[6] I am also convinced that my deep emotional responses to misogyny are not "over"-reactions. (In fact, to be told that they are, in being patronizingly "assured" that I am "making too much" of it, only infuriates me because I perceive this response to the depths of women's emotional responses to misogyny as another exhibition *of* the depth of misogyny.[7])

I do not regard my sexual identity as a superficial trait, like the color of my eyes or the length of my hair; and I do not believe that men wear their misogyny on their sleeve. That is, I do not believe that misogyny is entirely visibly apparent on the "surface" of flesh. In fact, it is difficult for me to imagine any superficial or "surface" shared trait of many men that would be capable of evoking these sorts of deep emotions in me. For example, probably as many men go bald as are misogynous. But I do not feel deep emotions about their balding heads and I do about their hating women.[8]

What makes all of my feelings about misogyny as deep as they are is the fact that in virtue of being a woman I am implicated in its depth (intermingled in the hatred) and my own feminist perception of its covert and culturally institutionalized depth—a depth I perceive as "surfacing" from "behind" so many scenes, so many screens. Exhibitions of misogyny are partially cloaked and surface as surfacings of depth whenever I perceive

- battered women;
- the "justice" that victimizes a rape victim by putting her on trial;
- the depiction of females in pornography;
- mother-in-law jokes;
- the male stranger (mechanic, sales clerk) calling me "honey";
- the "internalized inferiority" in the self-deprecatory manner of some women;
- that Simone de Beauvoir's name is not even mentioned in the *Encyclopedia of Philosophy.*[9]

(ad nauseam)

Again, imagine depriving these perceptions of their misogynist depths. With the exception of battered women, it is possible to perceive these "surfaces" not as surfacings of the depth of misogyny, as I tend to do, but either simply as surfaces (that is, as all "up front"—they just "are what they are"—with nothing malicious or hateful or "rearing its ugly head" "behind" their appearance) or as surfacings of different depths, in which case my emotional responses will tend to vary accordingly.

For instance, perceived superficially, mother-in-law jokes (aimed at *her* mother of course) may be perceived simply as jokes I find funny or amusing; the male stranger who calls me "honey" as breezily friendly or flirtatious; the "justice" at the rape trial as just a case of trying to get "the facts" straight; the pornography as a harmlessly titillating "art"—as an outlet or fabrication of male "fantasies" (that is, as having no intercourse with real-world violence toward women); the self-deprecatory passivity of females as innately and attractively "feminine"; and the exclusion of a world-famous woman philosopher from an important philosophical reference source as an innocuous and unintended "oversight."

When I deprive these perceptions of their misogynist depths or regard them superficially—that is, when I do not see through them or see past them to a history of the hatred and the oppression of women as being "behind" them—my deep feelings about them change considerably or disappear altogether.

I might mention, although it is beside my point of my thesis, that I do not believe that in each and every perceptual situation, there is only one true or "right" depth to be perceived. People do not always see "eye to eye"—"things" in precisely the same way or at or on the same level of depth. Furthermore, we can never perceptually penetrate completely through depth. Because perceptions of depth always do involve some occlusion, some stopping of our sight, and because all lived distances incorporate an individual's frame of reference and some opening of perception in the context (or the subtext) of one's life, there are margins and accommodations for errors or alternate intepretations of what "actually" is "there"—"behind" any perceived "situation." Epistemologically, I take this to be a merit, not a defect.[10]

So, for example, that someone else might perceive these "surfaces" as surfaces of different depths or, say, perceive misogyny itself as "the tip of the iceberg" and the surface of another depth,[11] does not undermine my thesis—which is only that deep feelings are evoked by perceptions of some (substantial or personally significant) depth; that the taking place of a perception of depth, that something be perceived as e-merging or un-folding from "behind" something else, is a sufficient condition for the evocation of a deep emotion. Still, it might be pointed out as an objection to my thesis, that we do occasionally appear to be genuinely and deeply emotionally moved by something manifestly superficial.

However, when this does occur, we are usually puzzled or baffled by it and we usually tend either to regard the depth of the feeling as an "overreaction" (as though the object of perception is not sufficiently depthful to justify or warrant the depth of the emotional response), as a case of emotional "disturbance" or pathology (again, the emotional response as inappropriate, not befitting the situation); or we interpret it as being indicative that there *is* something else[12]—some other, perhaps subconscious, depth behind it (or in a distanced contact with it) that the person does feel deeply about. In other words, we think that the emotional response is actually directed toward something else; that is, it is not so much an emotional dis-positioning or dis-placement (as we have been understanding this in Chapter 5) as it is that this emotional dis-positioning is itself "displaced."[13]

In any event, the consensus, on the part of pragmatic or phenomenologically inclined philosophers who have addressed the depths of emotional experience is that our deeper emotions are determined on the basis of increased proximity to the "self"; and that the deepest emotions permeate or overwhelm the self and are experienced by the whole of our being and by its being in a relation to (I would say, in "occlusive permeation" with) the moral, the creatively aesthetic, the metaphysical, or the divine dimensions of Existence.

In Max Scheler's view, for instance, "spiritual" feelings are the deepest. They are those that "bathe" or "permeate" "*everything* given in the inner world and the outer world" in their light or their darkness; and they are not, strictly speaking, "intentional."

In Scheler's depth stratification, they are exemplified by bliss and despair.

> we cannot be in despair 'over something' or blissful 'over something' as we can be glad or sad or happy or unhappy over something. *The use of these phrases is immediately felt to be an exaggeration* [my emphasis]. It can even be said that if this 'something' is given or if it is subject to explanation, we are certainly *not* yet blissful or in despair...*if* these feelings are there,....they...*fulfill*, as it were, our entire existence and our 'world,' to the *core of our person* [my emphasis]. We can then only '*be*' blissful or in despair. We cannot, in the strict sense of the world, 'feel' bliss or despair, nor can we even feel 'ourselves' to be blissful or in despair. According to the nature of these feelings, either they are *not* experienced at all, *or* they take possession of the *whole* of our being. Just as in despair there lies at the core of our personal existence and world an emotional 'No!'...so also in

'bliss,' at the deepest level of the feeling of happiness, there lies an emotional 'Yes!' Bliss and despair appear to be the correlates of the moral value of our personal being. And for this reason they are the metaphysical and religious self-feelings par excellence.[14]

A strikingly similar but condensed version of the same idea can be found in Dewey's *Art as Experience*:

Pleasures may come about through chance contact and stimulation; such pleasures are not to be despised in a world full of pain. But happiness and delight are a different sort of thing. They come to be through a fulfillment that reaches to the depths of our being—one that is an adjustment of our whole being with the conditions of existence.[15]

In addition, although he does not use the expression himself, probably the best and most thorough description of these "deepest" emotions has been accomplished by Quentin Smith. Smith's metaphysics of feeling relates "global feeling awarenesses" to "global importances" and regards the deepest ones as being "experienced as *emanated from and by* the important world-whole."[16] "Global affects" are "global awarenesses"—"a captivated intuition of a feature of the whole of created things, and . . . an intuition of a feature of the whole of myself, these-things-around-me, and everything-else."[17] In Smith's metaphysics, these Global Affects are identified, or exemplified, as being Rejoicing, Loving, and Reverence—our (deeply)-felt responses to the "World-Whole's" Fulfillment of Happening, Closeness, and Supremacy.[18]

I have little to add to the discussion of deep emotions or the depths of emotional experience that I have not already, but the following, in conclusion. Emotional experiences are differentiated in depth and are intimately related to their evocative "other sides." As we have noted throughout this book, our deepest emotions are those that we describe ourselves as being "in." We speak, for example, of being in awe or of standing in reverence, of being in mourning when we are deeply grieved, and in despair when we are deeply in sorrow, in terror, in agony or in ecstacy, in love, or in remorse. This *in* is an *in* of "in-mergion."

This *in* is not the *in* of a "container" or "receptacle" view of empty or "air" space. In experiences of emotional depth, we, as embodied beings, are "in" a sensitive space and experience ourselves as in-merged with-in a surface of sensibility, 'Flesh.' As I have tried to show, these "in-mergions" can be related to Merleau-Ponty's "en"-être thesis and connected through his reversibility thesis with depthful e-mergions of evocative significances—"like the finger of the glove that is turned inside out." We learn, through deep emotional experiences, that there really is "an indivision" of the world's flesh and our own and that there are times, as Marcel observed, when we have to transcend "the spatial and merely pragmatic distinction between what is here and what is somewhere else."

Through the "reversibilities" of deep emotional experience, we also come to understand the limits of the uni-directional and dichotomous thesis of "intentionality" as it is applied to emotions. Because it is trained on the proximally frontal and because it cannot incorporate its depth, intentionality is an insufficient "basis" for a comprehensive understanding of emotional experience. It is not that emotions cannot be or are not "directed" toward objects. It is that this notion that emotions are "directed" at or toward "objects" must itself be grounded in the space of embodiment and the space of distance, which in its turn is grounded in the space of depth.

The "deepest" of our emotional experiences are those "in" which the body-world boundary is de-bordered or altered to such an extent that intentional and dichotomous characterizations of the emotional experience break down—will obviously not suffice to cover the depth of the experience.[19] In the deepest of our emotional experiences, when or as we are "being as a winding," it is difficult or impossible to tell the "inside" and the "outside" apart from each other. Because they may "become" each other and "reverse," it is difficult to say "who" is perceiving and "who" is being perceived.

It also happens, often enough to deserve mention in relation to my thesis, that it is possible to have unspecified deep feelings—a sort of dimmed emotional awareness or "gut" feeling (a "firm" but "unsupported" belief) that is evoked, again, by some unspecified perceptual depth. I am referring to those times when we seem to be emotionally aware that there is something "there" that we are emotionally, or epistemically, responding to but that we cannot quite put our finger on, to the sense we sometimes have that there is "more" (depth) to something than "meets our eye." I think that this experience can be related to what William James called an *undifferentiated sense of reality* in "The Reality of the Unseen":

> It is as if there were in the human consciousness a *sense of reality,* *a feeling of objective presence, a perception* of what we may call *"something there,"* more deep and more general than any of the special and particular 'senses' by which the current psychology supposes existent realities to be originally revealed.[20]

We return here to Merleau-Ponty's notion of intuition as "auscultation or palpation in depth."

In terms of the Flesh ontology, any experience of what Merleau-Ponty calls, simply, the *Il y a*—the experience of the "There is," that of a pressing silence, of an inarticulate presence, the raw "material" of "Wild" Being (*Être Sauvage*)—would be a sufficient "ground" for deep, or the deepest, of our emotional experiences. Emotional depth would be the relation of an occlusive permeation between the Depth of Being and the Flesh of the world as It Is There Now—and the depth and flesh of our own being; that is, our being here and now. In the Flesh ontology, our bodies and the "body" of the world intermingle in the medium of a rich, inexhaustible Present, a Presence that cannot be entirely "grasped" or "pinpointed," because we are "in" it, we are of it.

In disclosing a number of literal senses for the expression *emotional depth*, I have relied primarily on Gibson's and Merleau-Ponty's rethinking of depth in terms of surfaces and surface recessions. I have modeled my interpretation of Merleau-Ponty's ontological notion of "chiasms," which is related to his sense of depth as "proximity through distance," after the optic chiasm, which achieves a certain "unity through disparity" and creates "blind spots." In extending their understandings of depth and its paradoxes into the emotional realm, I have tried to gesture in the direction of a "surface" theory of emotional perception, following the advice that any discussion of depth must "take occlusions into account."

Any text trying to "center" itself on Merleau-Ponty's notion of incomplete reversibility is necessarily incomplete. This study is not exhaustive. There are blind spots in this book—some I am aware of and others I am not. Depth is still new. Part of the novelty, and the enigma, of depth is that something more always remains—to be seen and to be said—about it.

Notes

Introduction

1. Noteworthy exceptions are Max Scheler's discussion of the (depth) stratification of emotional life in *Formalism in Ethics and Non-Formal Ethics of Values*, trans. Manfred S. Frings and Roger L. Funk (Evanston, Ill.: Northwestern University Press, 1973), p. 330; and to a lesser extent, John Dewey's discussion of the deepening of emotional feeling in *The Early Works of John Dewey 1882–1898*, vol. 2, *1887 Psychology* (Carbondale: Southern Illinois University Press, 1967), pp. 246–247.

2. Maurice Merleau-Ponty, *Phenomenology of Perception*, trans. Colin Smith (London: Routledge and Kegan Paul, 1962).

3. James J. Gibson, *The Ecological Approach to Visual Perception* (Hillsdale, N.J.: Lawrence Erlbaum Associates, 1986).

4. Maurice Merleau-Ponty, *The Visible and the Invisible*, ed. Claude Lefort, trans. Alphonso Lingus (Evanston, Ill.: Northwestern University Press, 1968).

Chapter One

1. For an analysis of criteria of emotional depth, see Quentin Smith, "Scheler's Stratification of Emotional Life and Strawson's Person," *Philosophical Studies* (Ireland) 25 (1977): 103–127.

2. It is of course true that we sometimes appeal to our own honor (e.g., in taking an oath, we may swear "on our honor"). But this is an appeal to the integrity of our reputation—to "what others know of us." Nietzsche suggests that this is "deeper."

> *What others know of us*—That which we know of ourselves and have in our memory is not so decisive for the happiness of our life as is generally believed. One day it flashes upon our mind what *others* know of us (or think they know)—and then we acknowledge that it is the more powerful. We get on with our bad conscience more easily than with our bad reputation.

Friedrich Nietzsche, *Joyful Wisdom*, trans. Thomas Common (New York: Frederick Unger Publishing Co., 1960), p. 87.

3. I am trying to avoid the hierarchical connotations of the expression *highest*.

4. On the level of more down-to-earth interactions with others, the spirit of Martin Buber's twofold "I-Thou" relation is a example of reverential encountering. Martin Buber, *I and Thou*, trans. Walter Kaufmann (New York: Charles Scribner's Sons, 1970).

5. Heidegger maintained that for curiosity nothing is "closed off." "Curiosity has nothing to do with observing entities and marvelling at them....To be amazed to the point of not understanding is something in which it has no interest." Martin Heidegger, *Being and Time*, trans. John Macquarrie and Edward Robinson (New York: Harper and Row, 1962), p. 216.

6. Gabriel Marcel, *Mystery of Being*, trans. G. S. Fraser (Chicago: Henry Regnery Co., 1960), vol. 1, pp. 236–237.

7. My thinking at the time was that construction paper would be more "shock absorbent" than ordinary paper and that the heaviness of the paper would reflect the "weight" of the experience.

8. Although I am not trying to make any connection between the emotions I experienced and the colors I selected to write on, I did find myself selecting culturally conventional emotional color schemes (e.g., blue for serenity and "seeing red" in anger).

9. For a discussion of "felt feelings," see Chapter 6.

10. Albert Camus, *The Stranger*, trans. Stuart Gilbert (New York: Random House, 1946), p. 129.

11. Ibid., p. 120.

12. He tells us for example that "really one can't be sure" whether it is a "damned or crying" shame that twice a day for eight years, a neighbor beats his dog. Despite the number of times Meursault has observed this maltreatment, it does not seem, to him, to amount or add up to a morally disgraceful or repugnant pattern of behavior on his neighbor's part—one that ought not to be continued in the future; and Meursault is not sickened or disgusted by it.

13. Also, except for finding a neighbor's story about how he beat a woman "til the blood came" "interesting," he has no other "opinion." The story is interesting in the same sense that the telegram informing him of his mother's death is "interesting" for Meursault. Whatever is right before his eyes, whatever is happening in a punctiform "now" is all that (momentarily) occupies his attention. He has no qualms about writing a letter for this man to entrap this woman and no moral sense of culpability or emotional sense of revulsion when the letter eventuates, as he knew it would, in the woman's being brutally beaten, once again, by this man. Meursault hears her piercing, bloodchilling screams

and sees Raymond "knocking her about," but when "Marie said, wasn't it horrible!" Meursault "didn't answer anything." The scene moves, without skipping a beat in the momentary time-space Meursault inhabits, to the next present: "Marie and I finished getting our lunch ready. But she hadn't any appetite, and I ate nearly all. She left at one, and then I had a nap" (ibid., pp. 32–46). Even when it comes to light that the Arab he kills is this battered woman's brother, we do not find Meursault remorsefully pondering the fact that his letter writing has something to do, through the spatiotemporal involvements of interpersonal relationships, with the fact that he is on trial for his life. Although he admits that this is a "shrewd" plausible way of "treating the facts" (p. 125), he does not seem to have a sense for the ways in which, over time, "one thing leads to another."

14. Ibid., p. 87.

15. Ibid., p. 127.

16. Merleau-Ponty, *Phenomenology of Perception*.

17. Camus, *The Stranger*, p. 98.

18. Ibid., p. 100.

19. Ibid., p. 132.

20. Ibid., p. 112.

21. Ibid.

22. Ibid., p. 116.

23. Ibid., p. 137.

24. Ibid., p. 143.

25. In a sense of depth to be developed from Merleau-Ponty's Flesh ontology—a depth I call the depth of distanced contact.

26. Aldous Huxley, *Brave New World* (New York: Harper and Row, 1932), p. 52.

27. Ibid., p. 163.

28. Ibid., p. 140.

29. Ibid., p. 46.

30. Ibid., p. 65.

31. George Orwell, *Nineteen Eighty-Four* (New York: Harcourt, Brace and World, 1949), p. 40.

32. Ibid., p. 54.

33. Ibid., p. 30.

34. Ibid., p. 56.

35. Ibid., pp. 28 and 29.

36. Ibid., p. 225.

37. Ibid., p. 230.

38. Ibid., pp. 232 and 233.

39. Ibid., p. 235.

40. Ibid., p. 236.

41. Ibid.

42. Ibid., p. 237.

43. Ibid., pp. 239 and 240.

44. Ibid., p. 239.

45. Ibid., pp. 238–239.

46. William Styron, *Sophie's Choice* (New York: Random House, 1976), p. 484.

47. Ibid., p. 495.

48. "Dark space" or "pure depth" is a phenomenological category I later discuss. I believe this spatial category played a significant role in the development of the Flesh ontology's thesis of the invisible ground of visibility (and the intangible ground of tangibility, etc.) and that it is related to the depths of emotional experience.

49. Sophocles, *Oedipus the King* in *The Oedipal Plays of Sophocles*, trans. Paul Roche (New York: New American Library, 1958), pp. 76–77.

50. Jean-Paul Sartre, *Being and Nothingness*, trans. Hazel E. Barnes (New York: Washington Square Press, 1966), pp. 301ff.

Chapter Two

1. James J. Gibson, *The Ecological Approach to Visual Perception* (Hillsdale, N.J.: Lawrence Erlbaum Associates, 1986).

2. Maurice Merleau-Ponty, *Phenomenology of Perception*, trans. Colin Smith (London: Routledge and Kegan Paul, 1962); "Eye and Mind," trans. Carleton

Dallery, in *The Primacy of Perception*, ed. James M. Edie (Evanston, Ill.: Northwestern University Press, 1964); "The Philosopher and his Shadow," trans. Richard C. McCleary, in *Signs* (Evanston, Ill.: Northwestern University Press, 1964); *The Visible and the Invisible*, ed. Claude Lefort, trans. Alphonso Lingis (Evanston, Ill.: Northwesternn University Press, 1968).

3. "[T]he ideas of space, outness, and things placed at a distance are not, strictly speaking, the object of sight." George Berkeley, "An Essay Towards a New Theory of Vision" in *Berkeley Essays, Principles, Dialogues*, ed. Mary Whiton Calkins (New York: Charles Scribner's Sons, 1929). Also see Margaret W. Matlin, *Perception* (Boston: Allyn and Bacon, Inc., 1983), pp. 125–126.

4. Gibson, *Ecological Approach*.

5. Ibid., pp. 148, 149, 156.

6. Ibid., p. 117.

7. Ibid., p. 148.

8. Ibid., p. 307.

9. Ibid., p. 17.

10. Ibid., p. 51.

11. Ibid., pp. 50, 51.

12. Ibid., p. 160.

13. Ibid., p. 117.

14. Ibid., p. 148.

15. Ibid., pp. 72, 79.

16. Ibid., p. 1.

17. Ibid., p. 193.

18. Ibid., p. 105.

19. Ibid., p. 77.

20. Ibid., p. 76.

21. Ibid., p. 80.

22. Ibid., p. 308.

23. Ibid., p. 209.

24. Ibid., p. 189.

25. G. A. Kaplan, "Kinestic Disruption of Optical Texture: The Perception of Depth at Edge," *Perception and Psychophysics* 6 (1969): 193–198.

26. Gibson, *Ecological Approach*, p. 190.

27. Ibid., pp. 80–84. Cf. Anthony J. Steinbock, "Merleau-Ponty's Concept of Depth," *Philosophy Today* 31 (Winter 1987): 339.

28. Ibid., p. 117.

29. Ibid.

30. Ibid., p. 85.

31. This is evidenced, for example, in invariant horizon ratios whereby one can see one's own eye height on terrestial objects or in the necessity to climb higher ground for the horizon to rise above them. Ibid., pp. 164, 165.

32. Ibid., p. 127.

33. Ibid.

34. Ibid., p. 129.

35. E. J. Gibson and R. D. Walk, "The Visual Cliff," *Scientific American* 202 (1960), pp. 64–71.

36. Gibson, *Ecological Approach*, p. 157.

37. Ibid.

38. Ibid., p. 164.

39. Merleau-Ponty, *Phenomenology of Perception*, p. 247.

40. Ibid., p. 250.

41. Ibid., p. 248. For an extensive commentary on this argument, see Joseph A. Kockelmans. "'Merleau-Ponty on Space Perception and Space," *Phenomenology and the Natural Sciences. Essays and Translations*, Theodore J. Kisiel and Joseph A. Kockelmans (Evanston, Ill.: Northwestern University Press, 1970), pp. 274–311.

42. Merleau-Ponty, *Phenomenology of Perception*, p. 252.

43. Ibid., p. 252.

44. Ibid.

45. Ibid.

46. John F. Bannan, *The Philosophy of Merleau-Ponty* (New York: Harcourt, Brace and World, 1967), p. 95.

47. Merleau-Ponty, *Phenomenology of Perception*, p. 253.

48. Ibid., p. 254.

49. Ibid., p. 251.

50. Ibid., p. 253.

51. Ibid., p. 284. For phenomenological descriptions of other emotional "directions," see Quentin Smith, *The Felt Meanings of the World* (West Lafayette, IN: Purdue University Press, 1986).

52. As Merleau-Ponty points out, temporary deprivation of this significance, in cases of "visual vertigo," for example, can evoke an appearance of unreality, an intellectual experience of disorder or a "vital" emotional experience of, for example, giddiness or nausea. Ibid., p. 254.

53. Ibid., pp. 254–267.

54. This question occurs quite naturally to a reader of his chapter on space, given the placement of his focused discussion on depth and despite his own conclusion that "in principle" there is no occasion to ask what is the level of all levels.

55. Ibid., p. 255.

56. Kockelmans, "Merleau-Ponty's View," pp. 84–85.

57. Merleau-Ponty, *Phenomenology of Perception*, p. 255.

58. Ibid., p. 256.

59. Ibid., p. 259.

60. Ibid., p. 257.

61. Ibid., p. 261.

62. Ibid., pp. 259–261.

63. Ibid., p. 264.

64. Ibid., p. 261.

65. Ibid., p. 262.

66. Merleau-Ponty, *Phenomenology of Perception*, pp. 264–265. It should be noted that Merleau-Ponty's view of experienced depth as an "original" dimension, as one that makes possible unity through disparity or identity through difference and as distinguishable from space of juxtaposition was consistent with an already established phenomenological position. We find a similar view in the works of Gabriel Marcel, *Mystery of Being*, vol. 1, trans. G. S. Fraser (Chicago:

Henry Regnery Co., 1960); Martin Heidegger, *Being and Time*, trans. John Macquarrie and Edward Robinson (New York: Harper and Row, 1962); Eugene Minkowski, *Lived Time*, trans. Nancy Metzel (Evanston, Ill.: Northwestern University Press, 1970); and Erwin Straus, *The Primary World of Senses*, trans. Jacob Needleman (London: The Free Press of Glencoe, 1963). Cf. Erwin Straus: "In experiencing, the being separated is gathered together, united and yet left as being separated" (p. 166). "The relation between nearness and remoteness is not that of spatial places which are next to or near each other" (p. 382).

67. Merleau-Ponty, *Phenomenology of Perception*, p. 265.

68. Straus, *Primary World*, p. 165.

69. Ibid.

70. Merleau-Ponty, *Phenomemology of Perception*, p. 275.

71. Straus, *Primary World*, p. 387.

72. Ibid., p. 384.

73. Ibid., pp. 384–385.

74. Merleau-Ponty, *Phenomenology of Perception*, p. 286.

 75. Glen A. Mazis, *Emotion and Embodiment: Fragile Ontology* (forthcoming with Peter Lang publishers, 1993). To my knowledge, this text is the first extensive work that explores the ramifications of Merleau-Ponty's thought for an understanding of emotions. Mazis' quote continues:

> E-motion seems to entail both the motion away from the person to his or her world, and away from the world to the person. In the etymologies of words used as synonyms for the emotions, one finds terms indicating literally a movement 'into the subject' *and* 'away from the subject'. . .the motion of e-motion undercuts any division into 'subject' and 'object,' 'active' and 'passive.' There is an indeterminacy in e-motion, which is really an interconnectedness that is a mutual enriching circularity: an expression of the subject and an impression of the object, or actually rather, a *circulation* of meaning *within the circuit of both*.

In Mazis's text, e-motion is understood as "this movement of body and world, reversing itself and turning back on itself within a circular movement." I take this opportunity to thank Glen Mazis for generously sharing portions of his work with me.

76. Straus, *Primary World*, p. 384.

77. Quentin Smith, *The Felt Meanings of the World: A Metaphysics of Feeling* (West Lafayette, Ind.: Purdue University Press, 1986), p. 45.

78. Merleau-Ponty, *Phenomenology of Perception*, p. 275.

79. As he appears to suggest, for example, on p. 284.

80. Ibid., p. 256.

81. Ibid., p. 267.

82. Cf. Straus, *Primary World*, p. 384: "Nearness and remoteness disappear for me when I am sunk in reflection."

83. Merleau-Ponty, *Phenomenology of Perception*, p. 283.

84. Minkowski, *Lived Time*, p. 406.

85. Ibid., p. 405.

86. Ibid., p. 430.

87. Ibid.

88. Ibid., p. 429.

89. That we cannot become "one" with distance-depth is phenomeno-logically apparent. The here and the there must be kept apart in their unity, for we experience the there "over there," *from* here, not *over* here.

90. Minkowski, *Lived Time*, p. 429.

91. Ibid., p. 52.

92. Practically speaking, there is some dark space in lived distance, since we experience ourselves as intermingled with but apart from something else. There is, however, no distance in "pure depth."

93. Minkowski, *Lived Time*, pp. 432–433.

94. Merleau-Ponty, *Phenomenology of Perception*, p. 287.

95. Ibid., p. 291.

96. Ibid., p. 286.

97. Merleau-Ponty, "Eye and Mind," in *The Primacy of Perception*, p. 180.

98. Merleau-Ponty, "The Philosopher and His Shadow'" in *Signs*, pp. 166–167.

Chapter Three

1. Despite the brevity of the chapter and the fragmentary nature of the notes left behind in the wake of Merleau-Ponty's sudden death, it is clear that

he was engaged in an ambitious undertaking; viz., the development of an ontology of perception which revisions and linguistically reformulates the Cartesian problematic in order to solve it (Merleau-Ponty, *The Visible and the Invisible*, 232–233) by thinking of the mind as "the other side of the body" (ibid., p. 259)

Given its purported philosophical significance ("the solution of the problem of the 'relations between the soul and the body'," ibid., p. 233) and Merleau-Ponty's own confidence in it (he believed that the 'reversibility' of the Flesh was "the ultimate truth," ibid., p. 155), the Flesh ontology calls for understanding. However, because he never finished articulating this ontology and because it is cast in novel terms (to avoid lapsing into "subject-object" or dichotomous language), it is difficult to fully or fairly assess it; and *The Visible and the Invisible* remains even more (widely) open to interpretation than his other texts.

The few extensive English-language commentaries we have to date have proceeded along different interpretive lines. Remy C. Kwant's *From Phenomenology to Metaphysics* (Pittsburgh: Duquesne University Press, 1966) regards "en-être" to be the pivotal notion; others (e.g., Margaret Whitford, *Merleau-Ponty's Critique of Sartre's Philosophy* [Lexington, Kentucky: French Forum, 1982]) contrast it with Sartre's *Being and Nothingness* ontology; some (M. C. Dillon, *Merleau-Ponty's Ontology* [Bloomington: Indiana University Press, 1988] and David Michael Levin, *The Body's Recollection of Being* [London: Routledge and Kegan Paul, 1985]) try to show its value in countering nihilistic "deconstruction"; and several interpretive commentaries (in Garth Gillan, ed., *The Horizons of the Flesh* [Carbondale: Southern Illinois University Press, 1973]; Calvin O. Schrag, *Communicative Praxis and the Space of Subjectivity* [Bloomington: Indiana University Press, 1986]) proceed on the basis of its conceptions of language, meaning and intersubjectivity.

2. From the following working note in *The Visible and the Invisible*, p. 220:

> Say that the things are structures, frameworks, the stars of our life: not before us, laid out as perspective spectacles, but gravitating about us.
> Such things do not presuppose man, who is made of their flesh. But yet their eminent being can be understood only by him who enters into perception, and with it keeps in distant-contact with them—

3. For example, Sartre's conception of Being (in *Being and Nothingness*) as undifferentiated full positivity ("it is what it is") is criticized for lacking an organization in depth—for distorting Being by conceiving it as essentially leveled-out or "flat."

> Because he who questions about being is a nothing, it is necessary that everything be absolutely outside him, at a distance, and one could not conceive of a more or less in this remoteness which is by principle. He who questions, having been once and for all defined as *nothing* is installed at infinity; from there he apperceives all things in an absolute equi-

distance: before what is not, they are all, without any degrees of Being, of the absolutely full and positive. (*The Visible and the Invisible*, p. 67)

We also read in a working note to the text:

The problem of negativity is the problem of depth. Sartre speaks of a world that is. . . in itself, that is, flat, and for a nothingness that is absolute abyss. In the end, for him, depth does not exist, because it is bottomless.— For me, the negative means absolutely nothing, and the positive neither (they are synonymous) and that not by appeal to a vague "compound" of being and nothingness, the structure is not a "compound." (Ibid., p. 237)

Sartrian ontological space is essentially that of dialectically opposed *juxtaposition*: the fullness of Being alongside the emptiness of human reality. The conceptual relation "between" them is essentially one of retreat, repulsion, mutual exclusion. If human reality is a "hole" relegated, albeit parasitically, to the margins of Being, with nothing "in between," Sartrian ontology cannot be unified as a totality because it has, on principle, excluded what it would need to include (ibid., p. 74).

On the other hand, Merleau-Ponty's ontological space is unified as space of disparate unity. The two sides of Being are not related as juxtaposed "partes extra partes" but as "belonging to" or implicating each other. They intermingle. There is always, already the depth of Flesh between them. As Merleau-Ponty puts it, the structure is "not a compound."

One reason Merleau-Ponty thinks that Sartre's ontology of pure negativity and pure overpositivized Being "ignores density, depth, the plurality of planes, the background world" is that it misconstrues the nature of bodily being—in admitting that the body has an "other" phenomenal side but in disavowing that there is any contact or communication between it and the "objective" side (see Dillon, *Merleau-Ponty's Ontology*, pp. 139–150). For Sartre, these two "sides" are, so to speak, "faced off" squarely against each other, in incommensurable opposition. In Merleau-Ponty's "ontology from within," they cofunction and remain in touch or in contact with each other. Whereas Sartre, presumably because of the mutually exclusive logic of Being and Nothingness, decides, in the end, to place bodily being wholly on the side of the en-soi, Merleau-Ponty believes that "if this contact really is ambivalent, it is for us to accommodate ourselves to it, and logical difficulties cannot prevail against its description," (*The Visible and the Invisible*, p. 75). So, Merleau-Ponty's ontology improves on Sartre's by providing an ambiguous conception of "between space"—and this "idea of proximity through distance."

It is obvious, however, that Sartre's conception of (full) Being (to the brim) does have the depth of (superfluous) voluminosity, a sort of "de trop" density that is the source, presumably, of our "nausea" with respect to it. However, there is no "more or less" in this superfluidity—it is all too much—it is not tempered by differentiated divergencies in depth or the relativities of distant contact. For the only distance in Sartre's ontology is that of an abstract, principled, abysmal removedness; an 'equi-distance' that does not vary relative to an embodied, mobile percipient-perceptible. Again, this "high altitude" thought of an invariable equidistance creates, through its abstractions, an ontologically "flat" conception of Being and no conception at all of human reality. On one side of the ontology, it is all the same; a montonous, flat Being. On the other side of the ontology, there is no depth to the being of percipience, because there is no depth at all to a transparent and isolated "hole"—to the being of a nothing. Human bodily reality, and the self-evidence of its percipience, cannot "belong to" Being in the way that Merleau-Ponty's "hollows or fissures" of percipience can because it has no bodily place to *be*.

4. The "relation between thought and its object,...contains neither the whole nor even the essential of our commerce with the world..." He believed that this relation must be situated "back within a more muted" and already accomplished initiation to the world that he describes as the "opening to the world" or as "perceptual faith" (*The Visible and the Invisible*, p. 35).

5. Ibid., p. 123:

When I find again the actual world such as it is, under my hands, under my eyes, up against my body, I find much more than an object: a Being of which my vision is a part, a visibility older than my operations or my acts. But this does not mean that there was a fusion or a coinciding of me with it: on the contrary, this occurs because a sort of dehiscence opens my body in two, and because between my body looked at and my body looking, my body touched and my body touching, there is overlapping or encroachment, so that we must say that the things pass into us as well as we into the things.

6. Ibid., p. 231.

7. Ibid., pp. 136–137.

8. Kwant, *From Phenomenology to Metaphysics*, p. 221.

9. It is beyond the scope of this book to discuss the influence of Merleau-Ponty's *The Visible and the Invisible* ontology on postmodernism and its technique of "deconstruction." In hindsight, Merleau-Ponty's does appear to be a "deconstructive ontology"; and the similarities between Merleau-Ponty's conception of depth and Jacques Derrida's notion of *différance* are striking. Some grasp of Merleau-Ponty's ontology also enhances understanding of contemporary French feminism. See Chapter 6.

10. As it happens, however, Merleau-Ponty's conception of Flesh (in its inaugural sense) is similar to the Chinese notion of the "'Tao'" (Lao Tse, *Tao Te Ching*, trans. Gia-Fu Feng and Jane English [New York: Random House, 1972]) and Flesh as "Between Space'" is similar to the Japanese conception of "'Ma."

11. Merleau-Ponty, *The Visible and the Invisible*, p. 139.

12. Ibid., p. 140.

13. See ibid., p. 236.

14. This account appears to be a development of that "out of place" passage about the "opening of perception" in the *Phenomenology of Perception*.

15. Kwant, *From Phenomenology to Metaphysics*, p. 61.

16. Merleau-Ponty did not believe that the emergence of percipience came about through an "incomprehensible accident." ("The flesh (of the world or my own) is not contingency, chaos, but a texture that returns to itself and conforms to itself." See *The Visible and the Invisible*, pp. 146–147).

17. Ibid., pp. 137, 138.

18. Cf. Immanuel Kant on the sides of the body in his 1768 essay, "On the Distinction of Material Regions in Space," trans. Handyside, in *Kant's Inaugural Dissertation and Early Writings on Space* (Chicago, 1929).

19. "Where are we to put the limit between the body and the world, since the world is flesh?" Merleau-Ponty, *The Visible and the Invisible*, p. 138.

20. Intentionality, insofar as it connotes that such consciousness is always "of" or "about" or "directed toward" an object, also seems to connote that consciousness and objects lie "out"-side each other.

21. Merleau-Ponty, *The Visible and the Invisible*, p. 210.

22. Ibid., p. 143: "what is proper to the visible is, we said, to be the surface of an inexhaustible depth."

23. Ibid., p. 259.

24. "For if the body is a thing among things, it is so in a stronger and deeper sense than they: in the sense that, we said it *is of them*, and this means [on the sentient "side" of bodily flesh] that it detaches itself upon them, and accordingly, detaches itself from them" (ibid., p. 137).

25. Ibid., p. 259.

26. Ibid., pp. 232, 233, 234.

27. Gaston Bachelard, *Poetics of Space*, trans. Marie Jolas (New York: Orion Press, 1964), p. 222.

28. Because they are embedded too deeply with*in* the perceptible for our powers of perception to completely uncover (and not because they are imperceptible in the way that "invisible" ghosts are or because of their belonging to some transcendently Platonic realm removed from this worldly one), ideas or essences are thought as invisible (in the visible).

29. Merleau-Ponty, *The Visible and the Invisible*, p. 219–220.

30. A consequence of the ontology's view of percepience being limited by imperceptibility is that percipient-perceptibles are, of necessity, epistemologically limited. We adhere to the density of Flesh. To some extent, human being, as bodily being, must always be a being "in the dark." However much we think we "know" or "clarify," we are not transparent. We do not "see-all-the-way-through"—even our own depth.

Nevertheless, our perceptual-epistemic limitations do not mean, for Merleau-Ponty, that we are ever "out of touch" or without contact with the depth of the Flesh of Being (for, as perceptible bodily beings, we belong to the Flesh of the world and, by implication, to its depth). The limitations of percipience imply only that its underlying contact with Flesh (its belonging to its depth) may be of a fundamentally obscure or hidden nature. If this underlying contact is itself hidden or imperceptible (and Merleau-Ponty apparently believed that it was), then inasmuch as our percipience belongs (ultimately) to (perceptible) Flesh (too), the implications are only that self-permeating (dense) Flesh can be partially hidden from itself; that is, as a textural unity it has retained its characteristically self-occlusive nature and that this obscurity or hiddenness "is itself a characteristic of Being, and no disclosure will make us comprehend it" (ibid., p. 122). But even that does not mean that we cannot be "at one" with it or that we do *not* "belong to it." Self-occlusion or Hiddenness may characterize Being; but this feature of Being need not lead either to ontological dualism or to "mysticism." Cf. Kwant, *From Phenomenology to Metaphysics*, pp. 239–241.

31. An excellent discussion of this aspect of Merleau-Ponty's later philosophy can be found in Anthony Steinbock's article, "Merleau-Ponty's Concept of Depth," *Philosophy Today* 31 (Winter 1987): 337–351.

32. Merleau-Ponty, *The Visible and the Invisible*, p. 137.

33. Ibid.

34. In optics, the chiasm refers to the crossing over of the two optic nerves so that portions of each "wind up" on the other side. Together with eye (con- or di-)vergences and through its "windings" and reversals, the optic chiasm coordinates or mediates between the two (disparate but) overlapping optical regions to ensure the integrity of the left and right "sidedness" of a unified visual field. Obviously, because these regions overlap, they are not "brought together" juxtapositionally, but through a convergency of divergencies (i.e., a unity through disparity), just as when our two (distanced and sensitive) eyes see two things together (through converging) *at the same time*, we see one (sensible) thing. Only because our eyes are spread apart as they are can we unify our visual field as we do; and it is only the "sidedness" of the unified region that the optic chiasm keeps apart—while it joins them together.

35. Merleau-Ponty, *The Visible and the Invisible*, pp. 214–215.

36. Ibid., p. 144.

37. Ibid., p. 155.

38. Depth as "urstiftung."

39. Dillon, *Merleau-Ponty's Ontology*, p. 172.

40. Merleau-Ponty, *The Visible and the Invisible*, p. 264.

41. Ibid., p. 263.

42. Ibid., p. 136.

43. Ibid., p. 142.

44. So there is even, in this ontology, a reversible circle of visibility. For example, by seeing the visibility of other seers, I see, through my own eyes, that seeing is visible and that the visibility of my own seeing is open to other visions. Through "reversibility," I see my own visibility through my own vision, appearing to myself "completely turned inside out under my own eyes" (ibid., p. 143).

45. Kwant, *From Phenomenology to Metaphysics*, pp. 68–70.

46. I take this example from Kwant.

47. Merleau-Ponty, *The Visible and the Invisible*, p. 134.

48. Ibid., p. 134.

49. Ibid., p. 147.

50. Ibid., p. 141.

51. As when we are, for example, re-turned and re-moved (in Mazis's sense) to a "first perception" or when we are making, in Mary Daly's sense, a transformative "leap" of perception. See Chapter 7.

52. Merleau-Ponty, *The Visible and the Invisible*, p. 134.

53. Ibid., p. 148.

54. That Merleau-Ponty was still thinking about how perception can be "formed in the things" can be seen in his working note of May 20, 1959. That he refers this paradox to "Being" can be seen on page 136 of the text.

55. Ibid., p. 138.

56. Ibid., p. 140.

57. Ibid., pp. 134–135.

58. Ibid., p. 140.

59. Merleau-Ponty, *Phenomenology of Perception*, p. 277.

Chapter Four

1. For a discussion of the reversibilities of time, see Glen Mazis, "The Depth of Memory as the Depth of the World," in *The Horizons of Continental Philosophy*, ed. Hugh Silverman and others (Dordrecht: Kluwer Academic Publishers, 1988).

2. Anthony J. Steinbock, "Merleau-Ponty's Concept of Depth," *Philosophy Today* 31 (Winter 1987): 339–340.

3. Merleau-Ponty, *The Visible and the Invisible*, p. 219.

Chapter Five

1. For a critique of this notion of emotional depth, see Henri Bergson, *Time and Free Will*, trans. F. L. Pogson (New York: Macmillan Co., 1910). For a critique of Bergson's notion, see Max Scheler's *Formalism in Ethics and Non-Formal Ethics of Values* (Evanston: Northwestern University Press, 1973).

2. As it is thought in Freudian or psychoanalytic discourse.

3. I do not wish to hold with William James, for example, that an emotion is a bodily feeling.

4. For a survey of answers to this question, see Robert Solomon and Cheshire Calhoun, eds., *What Is an Emotion?* (New York: Oxford University Press, 1984).
I am partial to the inclusive nature of "contextual" approaches to emotion because they intervolve situational "sides" and other psychological categories, such as feeling with behavior, perception, attention, motivation, imagination, choice, purposeful ends, beliefs or "cognitions," social and linguistic settings, in their understanding of *emotion*.

5. John Dewey, from *The Theory of Emotion* in Calhoun and Solomon, *What Is an Emotion?* p. 171.

6. John Dewey, *Art as Experience* (New York: Capricorn Books, 1958), p. 15.

7. Quoted in Maurice Merleau-Ponty, "The Film and the New Psychology" in *Sense and Non-Sense*, trans. Hubert L. Dreyfus and Patricia Alien Dreyfus (Evanston, Ill.: Northwestern University Press, 1964), p. 53.

8. Quentin Smith, *The Felt Meanings of the World, A Metaphysics of Feeling* (West Lafayette, Ind.: Purdue University Press, 1986).

9. Glen Mazis, *Emotion and Embodiment: Fragile Ontology* (forthcoming by Peter Lang Publishers).

10. "the experience of our own body...discloses beneath objective space...a primitive spatiality....To be a body, is to be tied to a certain world, as we have seen; our body is not primarily *in* space: it is of it." Merleau-Ponty, *Phenomenology of Perception*, p. 148. Cf. p. 140.

11. "my body appears to me as an attitude directed towards a certain existing or possible task. And indeed, its spatiality is not, like that of external objects or like that of 'spatial sensations,' a *spatiality of position*, but a *spatiality of situation*" (ibid., p. 100).

12. In her novel, *The Mind-Body Problem* (New York: Random House, 1983), p. 22, Rebecca Goldstein has conveyed this notion in terms of a "mattering map":

> People occupy the mattering map....The map in fact is a projection of its inhabitants' perceptions. A person's location on it is determined by what matters to him, matters overwhelmingly, the kind of mattering that produces his perceptions of people, of himself and others....One and the same person can appear differently when viewed from different positions, making interterritorial communication sometimes difficult. And then some of us do an awful lot of moving around from region to region.

13. Merleau-Ponty, *Phenomenology of Perception*, pp. 285–286.

14. Ibid., p. 151.

15. Ibid, pp. 184–185. Also see "The Film and the New Psychology," pp. 52–53.

16. Together with Max Scheler (in *The Nature of Sympathy*, trans. Peter Heath [West Haven, Conn.: Yale University Press, 1954]), whose position this is and to which Merleau-Ponty is evidently subscribing.

17. Neither are they "a mosaic of affective states, of pleasures and pains each sealed within itself, mutually incomprehensible, and explicable only in terms of the bodily system." Merleau-Ponty, *Phenomenology of Perception*, p. 154.

18. I mean by this one that strictly identifies emotion with behavior or one that construes emotions as a determined and publicly observable behavioral "response" of a physiological body-object to the reinforcing elicitations of "stimuli" (ibid., pp. 188 and 189): Merleau-Ponty construes emotions as "contingent in relation to the mechanical resources contained in our body," is aware that the body's "psycho-physiological equipment leaves a great variety of [behavioral] possibilities open," and affirms that "the use a man is to make

of his body is transcendent in relation to that body as a mere biological entity."

19. "One can see what there is in common between the gesture and its meaning. . . in the case of emotional expression and the emotions themselves: the smile, the relaxed face, gaiety of gesture really have in them the rhythm of action, the mode of being in the world which are joy itself." Ibid., p. 186.

20. Ibid., p. 147.

21. In Marcel Proust's description of this phrase in *Swann's Way*, trans. C. K. Scott Moncrieff (New York: The Modern Library, 1928), pp. 298–303, 498–505.

22. It is clear that Merleau-Ponty is quite taken with this description of Proust's. He frequently and endorsingly refers to it in the *Phenomenology*; and even in *The Visible and the Invisible*, Merleau-Ponty continues to affirm that "no one has gone further than Proust. . . in describing an idea that is not the contrary of the sensible, that is its lining and its depth" (p. 149).

23. Merleau-Ponty, *Phenomenology of Perception*, p. 134.

24. Ibid., p. 157.

25. So far as I can determine, what appears to be wrong about Gibson's theory of affordances is that his "mobile" observers are not intrinsically affective or emotional beings, except perhaps in some Heideggerian sense of being "concerned" about their environment. Also, Gibson fails to take his own advice about occlusions into account in discussing his affordances. That is, he does identify these meanings with depth, but then regards them as "all up front"— "directly" and immediately perceived. As we shall see in the following sections, Merleau-Ponty's account of "living meanings" are like Gibsonian affordances that take occlusions into account.

26. I further address the puzzling question of how we do this later.

27. Merleau-Ponty, *Phenomenology of Perception*, pp. 189, 188.

28. The Flesh ontology, by the way, although preserving a sense for this mystery, does not speak in terms of "miracles" and does indeed seek to elucidate such phenomena.

29. The body "defined in terms of its property of appropriating, in an indefinite series of discontinuous acts, significant cores which transcend and transfigure its natural powers." Merleau-Ponty, *Phenomenology of Perception*, p. 193.

30. Ibid., p. 194.

31. Ibid., p. 189. This "irrationality" or "genius for ambiguity" is one variation in the phenomena of emotional expressivity of the *Phenomenology's*

thesis of the "paradox of perception." This thesis concerns the puzzle of how something can appear to be resting, densely, "in itself"—"transcendently" more than simply a correlate of my perceptual capacities—at the same time that it appears "immanently" present to my perception, as "my perception" or "for me." This puzzle is set forth in ibid., pp. 299 ff., in terms of how there can be the perceptual constancies, perceptually invariant sizes or shapes to objects throughout apparent variations of perspectives—"Or, more concisely still, how can there be objectivity."

A corrolary here is how there can be emotional objectivity: emotional objectivity *not* in the sense that intentionality construes it, as emotions having "objects," but in the sense of how there can be in the appearance of emotional significance an objectively "constant" emotion "in" or "on" an indefinite number of facial expressions and anatomies that is nevertheless accurately apprehended. For discussions of this aspect of emotion, see Joel R. Davitz, ed., *The Communication of Emotional Meaning* (Westport, Conn.: Greenwood Press, 1976).

32. Merleau-Ponty, *Phenomenology of Perception*, p. 197.

33. "Indicative" not in the sense of being a sign of something else but "indicative" in its demonstrative sense, that is, the gesture's "showing" of meaning.

34. Ernst Cassirer, *The Philosophy of Symbolic Forms*, vol. 3, trans. Ralph Manheim (New Haven, Conn.: Yale University Press, 1957), pp. 151–152.

35. It is a mistake to think that these two (the latently perceptible significance of a gesture and the percipient feeling of a gesture) are unrelated. For we surely can and do, also, feel our gestures (a smile, a frown) on the "other side of our body." See Paul Ekman and others, eds., *Emotion in the Human Face* (New York: Pergamon Press, 1972).

36. The passages from Proust also provide some sense for what Merleau-Ponty might have had in mind with his claim that feelings are invented like words. In art of course emotions are both created and communicated. An artwork can be said to be ("in itself" or "objectively") melancholy, hopeful, blissful, sorrowful, gloomy, and so forth; and our commerce with art can be said to educate us emotionally (for good or ill). Although he does not explain this phenomena, in any comprehensive theory of art (as Susanne Langer does with her thesis that art is the form [essence-idea] of a feeling (Susanne K. Langer, *Feeling and Form* [New York: Charles Scribners Sons, 1953]), Merleau-Ponty is obviously sensitive to the emotional content of art in his writings and philosophically appreciative of the "bedrocking" epistemological value of artistic endeavoring. See Merleau-Ponty, *Signs*, p. 22.

37. Merleau-Ponty, *Phenomenology of Perception*, p. 189.

38. Cf. Buytendijk's assertion that "the profoundest basis of the phenomenon of feeling" is the "fact that we find ourselves as subjects...only

by standing apart and viewing ourselves in the situations in which we are involved." F. J. J. Buytendjik, "The Phenomenological Approach to the Problem of Feelings and Emotions," in *Phenomenological Psychology: The Dutch School,* ed. Joseph J. Kockelmans (Dordrecht: Kluwer Academic Publishers, 1987), p. 121.

39. Merleau-Ponty, *The Visible and the Invisible,* p. 149.

40. Ibid., p. 152.

41. Ibid., p. 149. Gibson acknowledges an analogous difficulty in recognizing the radical nature of his hypothesis that affordances or "meanings of things in the environment" are directly perceptible and that the undeveloped aspect of his hypothesis is "how we go from surfaces to affordances." Gibson, *The Ecological Appraoch to Visual Perception,* p. 127.

42. Merleau-Ponty, *The Visible and the Invisible,* p. 155. Although he does identify essences with invisibility (no essence or idea is directly perceived—it is in the visible), Merleau-Ponty does not identify essence with meaning.

It was Merleau-Ponty's belief that the (unified and self-occlusive) voluminosity of what "There Is" would always exceed whatever might be spoken of it. From the (inarticulated) depth of Flesh, there would always be more meanings of an essence to unfold in expression, would always be more of an invisible essence for (the flesh of) language to reveal. Depth, as either in-visible essence or as ontologically "pure" or "dark" space, is taken to be inexhaustible in this regard. The meanings of language disclose the world's intelligibility, but its full disclosure is ontologically limited. Invariably, there are hidden or concealed sides to any express(ed) articulation of meaning.

43. Ibid., p. 149.

44. Ibid., pp. 149–151.

45. Language plays a crucial mediating role in the Flesh ontology: as a "bond" between the Flesh and the idea or a distanced contact between Being and Essence, Being and Truth, Essence and Meaning, Visibility and Invisibility.

46. Merleau-Ponty, *The Visible and the Invisible,* p. 155.

47. Ibid., p. 151.

48. Ibid., p. 87.

49. Toni Morrison, *Sula,* quoted in Mary Daly, *Pure Lust* (Boston: Beacon Press, 1984), p. 379.

50. William James, "What is an Emotion?" [1884], quoted in Calhoun and Solomon, *What Is an Emotion?* p. 132.

51. Merleau-Ponty, *The Visible and the Invisible,* p. 149.

52. I appropriate this expression from Stephan Strasser, *Phenomenology of Feeling*, trans. Robert E. Wood (Pittsburgh: Duquesne University Press, 1977).

Chapter Six

1. Merleau-Ponty, *The Visible and the Invisible*, pp. 264–265.

2. This expression will be explained in the next section.

3. As we have already discussed, Merleau-Ponty attributes reversibility not to a fusion, but to an écart, a divergency, a dehiscence, a fission. *The Visible and the Invisible*, pp. 123, 143.

4. Ibid., p. 263.

5. Ibid., p. 136.

6. Richard A. Cohen, "Merleau-Ponty, The Flesh and Foucault," *Philosophy Today* 28 (Winter 1984): 330.

7. Dillon, *Merleau-Ponty's Ontology*, p. 172.

8. See Chapter 1.

9. This is not to say that we are not, and in a significant sense, "attached" to each other. However, it is to say that whatever unity we do experience ourselves achieving is "formed across incompossibilities." See M. C. Dillon, "Erotic Desire," *Research in Phenomenology* 15, (1985).

10. See page 73.

11. Merleau-Ponty, *The Visible and the Invisible*.

12. Where purposeful movements "are guided beforehand by the circumspection of concern." Martin Heidegger, *Being and Time*, trans. John Macquarrie and Edward Robinson (New York: Harper and Row, 1962), pp. 134–143.

13. See the next section for a discussion of their "cross overs."

14. Merleau-Ponty, *Phenomenology of Perception*, p. 316.

15. Merleau-Ponty, *The Visible and the Invisible*, p. 256.

16. "As a thing is 'in' a vessel." Aristotle, *Physics*, IV:2, 210a.

17. See the Chapter 8 discussion of Scheler.

18. Merleau-Ponty, *The Visible and the Invisible*, pp. 219–220.

19. The "rapture of the deep" is discussed in a similarly Skin-Deep vein by Alphonso Lingis, *Excesses* (Albany: State University of New York Press, 1983), pp. 1–16. The rapture of the deep, he says, is "all in surface effects. . .not different in delight from the delight before the fugitive inventions in foam and spray of the waves at the surface."

> Yet why must it be that men always seek out the depths, the abyss? Why must thought, like a plumb line, concern itself exclusively with vertical descent? Why was it not feasible for thought to change direction and climb vertically up, ever up, towards the surface? Why should the area of the skin, which guarantees a human being's existence in space, be most despised and left to the tender mercies of the senses?. . .
>
> If the law of thought is that it should search out profundity, whether it extends upwards or downwards, then it seemed excessively illogical to me that men should not discover depths of a kind on the 'surface,' that vital borderline that endorses our separateness and our form, dividing our exterior from our interior. Why should they not be attracted by the profundity of the surface itself?

Quoted in *Excesses*, p. 7, from Yukio Mishima's *Sun and Steel*.

20. Ashley Montagu, *Touching The Human Significance of the Skin*, Third Edition (New York: Harper and Row, 1986), p. 125.

21. Cf. Merleau-Ponty, *Phenomenology of Perception*, p. 93: "When I press my two hands together, it is not a matter of two sensations felt together as one perceives two objects placed side by side, but of an ambiguous set-up in which both hands can alternate the roles of 'touching' and being 'touched.' "

22. Calhoun and Solomon, *What Is an Emotion?* p. 4.

23. Ibid., p. 16.

24. For a discussion of somatophobia, see Elizabeth V. Spelman, "Woman as Body," *Feminist Studies* 8, no. 1 (1982): 109–131.

25. Alison M. Jaggar, "Love and Knowledge: Emotion in Feminist Epistemology" in Ann Garry and Marilyn Pearsall, *Women, Knowledge and Reality* (Boston: Unwin Hyman, 1989).

26. Robert Solomon, *The Passions* (Garden City, N.Y.: Anchor Press/Doubleday, 1976), pp. 172ff.

27. Calhoun and Solomon, *What Is an Emotion?* p. 9; and Ronald deSousa, *The Rationality of Emotion* (Cambridge, Mass.: The MIT Press, 1987), p. 37. The view that emotional feelings are not substantial enough for analysis has been challenged by Quentin Smith in *The Felt Meanings of the World* (West Lafayette, Ind.: Purdue University Press, 1986), p. 40.

Smith's "essentially metaphorical" descriptions of "feeling-sensations" and his typecasting of them in terms of "internal and typological character" of "flowing in a certain direction and manner" are refreshingly recognizable. For example, he depicts hilarity as flowing "upwards in a manner of *quick, staccato surges*"; and fear as flowing *"backwards* in a shrinking and cringing manner" (ibid., p. 45). Although Smith has broken significant ground in challenging the traditional bias against emotional feeling, I still find that some of his descriptions are too linear, too flat, and too cerebral because they are referred to mental feelings rather than bodily experience. His description of humiliation as "flowing downward in a plummeting manner" is an instance of such a "linear" rendering. It ignores the depth of flesh: its hot, flushed appearance in the embarrassment of cheeks, the belittling sense of feeling "small" in relation to one's surroundings.

28. Where they contract the notorious difficulties of the James-Lange theory (William James and Carl George Lange, *The Emotions* [New York: Hafner Publishing Co., 1967]). See, for example, Walter B. Cannon, "The James-Lange Theory of Emotions: A Critical Examination and an Alternative Theory" in Magda B. Arnold, *The Nature of Emotions* (Baltimore: Penguin Books, 1971); and Stanley Schachter and Jerome E. Singer, "Cognitive, Social, and Physiological Determinants of Emotional States," *Psych Review* 69 (1962): 379–399.

29. So-named "without prejudice" by Elizabeth Spelman in "Anger and Insubordination" in Garry and Pearsall, *Women, Knowledge and Reality*.

30. I am grateful to the editors at *Hypatia* (Bloomington, Indiana: Indiana University Press) for their valuable comments on an early draft of this chapter.

31. *"Emotion, feeling, affect* and *touch* are scarcely separable from one another" Montagu, pp. 287–288. However, one way in which tactile and affective feelings diverge is referential: "As commonly understood feeling refers to the sensations arising within the organism as a whole. One *feels* well or not. The state is an affective one" (ibid., pp. 287–288). Whereas our emotional feelings are usually attributed to our "selves," tactile feelings are usually referred to the object touched through our touch. For example, it is the sandpaper that feels, texturally, abrasive to my touch; while it is "I" who feel, emotionally, irritated.

32. For example, as infants, we learned about love, directly and immediately, through our mother's touch. If we reflect on our lived experiences of embraces or caresses, it appears to be an artifical imposition—a product, perhaps, of a somatophobic, dichotomous (and hierarchical) philosophy of "mind" (over body) to theoretically abstract out of this experience discrete tactile "sensations"—to disparage the emotional feelings that are a part of this experience as diminutive "feels" and to posit, at some isolated remove "cognitions" that interpret or "judge" these dumb sensations to be love. One wonders how they could; and the cognitivist theory does not explain.

An alternative view may be to simply regard the love as affectively felt to be "there"—on the Surface—communicated through the medium of flesh in a tactile experience. Our bodies can distinguish a gentle, loving touch when it feels one; and when it feels one, the love is not apprehended apart from the tenderness of its "touch."

33. "What Is Music?," written, produced and directed by John Angier, PBS's *NOVA*, 1989.

34. Ibid.

35. We must acknowledge that "lived experience" is not entirely a-linguistic. It may be that the language of tactility structures our lived experience of emotional feeling.

36. I do not want to say that this is the only way in which apprehension might be felt. In apprehension, we might feel our stomach "churning" or our heart racing instead. Still, we cannot describe our feelings without describing what is felt; and some of what is felt is a vessel or motor inside our body—"churning" our stomach or "racing" our heart.

37. Merleau-Ponty, *The Visible and the Invisible*, p. 137.

38. Or our saying that we are is why we experience ourselves as being...

39. Cf. Quentin Smith's description of humiliation as "flowing downward in a plummeting manner" which I discuss in note 27.

40. In his excellent article, " 'Seeing' and 'Touching,' or, Overcoming the Soul-Body Dualism" (in Anna-Teresa Tymieniecka, ed., *Soul and Body in Husserlian Phenomenology* [Dordrecht: D. Reidel Publishing Co., 1983] pp. 87, 90), Tadashi Ogawa has called some attention to this phenomenon.

41. This is taken to be the result of Schachter and Singer's experiments, noted previously.

42. Elizabeth Spelman wonders about how we may identify anger in "Anger and Insubordination" in *Women, Knowledge and Reality*, pp. 270–271.

43. See Jaggar, "Love and Knowledge" in *Women, Knowledge and Reality* and Elizabeth V. Spelman and John M. Connolly, "Emotion and the Thought of Nuclear Holocaust" in *Twenty Questions: An Introduction to Philosophy*, 2d ed., ed. G. L. Bowie, Meredith W. Michaels, and Robert C. Solomon (New York: Harcourt, Brace, Jovanovich, 1992), pp. 381–383.

44. Young, Iris Marion, *Justice and the Politics of Difference*, pp. 136–137. Copyright © 1990 by Princeton University Press. The extracts in this chapter are reprinted by permission of Princeton University Press.

45. Merleau-Ponty, *The Visible and the Invisible*, p. 134.

46. Montagu, *Touching*, p. 124.

47. Ibid., p. 3.

48. For an account of divergent perceptions on this score, see especially Doris Davenport's "The Pathology of Racism: A Conversation with Third World Wimmen" in Cherrie Moraga and Gloria Anzaldua, eds., *This Bridge Called My Back: Writings by Radcal Women of Color* (Watertown, Mass.: Persephone Press, 1981), pp. 85–90.

49. Arthur Brittan and Mary Maynard, *Sexism, Racism and Oppression* (New York: Basil Blackwell, 1984), p. 13.

50. I am indebted to Uma Narayan for sharing her story about the meaning of *"flesh" colored* with me.

51. Thomas F. Slaughter, Jr., "Epidermalizing the World: A Basic Mode of Being Black," in *Philosophy Born of Struggle*, ed. Leonard Harris (Dubuque, Iowa: Kendall/Hunt Publishing Co., 1983), p. 284.

52. Young, *Justice*, p. 60.

53. Slaughter, "Epidermalizing the World," pp. 283–284.

54. Ibid., p. 284.

55. Ibid.

56. Ibid., p. 286.

57. Ibid.

58. Brittan and Maynard, *Sexism, Racism and Oppression*, p. 105.

59. Ibid., p. 106.

60. Young, *Justice*, p. 124.

61. Ibid., p. 123.

62. Ibid., pp. 123–124.

63. Ibid., p. 124.

64. Ibid., p. 123.

65. Julia Kristeva, *Powers of Horror: An Essay in Abjection* (New York: Columbia University Press, 1982).

66. Young, *Justice*, p. 123.

67. Ibid, p. 144.

68. Ibid., p. 144.

69. Ibid., p. 144.

70. Judith Butler, *Gender Trouble: Feminism and the Subversion of Identity* (New York: Routledge, Chapman and Hall, 1990), pp. 133–134.

71. Young, *Justice*, pp. 143–144.

72. Ibid., p. 146.

73. I wish to thank Alice for sharing her experiences with me and for calling my attention to these lived, bodily experiences.

74. See Anne Wilson Schaef, *Women's Reality* (New York: Harper and Row, 1981), pp. 62–63.

75. Brittan and Maynard, *Sexism, Racism and Oppression*, pp. 219–220.

76. Jaggar, "Love and Knowledge," p. 141.

77. Spelman, "Anger and Insubordination," p. 264.

78. Ibid., pp. 264–267.

79. Ibid., pp. 270–272.

80. Matlin, *Perception*, pp. 205–207; cf. Montagu, *Touching*, p. 221. Insofar as emotional feeling is intermingled with tactility and because women in our culture are not conditioned to deny or suppress their emotional feelings whereas men in our culture are, there do appear to be some grounds for supporting the belief that women are more emotionally perceptive than men.

81. Young, *Justice*, p. 125.

82. Montagu, *Touching*, p. 3.

83. Simone de Beauvoir, *The Second Sex*, trans. and ed. H. M. Parshley (New York: Alfred A. Knopf, 1952; Vintage Books Edition, 1989). See particularly pages 416, 450, and 529–530.

84. See Elaine Marks and Isabelle de Courtivron, *New French Feminisms: An Anthology* (New York: Schocken Books, 1981).

85. Luce Irigaray, *Speculum of the Other Woman*, trans. Gillan C. Gill (Ithaca, N.Y.: Cornell University Press, 1985), p. 48.

86. Luce Irigaray, *This Sex Which Is Not One*, trans. Catherine Porter (Ithaca, N.Y.: Cornell University Press, 1985), especially pp. 23–33 and 205–218.

87. Irigaray's reading and critique of Merleau-Ponty's chapter, entitled "The Intertwining—The Chiasm," in *The Visible and the Invisible,* can be found in Luce Irigaray, *Ethique de la Difference Sexuelle* (Paris: Minuit, 1985), pp. 143–171.

88. Irigaray, *This Sex Which Is Not One,* p. 26.

89. Ibid., p. 23.

90. Ibid., p. 205.

91. Ibid., p. 26.

92. Ibid., p. 26; cf. p. 209.

93. Ibid., p. 213.

94. Ibid.

95. Merleau-Ponty, *The Visible and the Invisible,* p. 148.

96. In addition to its exclusion of "fluidity," it must also be kept in mind that "dark space" is traditionally associated with women.

97. Irigaray, *This Sex Which Is Not One,* p. 113. Cf. Bertrand Russell's remark quoted on page 13 of Montagu's *Touching*: "a good speech is 'solid,' a bad speech is 'gas,' because we feel that a gas is intangible, not quite 'real.' "

98. Irigaray, ibid., p. 147.

99. Ibid.

100. Chantal Chawaf, "Linguistic Flesh," trans. Yvonne Rochette-Ozzello, in Marks and Courtivron, *New French Feminisms,* pp. 177–178.

101. An application of Merleau-Ponty's conception of Depth from the Flesh ontology in the social and political realm can be found in "Totalitarianism, Homogeneity of Power, Depth: Toward a Socio-Political Ontology" by Anthony J. Steinbock, published in *Tijdschrift voor Filosophie* 51, 4 (December 1989).

Chapter Seven

1. Gabriel Marcel, *Mystery of Being,* vol. 1, trans. G. S. Fraser (Chicago: Henry Regnery Co., 1960).

2. John Dewey, *The Early Works of John Dewey 1882–1898,* vol. 2, *1887: Psychology,* (Carbondale: Southern Illinois University Press, 1967), pp. 246–247.

3. We might compare this "deepened" anger with Max Scheler's discussion of love's "blindness"—the supposed imputatation of imaginary or illusory values onto a beloved. In *The Nature of Sympathy,* p. 160:

Such illusions do of course occur, but they are certainly not occasioned by love for the object, being brought about by the very opposite of this, namely the inability to free oneself from partiality to one's *own* ideas, feelings and interests. The lover's notorious propensity. . .to 'overvalue,' exalt and idealize the object of his love, is by no means always present where it is commonly alleged to be. It is usually only the 'detached observer' who arrives at this conclusion, because he fails to recognize the particular *individual* values present in the object, but discernible only to the sharper eye of love. The 'blindness' then, is all on the side of the 'detached observer.' Indeed, the essence of individuality in another person, which cannot be described or expressed in conceptual terms (*Individuum Ineffabile*), is *only* revealed in its full purity by love or by virtue of the insight it provides. When love is absent the 'individual' is immediately replaced by the 'social personality,' the mere focus of a set of relationships (being an aunt or an uncle, for instance), or the exponent of a particular social function (profession), etc. In this case it is the lover who actually sees *more* of what is present than the others, and it is *he* and not 'others', who therefore sees what is objective and real.

4. Cf. Freud's discussion of "the blindness of the seeing eye" in the Case History of Miss Lucy R. in Sigmund Freud, *The Standard Edition of the Complete Psychological Works*, v. 2 (London: The Horgarth Press and the Institute of Psycho-Analysis, 1955), p. 117 note.

5. This particular sense of Mazis's can be likened to Dewey's sense of the unhealthy narrowing of feeling at the expense of its comprehensiveness, which results, so to speak, in a "hardening" of our emotional arteries and a pathological "split" in our nature.

6. Glen A. Mazis, *Emotion and Embodiment: Fragile Ontology* (forthcoming with Peter Lang Publishers, 1993).

7. Ibid., pp. 40–41.

8. Glen A. Mazis, "The Re-turn of E-motion," "Desire Itself Is Movement,". . ."Or Say That the End Precedes the Beginning," p. 22.

9. Ibid., p. 24.

10. Ibid.

11. Ibid. Cf. "the return of what would have been the same but is now different in the way things are always becoming different, in the becoming of becoming, or in what I would call the re-turn of the past" (ibid., pp. 26, 27).

12. Marvelously concrete accounts of them can be found in Clark E. Moustakas, *Turning Points* (Englewood Cliffs, N.J.: Prentice-Hall, 1977).

13. Mazis, "The Re-Turn of E-motion," "Desire Itself Is Movement," p. 6.

14. A description of falling in love:

The relationship of love when it permeates one's being changes the entire world.... Nothing remains the same. Colors, textures, sounds, food, all of life takes on a fresh, dazzling beginning. Rooms brighten and move; energy skyrockets. All at once the world is a beautiful place, and there is a sense of being able to do what one wants, a sense of great freedom, of visions and dreams. Nothing is impossible, when the spark of love fills life. All of one's senses come alive in the glory of the revelation, the glory of the fullness of intense feelings, in this new, completely enthralling relationship, in the limitless boundaries and sensations that love creates. (Moustakas, *Turning Points*, p. 24)

15. Whether or not the following scenario would be a deep emotional experience in the self-transformative sense would depend upon the extent to which one is identified with one's love or one's lover and whether one's concept of "self" or 'identity" is relational. Clearly, if Romeo and Juliet were to fall out of love with each other, that would be, for them both, an "identity crisis."

16. I appropriate this expression from Mary Daly. It is explained later.

17. Mary Daly, *Pure Lust* (Boston: Beacon Press, 1984), pp. 392ff.

18. This same phenomenon, which is analgous to what philosophers of science describe as "paradigm shifts," Mazis, also, tries to capture with his expression *seeing with fresh eyes.*

19. It is this dimension of Merleau-Ponty's thought that Mazis has so skillfully incorporated into his notion of the re-turn of the past *as* a seeing with "fresh eyes." Mazis says, for example, that

within each perception, there is still the novelty, the freshness, of our first perception. I am still attempting to discover the meaning, the identity, of those things, of those people, and even of myself, that have surrounded me during my life, and it is in this sense that, "The event of my birth has not passed completely away, it has not fallen into nothingness in the way that an event of the objective world does.... There was henceforth a new 'setting,' the world received a fresh layer of meaning... another account has been opened. My first perception, along with the horizons which surrounded it, is an ever-present event, an unforgettable tradition; even as a thinking subject, I still am that first perception..." When we experience the novelty of the old, it is we, the perceiver, who has been moved backward to our beginnings, or rather some part of us has never fully left those beginnings. At each moment, we are turned back toward the beginnings as that which is turned toward the future in a fresh way....

Mazis, *Emotion and Embodiment*. The quotation is from *Phenomenology of Perception*, p. 407.

20. Anthony J. Steinbock, "Merleau-Ponty's Concept of Depth," p. 339.

21. I prefer this expression to the more mechanical expression *adjustment*. It suggests a certain "fitting of significance" between our selves and our situation and has an etymological relation to *attitude*.

22. Sophocles, *Oedipus the King*.

23. The only intention of "double-speak" is to manipulatively obscure, by talking and thinking *over*, the truth with false-*hoods* and deception, so that its "real" nature or the nature of reality that might be dis-closed through it is camouflaged.

24. George Orwell, *Nineteen Eighty-Four*, p. 213.

Chapter Eight

1. John Dewey, *1887 Psychology*, p. 246.

2. Max Scheler, *Formalism in Ethics*, p. 331. Also see Quentin Smith, "Scheler's Stratification of Emotional Life and Strawson's Person" *Philosophical Studies* (Ireland) 25 (1977), pp. 103–127.

3. Jean Paul Sartre, *The Emotions: Outline of a Theory*, trans. Bernard Frechtman (New York: Philosophical Library, 1948), p. 82.

4. Cf. Robert M. Gordon, *The Structure of Emotions* (Cambridge: Cambridge University Press, 1987), pp. ix, 13ff, on "causal depth."

5. Cf. Sartre, *The Emotions*, pp. 59–61: "this is not a game. We are driven against a wall, and we throw ourselves into this new attitude with all the strength we can muster. . . . If emotion is a joke, it is a joke we believe in."

6. Several of the ways in which the depth of misogyny can surface from "behind" women's perceptions in the "ordinary" course of their lives are addressed in Marge Piercy's "Rape Poem" in *Circles on the Water* (New York: Alfred A. Knopf, 1989), pp. 164–165.

7. I perceive it as a "gaslighting" technique—intimating, as it does, that real, actual perceptions of its depth are "all in our heads"—are not really as extensively and as tangibly "there" as we perceive them to be or, if they are, that they are not really "as bad as all that."

8. That balding men might and do feel deep emotions about their baldness or even that other women might is not a counterexample to my thesis but can be intepreted as an instance of it. See later.

9. In addition, although it is reported, in passing (under the "History of Aesthetics"), that "Mrs." Langer "has developed in detail a theory of art" and

that her books "have been much discussed," there is "no entry" either for Susanne K. Langer or for any further discussion her philosophy in this "Encyclopaedia" or for hundreds of other women philosophers.

10. Cf. Merleau-Ponty's notion of the "hyperdialectic" that is "autocritical" (*The Visible and the Invisible*, p. 94). This dimension of Merleau-Ponty's thought and its relation to depth psychology can be found in: Dorothea E. Olkowski, "Merleau-Ponty's Freudianism: From the Body of Consciousness to the Body of Flesh," *Review of Existential Psychology and Psychiatry* 18 (1982–1983): 97–116.

11. For example, misogyny may have its roots in a deeply seated fear on the part of males of being identified with women or, as Dorothy Dinnerstein speculates in *The Mermaid and the Minotaur* (New York: Harper and Row, 1976), its depth-source may be seen as the exclusively female "mothering" of infants in most cultures.

12. That balding men might have deep emotional responses to their balding might be construed this way. That is, there is something else, some other depth, that they feel deeply about: their body in relation to the ground, of time (as a visible sign of aging) or to the ground of Flesh, of perceptibility (a concern about their own attractiveness or sexual desirability such as their appearance for others).

13. Sartre's example (in *The Emotions*, p. 43) of the woman who is so deeply afraid of bay trees that she faints and a psychoanalyst discovering "in her childhood a painful sexual incident connected with a laurel bush" is a good example here.

14. Scheler, *Formalism in Ethics*, pp. 343–344.

15. John Dewey, *Art as Experience* (New York: Capricorn Books, 1858), p. 17.

16. Quentin Smith, *The Felt Meanings of the World*, p. 125.

17. Ibid., p. 140.

18. Part II of his text is devoted to a discussion of these "pure" affects and their "impure" appreciations.

19. Of course some of this nondichotomous depth or debordering is taking place in any emotional experience, as I tried to point out through my notion of emotional dis-positionings. Also see, for example, William James, "The Place of Affectional Facts in a World of Pure Experience," from *Essays in Radical Empiricism* in Bruce Wilshire, ed., *William James: The Essential Writings* (Albany: State University of New York Press, 1984), pp. 203–206. Ultimately, I believe that we can tell these depths apart from each other—distinguish them from each other—only by undergoing them or going through their openings. There is no "higher" court of appeal or "objectively" measurable criterion on which we might base an emotion's "depth."

20. William James, "The Reality of the Unseen" in *The Varieties of Religious Experience* (Cambridge, Mass.: Harvard University Press, 1985) p. 55.

Index